rder

d

Neil Fraser

Function Books

Published by Function Books
#40, London, N22 6AD
www.functionbooks.com

Designed by Steve Hutchins.

For Suki, Eva and Louis, with love

CONTENTS

Acknowledgments

ACKNOWLEDGMENTS

For making this happen, my thanks go to Shane Billingham, without whose drive and enthusiasm it is unlikely that this book would have seen the light of day. Thanks to Richard Hardy for his honest and insightful comments on the text; I couldn't have wished for a more generous editor. Thanks also to Steve Hutchins for the fantastic cover design and work on the layout. Being last in line on the deadline chain can't have been easy and his hard work and patience have been much appreciated. Thanks to Jenni Munro-Collins and Richard Durack at the Newham Archives. Jenni was very helpful in the early days when my interest in the history of Newham first arose, and latterly when this became a reality. Jenni and Richard were also very generous with their time in assisting with a last minute request for archive images. It was always my intention to include more histories from local people but time constraints and having to work around a teaching job and two small children made this an impossibility this time around; perhaps in the future. Thank you though to Keith who owns the flower stall on the market in Stratford Shopping Centre, who kindly spared the time to chat at the end of a working day and provided some useful details that I was able to use in the chapter, Dream Machine. Also thank you to Erwan, who took time out to give me a potted history of the Friends of Abbey Gardens. Thanks to

Keith Sargent and Andy Milligan for pointing us in the right direction. Finally, thanks to all the people who know me and offered words of encouragement and support, including Mum and Dad, and my partner, for her patience and her inventiveness in finding new ways to keep my two young children occupied so I could write at the weekends.

CHAPTER 1

The Circus is Coming

This isn't a history book, though there is a lot of history in it. Some of this is what you might call 'big history', such as how the industrial revolution completely transformed the landscape you are going to read about. Some of it we can call 'small history'; stuff that rarely makes the history books, like the lives and deaths of people who weren't kings or queens, or famous statesmen, or scientists – ordinary people who don't make history because history is done to them. Stuff like ghost stories, or peculiar incidents. These stories are frequently more interesting than the 'big history'.

This story starts with some people celebrating the fact that London was awarded the right to host the 2012 Olympic Games. Images of these people in Trafalgar Square show lots of cheering faces and flags and branded clothing, to remind us, in case we aren't paying attention, that celebrating the spectacle is somehow patriotic. Or something like that. People waved flags because they were given flags, and cheered because that is part and parcel of the spectacle these days, for those lucky to be part of it. This was history. Very small history – it was after all just the result of a vote, of a selection of men and women who had been wined and dined at various cities around the world and then pressed a button to say who they thought should get to host the Olympics.

And the winner was London. More specifically it was Stratford. Those cheering and waving flags in Trafalgar Square weren't celebrating a victory for Stratford – indeed it is debatable whether it was a victory at all, as we will see. They were celebrating the moment of the spectacle that had been created around them, and of course the right to create an even bigger spectacle in what was then seven years into the future. But then, the very next day, not even twenty four hours later, a series of explosions on the London tube network brought the party to an end. The hangover was palpable.

When I had arrived back in Stratford from work the evening before and walked through the remnants of the celebrations outside the station, I noticed that the manager of the supermarket in the shopping centre had entered the celebratory mood by offering a 50% discount on some already cheap red wine. Seeing the usual post-work queues, I resisted and continued to walk through the shopping centre, trying to gauge the mood. Apart from the special offer in the supermarket, and the litter of the celebration outside the station, it was difficult to tell this day from any other. The last of the market traders were packing up, dragging their packed carts towards the exit corridor between the shops. Nobody seemed to be smiling more broadly, or whistling more cheerfully. People were just on their way home after another day's work.

I took out my phone and called my partner, who was in Scotland. Like me, she had been hoping that the Games went to Paris, if for no other reason than just as we were considering buying a house in the area, the property prices were obviously going to jump overnight. My call went to voicemail and I left a message, by which time I was out the other side of the centre and walking past the Gurney memorial on Stratford Broadway, towards the pedestrian crossing. As I stood waiting for the green man I looked over at the Eddie, wondering how busy it might be inside, and as I crossed the road I caught a glimpse of a familiar figure through one of the pub windows. Angry Bob. It was time for a pint. After all, an extra £10,000 was going to be added to property asking prices within a matter of days.

Bob was sitting at the bar, at his usual spot next to the tubular metal pillar. I stood next to him, nudged his arm. He greeted me without a smile. Not because he didn't like me, or because he was unhappy, but because somewhere inside his psyche he believed that smiles were a finite resource and that he had better err on the side of caution, lest they all get used up before something really worth smiling about happened. Or something like that. I nodded at his almost empty pint pot.

"Same again thanks," he said, and while I waited to get served we talked about the inevitable. Bob was more upset than me, but not because of property prices (eventually he would be glad that they went up, as he got more when he came to sell up and move out), but just because. Because.

"Nothing good will come of it." That's why. No further explanation is needed. He says it like it is a bet, and he has the patience to wait seven years to collect on his statement. All that is missing is a *mark my words*.

Bob was a person who spoke as if he liked his words marked. Maybe that is why he ended up being called Angry Bob. If there was anger it was measured, calm, a bit like that of his hero, the Man with No Name. I could imagine Bob denouncing the latest Olympic spin with a few carefully chosen words (no more), followed by a sideways spit onto the ground and a cold, unflinching stare. The main reason he was called Angry Bob though, was that the other Bob I knew was called Happy Bob, on account of permanent good humour. I might just as easily christened him Printer Bob, because this was his trade, and was how I came to know him. We got talking one night in the Eddie when I overheard him talking about an obviously awkward client. A friend of mine was setting up a courier business and needed something printed on the side of his van, so after confirming that this was something within his capabilities, I asked for Bob's business card. *Robert S. Ham. Printer.*

We were both surprised but not surprised that London had emerged clutching the golden Olympic ticket.

Despite both bookmakers and common sense dictating that it would be granted to Paris, there had been a feeling that it was always going to be this way, that hidden hands had been working silently. We mulled over the impact of the Olympics coming to Stratford, Bob focusing on the area becoming a building site for the next seven years, me on the price of property going up. Montreal was mentioned – *Have they paid that off yet?* Outside darkness was descending.

After a couple of pints Bob reached down and pulled up from the floor by his feet an orange plastic bag. Even above the echoing din of the pub, I could hear the clink of bottles and the thud as he put the bag onto the bar in front of us. He pulled the plastic down like a pair of trousers to reveal two wine bottles.

"So," I said, and smiled. "You took them up on the offer. I didn't think you even drank wine."

"I don't. But…" he paused to quietly belch, "two for the price of one. You can't pass up an offer like that. Here, take one." He picked up a bottle by the neck and held it out, slid off his stool and drained his glass.

"You know about Stratford City?" he said, fumbling into his jacket. I said I had seen the model of it in the library.

"Well, that won't get a mention from now on. You can guarantee that." He held out a hand, which I shook, then saluted and was gone. He was kind of right about Stratford City. The pro-Olympic crowd would try to bury it. Then, later, it would be brought back to the surface, bent out of shape and re-badged. With Bob gone, there was nothing left for me to do but finish my own drink, and walk the short distance home, thinking about what he said about Stratford City, about how selective history can be, and who gets to write it. The following day three sevens would clash and the narrative would change.

I woke the next morning with a bad head, and the slow-motion realisation that I had slept through my alarm. On the table downstairs stood a two-thirds full bottle of wine, a red-rimmed wine glass and a plate with two crusts of the pizza I had stuck in the oven upon returning from my drink with Bob. The wine was responsible for rendering my alarm subliminal. Red wine always has the kind of soporific effect that leads to sleep at depths unfathomable by sound. I set off on the walk to the station under a moody grey sky, a fine rain misting down. As I left Stratford Shopping Centre (a welcome respite from the weather), crossed Great Eastern Road and approached the rain-slicked concourse of the station, all seemed unusually quiet. It was around 9am and though the main rush hour was over, there was a stillness and emptiness that suggested something was amiss. It was usual to see one, even two Central Line trains pull into the westbound platform before you could cross the road, walk over the concourse and enter the station, but that morning, nothing. The station itself was more or less deserted and the few people lingering outside were talking into mobile phones, a sure sign that services had been suspended. I could hear an announcement over the station PA, but it was unclear. When I reached the entrance I discovered that all lines had been suspended. There was no explanation. I was not even able to enter and take a main line train to Liverpool Street, as the station itself had been closed, so I phoned work with my excuse and said I would find a bus. By the time a 25 got anywhere near the centre of the city on congested morning roads the tube lines would probably be up and running again.

But the bus stop was already swollen with people and when three of the long "bendy buses" had sped past, spitting rain water at the pavement, I decided to walk the short distance to Maryland station to try and catch an overground train. Again I arrived to find the ubiquitous commuter on a mobile phone outside, and stepping into the station saw on the screens that all overground lines had also been suspended. Outside the rain was beating harder, and a strange atmosphere descended as it became clear that something serious had occurred. Defeated in my objective I returned home to take stock and dry out. I turned on the television and phoned work once more, just as reports on the news mentioned power surges that had hit the underground network and resulted in the suspension of all services. The ensuing news reports told a now familiar tale: power surges or not, there had been explosions on the underground.

If I had not been late for work – due to the wine which Bob had only bought because it was on offer, which was in turn due to London winning with its Olympic bid – then I would, in all likelihood, have been on the Piccadilly line somewhere in the vicinity of one of these explosions, albeit going in the opposite direction to the fateful train. Instead I spent the day indoors while it rained outside and rolling news reports pieced together a narrative for the morning's events. On the dining room table was a newspaper I had bought on the way to the station. The front page celebrated the capture of the Olympics with a picture of cheering school children in the designated party area outside the train and bus stations. Games On! was the simple headline, picked out in Union Jack colours. The Olympic rings appeared in the newspaper's red mast, along with the slogan "Make Poverty History" (the feel-good slogan that had made it onto the agenda at the G8 summit, which in reality often involved lots of privatisation in poor countries for the benefit of Western firms). The following day, and for many days and weeks afterwards, the Olympic story was reduced to the proverbial fish and chip wrappers. Sure, it would return – there were still seven years left to play with it – but for now it was dead and buried.

Two days later I had the distinctly odd experience of travelling on a virtually empty Central Line train, which normally would have been packed with people heading into the West End to work or shop. On the windows of the carriages were the "Back the Bid" stickers that had appeared in the run up to the IOC decision day, the same marketing campaign that had seen a series of posters depicting giant sized athletes leaping, vaulting or Fosbury-flopping over famous London landmarks, none of which were located anywhere near Stratford. The logo for this campaign was a flourish of ribbons in Olympic colours, the Olympic rings, and the text London 2012 and Back The Bid. The ribbon flourish also appeared on the side of the station. Around this time it is fair to say that local enthusiasm was, at best, decidedly lukewarm. Those locals who had an active interest in the area were most likely aware of the Stratford City project, plans, documents and a model of which could be viewed on the first floor of the local library.

In the pre-Olympic days such ambition might have seemed ludicrous to the average Londoner, many of whom weren't even aware of where Stratford actually was. Beyond the city environs most people, when asked, would have suggested it was the birthplace of Shakespeare. Although the typical person would have included West Ham United in their list of East End representations (it is actually situated in East Ham), geographically the mental map of the East End encompasses Whitechapel (Jack the Ripper), Bethnal Green (The Krays) and Bow (Bow Bells). Such is the almost mythological power of this area in our national consciousness.

Back then Stratford was strictly off-the-map. Only the most confused tourist would end up there. Residents in the middle class enclaves amid otherwise downtrodden Hackney tended to look down their noses at the area, which lacked the arty frisson of their own borough. Stratford was emphatically working class, with Plaistow, West Ham, East Ham, Canning Town and Barking to the east equally so. Middle class influence had been thin on the ground since what was once a collection of villages had been transformed into an industrial urban sprawl, thanks to the birth of the Royal Docks and the railways.

Yet the locals had a view from the ground that would have allowed them to see that the history of change in the area was ongoing. Those old enough would have seen the demolition of Angel Lane to make way for a new shopping centre in the mid-1970s. Those a bit younger would have seen the relocation of the library, a new cinema and a complete overhaul of the station. It is perhaps the station that has been pivotal in much of the changes that have taken place. An already good transport hub with one tube line and various overground lines, along with a bus station, meant that it was easy to reach many parts of London; the City and West End were twenty minutes away or less. The arrival of the Dockland's Light Railway (1987) and the Jubilee Line extension (1999) meant that Stratford was better served than perhaps any other London borough outside of zone 1, something not overlooked by the Olympic bid organisers.

One thing that did seem to get overlooked was reality. The reality of the Stratford City project, for example, was ignored in favour of the myth that the Olympics would be solely responsible for regenerating of the area. To add flavour to this fiction, Stratford and its environs were depicted as an urban wasteland of deprivation, and the land required for the Olympic Park as derelict and contaminated. That Newham is a borough of deprivation isn't in dispute, but the tone of some descriptions smacked of the abhorrent attitude once reserved of the old East End in Victorian times. There was the distinct sense that the sort of people talking about Newham in this fashion might be the sort of people who would employ their central locking systems as they drove through it, with sweating palms gripping the steering wheel. Ignoring reality would soon become a pre-requisite for all involved, and the monumental decision not to run the marathon through the East End streets towards the traditional stadium finish in Stratford told the world, if they were bothering to pay attention, everything they needed to know about the intent. The organisers were quick to highlight the fact that the Olympic boroughs were some of the very poorest in Britain, and certainly the most deprived in the capital, but when it came to allowing the residents of these areas see a bit of the Olympic spectacle for themselves, and the world to see the reality of the East End, any sense of altruism seemed to have withered on the vine. The unvarnished truth was the last thing anyone wanted.

One day in February, workers ending or interrupting their daily commute in the late afternoon and early evening noticed something different. On the way to work the approach to the station in Stratford had looked as dusty and scruffy as it always did, but by the afternoon it was as if a team of fairies had descended and redecorated while they were all busy with the 9-5 routine elsewhere in the city. Now the railings outside the train and bus stations, and the crossing on Great Eastern Street, had had a fresh coat of black paint: details had been picked out in gold. Flowers had appeared in small hanging baskets, rubbish had been swept away, and those ribbon flourishes of the bid branding seemed to have multiplied.

Continuing through Stratford Shopping Centre, which seemed more polished than usual, and emerging at the other end on the High Street revealed more of the same. Fresh paint and flowers everywhere, streets swept clean and so on. Then crossing the High Street and reaching the bottom of Tramway Avenue, this sheen of newness abruptly stopped. Here the paint on the railings was still old and peeling, the colour dull and no gold highlights anywhere. The railing opposite Brother's Fish Bar was still caved in where a car had hit it months before. The rubbish bin that had been set on fire by bored youths still stood in a contorted molten shape; the sprayed-on words "Bin Laden" were still imprinted on it, evidence of how seriously the war on terror was being taken. The pavement here was pock-marked with the black stains of long-discarded chewing gum. The road was dusty. Cigarette butts and scraps of rubbish decorated the outside of the job centre. Here, everything was just as it always was.

Not a derelict wasteland, as the ODC would repeatedly claim, but not the swept, polished and freshly painted segment that the IOC got to see. Their brief, choreographed visit in February 2005 came at the end of a marketing campaign urging everyone to Back the Bid, but backing wasn't needed. The Olympics would be done unto Stratford regardless, like some alien visitation. For the likes of us who lived there, the situation was out of our hands. The important people were at work now; the ones who lived elsewhere, but needed this place, this bit of land.

One of the only notes of caution that the IOC raised about the London bid was whether the transport system was up to the job. Anyone who has experienced the rush-hour platforms at Stratford will know that they are bad enough when the crowd knows where it's going. The thought of large numbers of disorientated tourists being thrown into the mix is somewhat interesting. Still, if the transport system itself remained a concern, no doubt the good humour of the London Underground staff would see them through, as demonstrated a few days after Jean Charles Menezes was shot dead on a tube train at Stockwell, when some wag wrote the following on the notice board at a station:

Service Information
Date: 26 July 2005
Time: All day
<u>*NOTICE TO ALL PASSENGERS*</u>
<u>*Please*</u> *do <u>not</u> run on the platforms or concourses. Especially if you are carrying a rucksack, wearing a big coat or look a bit foreign. This notice is for your own safety.*
Thank you

Terrorism and the Olympics. There seemed to be no getting away from them in 2005. In the run up to the decision, when the bidding was big news but the consensus was that Paris would most likely get the vote, I was asked at work to help some students prepare for their Communications test. In the first workshop a theme was needed as the subject matter on which to base a short letter. I led a discussion about what might be the impact of London winning the Olympic bid, with financial, social and other aspects taken into consideration. Afterwards the students were asked to write an imaginary letter to their local MP about what hosting the games might mean. They were encouraged to weigh up the factors that had been discussed, both positive and negative, and make up their own minds. One student wrote about how council tax might be increased and that the money would better be spent on the NHS or housing. Her argument then span somewhat out of control, propelled by media distortions while incorporating both elements of a recent project on sexual health and the dominant media agenda of terrorism. The nightmare scenario according to her, therefore, was that most of these terrorists might have an infection and may decide to have unprotected sex with different people. Information has become white noise, and for people who are constantly distracted, repetition is often the only way to clarity. The naysayers, with little opportunity to project their argument, were never going to be heard by the majority. Despite this, the Olympics was never going to get full support. Pretending that everyone agrees with you is one thing, believing it to be so is another.

A significant year for Stratford should have been two years earlier. In 2003 proposals were put forward for a huge development to be called Stratford City. It was the largest planning application ever received and in 2004 permission was granted. The plans included 4,500 new homes, offices, department stores and shops, premises for small businesses, schools, health centres, parks, community facilities and more besides. The area would be split into four zones, each of which would include homes, offices and shops. An arts and cultural centre was part of the plan, as well as a cinema, fitness clubs and nightclubs. Education was included with plans for nursery, primary and secondary schools and an adult learning centre. A health centre, youth facilities, crèche and recruitment centre were also to be developed. It was, in short, a proper piece of town planning that, on paper at least, was to provide for the local population in a fully integrated fashion. Then came the Olympics and Westfield. The Olympic planners reworked the Stratford City story as their own, promising a legacy. Westfield got to buy-out the Stratford City project – a reduced land area that would now contain the shopping mall, Olympic village and Stratford International station. A reduced, privatised version was thus the first legacy.

So the future of Stratford, though set to change dramatically, isn't going to be quite the one envisaged. The economic crash of 2008, an ongoing disaster that slowly unfolds to reveal more and more devastation, will have a further impact on any legacy. But change is change – it's all history, and this area has a lot of that packed into the last two centuries.

The Stratford rising from the ground along the High Street and on the former railway lands is a dream with more than one dreamer, a vision of a future that may or may not work out as intended. Once the dream begins, each dreamer begins to lose control of it. There is no way of knowing what will happen next. The people in Stratford are living in this dream.

Victorian men shared dreams of industry and altered the landscape east of the River Lea with a ferocity that took little else into account. Like a tidal wave the factories, railways and docks came, and the people came with them. The land sprouted houses and churches and schools, but not always pavements or sewers. Pollution came, and disease and poverty spread like stains.

Joan Littlewood dreamt of a theatre that would free people from their torpor. Although her vision was realised onstage, it wasn't shared by the people of Stratford who were still trapped inside the decaying dreams of those Victorian men of industry. So in order to break down the walls of the theatre she dreamt of a cultural space where the audience could become the players, and asked Cedric Price to help her design this 'Fun Palace'. But the authorities wouldn't give her the land and the dream was never realised.

In the middle of the 16th century the dreams of the people were of a different order. The Reformation man was absorbing himself with rationality, but the common man inhabited a world where the boundary between dreams and reality was permeable, and in this supernatural world spirits and demons were free to manifest themselves. Not ten years after Stratford Abbey was dissolved in 1538, it appeared to some that the devil had seized the absence of the Papal presence to make an appearance in the skies over London, and not only that but to land in Stratford. The commotion of this Satanic visit in 1547 was recalled some years later by William Fulke.

More than sixteen years ago, on May-day when many young folk went abroad early in the morning, I remember by six of the clock in the forenoon there was news come to London that the Devil the same morning was seen flying over the Thames. Afterward came word that he lighted at Stratford, and there he was taken and set in the stocks, and that though he would fain have dissembled the matter by turning himself into the likeness of a man, yet he was known well enough by his cloven feet.

I know some yet alive that went to see him and, returning, affirmed indeed that he was indeed seen flying in the air, but was not taken prisoner. I remember also that some wished he had been shoot at with guns or shafts as he flew over the Thames.

Thus do ignorant men judge of these things that they know not: as for this devil, I suppose it was a 'flying dragon' whereof we speak, very fearful to look upon, as though he had life because he moveth, whereas he is nothing else but clouds and smoke.[1]

Nothing changes. Clouds and smoke take on different forms. We think we are different from the men and women who saw the devil in Stratford, but we still allow ourselves to be possessed by the demons of other people's dreams. Here are some of those dreams and the stories of the people who populated them.

---

1 William Fulke, *A Goodly Gallerye,*(London, 1563)

CHAPTER 2

A Walk In The Park

"My name is Ozymandias, King of Kings:
Look on my Works, ye Mighty, and despair!"

Percy Bysshe Shelley

We were somewhere around the middle of Stratford High Street, on the edge of the proposed Olympic Park, when the bile began to rise in Angry Bob's throat and take control of his tongue. Saturday 27th May 2006 was a bleak day in Stratford. The sky was a shade of grey that suggested colour would never return, and the rain felt like morse-code. The walk down the High Street – a grimy tarmac ribbon framed by dirty buildings of differing shapes but uniform drabness – was long enough for Bob and me to wonder why we were bothering to do this in the first place. Bob was answering these doubts with a stream of consciousness vitriol directed at the various bodies he saw as being responsible for our excursion. I pointed out that nobody had forced us to leave the dry warmth of our homes on this foul morning, but he was having none of it. Bob was a man prematurely disappointed with the future. There was no question in his mind that the Olympics coming to town was a bad thing. Any good things would certainly be outweighed by this bad thing which, he explained, was made up of a combination of many different bad things, the prime one being 'greed'.

There were no signs of life on the High Street aside from us. As we slowly trudged along, leaning into the wind and rain, we might have looked like characters in a sparsely populated Lowry painting. All other breathing things were indoors (and hidden, as if simply being indoors wasn't enough; staying well away from windows was the only true sanctuary from the conditions outside), or safely encased in passing cars and the odd bus. Even the birds had stayed at home.

As we walked we passed several local landmarks, including the Stratford Rex, a building that even when in use had the ability to look shut down. On the corner opposite was the shell of the old Stratford Market railway station. Further down on the opposite side of the High Street, past early signs of transformation in the shape of new blocks of flats, the image of the Yardley flower girls remained on a side wall of a large building, a reminder of its previous existence as a box making and printing factory for the perfume and cosmetics company. This was a detail only the observant might notice and only the curious ponder, but another clue to the history of this stretch of road. Finally we reached the end of the High Street. Here the road is overshadowed by the Bow Flyover as it is intersected by the Blackwall Tunnel Northern Approach Road. Here the strata of history are laid bare.

The Bow Flyover opened in 1969 and takes traffic from Stratford and the London Borough of Newham to Bow Road and the borough of Tower Hamlets. Traffic heading south flashed past, entirely ignorant of life on either side. Here was the ugly brutalism of Twentieth Century road construction, ripping through swathes of flats and housing from an earlier era, much of it in the polluted dark brown of industrial times. To one side stood the building that was once the Bryant and May match factory. In this direction we looked into the almost mythical history of the East End, the one most people are familiar with – one of poverty and industry; little match girls and Jack the Ripper; the Kray Twins and the Siege of Sidney Street. This East End history has been so deftly packaged over time that our very idea of a cockney has become firmly located here, despite the cockney-defining Bow bells actually being located in what is now called 'the City'. Technically the City is where the East End begins, but ask most people in this wealthy business enclave to define themselves and their workplace, and you won't get anything remotely akin to rhyming slang by way of reply. People here refer to stairs as stairs, not hard fruit.

On the other side from Bow lies Newham, whose history is a blank slate to the vast majority of people. On one side of the flyover were billboards, the splashes of colour mirrored on the other side by the drive-in McDonalds. The landscape here was industrial and ugly. Walls and buildings decayed, while grass and weeds grew through the cracks in walls and the gaps in corrugated iron roofs. On the left was an open air gas container storage facility, beyond which lay our destination. To the right, running beneath our feet but hidden by concrete, was the River Lea. It is difficult to describe the banal ugliness of this spot, one perfectly framed by such grey and wet weather. Industrial Estate meets motorway flyover meets decaying, blackened Victorian brickwork meets polluted waterway; this makes it sound more interesting than it is in reality. Perhaps only J G Ballard might have found any artistic merit in it, and could certainly have used it as a setting for one of his post-apocalyptic novels of the early seventies.

So amid all this ugly, faceless concrete it is hard to imagine that, in the words of cliché, this was once all fields. Or more accurately fields, marshes and waterways. That is what the Romans would have seen here as they planned one of the first Roman roads in Britain, leading from London Bridge to Colchester, their initial capital city during the occupation. Indeed, a paved way had existed here even prior to the Romans' arrival, leading to the crossing point over the Lea river that gave Stratford its name[2]. Depending on the weather conditions, this crossing could be treacherous. According to legend Matilda, wife of Henry I, took a tumble here in 1110 on her way to Barking Abbey. As she fell into the water, several church spires and the odd windmill may have flashed before her eyes. Both types of landmarks were evidence that small settlements had grown here.

---

2 *Strat* meaning road, and *ford* being a crossing over water

But mostly, there were fields. The aristocracy made good use of this land for their own leisure, amongst other things. As this was still the main route into London from Colchester and the important trading city of Norwich, it was inevitable that a safer passage over the Lea would have to be devised. Matilda, perhaps still smarting from her drenching, ordered a new bridge to be built: a bow-shaped, three arch construction that was something of a marvel for the times. The bowed bridge leant itself to the new name for the area – Stratford-atte-Bow. Over time, in order to avoid confusion with Stratford Langthorne which was situated on the Essex side of the water, the crossing became shortened to Bow, while on the East side the name was eventually shortened to Stratford.

Bob, rant over, merely commented on the almost comical ugliness of our surroundings as we continued our walk along the edge of the Northern Approach Road, one of those stretches of pavement that exist seemingly to ridicule the mere pedestrian in the face of fast traffic. For a hundred yards or so we seemed to be trespassing in an area designed purely for vehicles. It was a dusty, dirty and noisy procession until we reached Hancock Road, which runs below the Approach Road as it rises and arcs to the right on its relentless passage towards the Blackwall Tunnel. Hancock Road exists in my memory as the location of a rather dodgy-looking nightclub called Echoes, which ran late night acid house and rave parties in the late 80's and early 90's. That and a Tesco supermarket. This was a supermarket that you had to drive to, and at the time it was built seemed huge – an early sign of the impending Tesco-isation of the landscape. As Bob and I approached, we made out a marquee erected beyond the supermarket car park, over the bridge at the end of Three Mill Lane. This was our destination.

A small crowd of people encompassing all ages was gathered outside the marquee. Inside were tables piled with cloth bags displaying the 'Walk The Olympic Park' logo, each containing a pamphlet that doubled as a route map, a bottle of water, a carton of juice, fruit and a snack bar. Down at this level, by the water, a different perspective is afforded. The contrast between it and the ugly industrialisation we had just left behind was quite startling. Before us lay the Three Mills.

Beyond an inlet of water was the Clock Mill and opposite, on the left, the House Mill. Mills have a long history in this area: eight were recorded in the Domesday book, with windmills added later. These mills were in the possession of the Abbey of Stratford Langthorne until the Dissolution of the Monasteries. In medieval times, when the site was known as Three Mills, flour was milled for the bakers of Stratford-atte-Bow who supplied bread to the City of London. For most of urban history, towns and cities have been fed by the produce of the surrounding land. Until the industrial revolution and later arrival of the railways, this was the predominant function of the land that we now call Newham.

In 1728 Peter Lefevre, a Huguenot, bought Three Mills in partnership with Daniel Bisson and others. The mills were operated in conjunction with a distillery on neighbouring Three Mills Island. A piggery was also established, and the animals fed on waste products. The current House Mill was built by Bisson in 1776 between two houses occupied by the miller and his family, hence the name. The current Clock Mill dates from 1817, although the actual clock tower dates from 1750. A third mill, a windmill, no longer survives.

Grain was transported to the mills along the waterways. During medieval times the tidal flows allowed for three to four hours of milling per tide. By 1938, with the addition of sluice gates, this was increased to 7-8 hours. The grain was then either transported for delivery, or taken to the distillery. It was illegal after 1820 for alcohol to be produced and rectified into gin on the same premises, so it was stored in a large bonded warehouse on the island. The convenience of this set-up led to the acquisition of Three Mills in 1872 by J&W Nicholson & Co. This Clerkenwell-based gin maker, founded during the Gin Craze in the 1730s, had provided the Gin palaces of central London with their fuel of ill-repute. Gin was big business. Despite the imposition of high taxes on the sale of gin via the Gin Act of 1736 trade was helped by the ban on imports of French wine and spirits. Before this the government had encouraged the distilling industry in order to prop up grain prices. Early supporters of such moves, including Daniel Defoe, soon changed their opinion when the devastating effects of the drink were felt, primarily among the poor. When the tax was abolished in 1743 the trade was free to flourish once more, and by 1750 over a quarter of all residences in St. Giles parish were gin houses. A year later Hogarth published his famous Gin Lane and Beer Street prints, which took an enlightened view of the problem. Like Dickens much later, Hogarth saw poverty, rather than gin, as ultimately responsible for the misery he so deftly depicted. Alcohol, for many, was a way of life. As social reformer Francis Place put it, "[the poor] have recourse to only two enjoyments: sexual intercourse and drinking... and drunkenness is by far the most desired as it is cheaper and its effects more enduring."

Booze continued to remain high on the list of working class enjoyments, though the popularity of gin waned over time. Although J&W Nicholson and Company did not sell The House Mill until 1966, it had ceased functioning as a mill by 1941, when the area was bombed during the war. The old water wheels and millstones that turned on the captured high tidal flows up the Thames Estuary and Bow Creek survive to this day, and House Mill is the largest remaining tidal mill in the world. The distillery is now a film studio where much of Lock, Stock and Two Smoking Barrels was filmed ("Shit film," according to Bob), as well as the Big Brother television series (don't start Bob on this one), an irony not lost on anyone who, upon getting too close to the perimeter, found themselves informed by the disembodied voices of bored security guards emanating from speakers on poles that they were close to trespassing. As experienced by Bob one afternoon. "Trespassing? Fucking trespassing?" he had said, when first relating this story. I imagined him waving an angry fist at the pole on the perimeter of the studio site. But that wasn't enough for Bob, and the next day he came back with a borrowed megaphone and shouted back at the film studios from behind a bush, telling 'them' their product was shit, and that the security guards should get a proper job or come out and face him. "But you were behind a bush!" I pointed out. "Only because they were talking through a speaker on top of a pole," he responded. At this point I decided to retire gracefully from the topic of conversation.

I was worried that Bob might try to tell this story again, such was his habit of repetition but thankfully he didn't. I wondered if his ranting into the wind on the High Street had sated his appetite for the day, as he didn't even pass comment on the small crowd of the curious we found ourselves in, and which our two fresh-faced looking tour guides ("Bloody students," according to Bob), were trying to herd together.

Although the route printed on the map suggested otherwise, our tour guides led us past the mill and round the perimeter of the Mills complex, the thin muddy path sandwiched between the high perimeter walls of the film studio and the Channelsea river. In the distance a westbound district line train rattled across the green painted iron bridge that spans the river, which widens considerably here. We passed a colourful flourish of graffiti on the wall, echoed in style by spray painted tags on the underside of the distant bridge. As the path curved around, we entered another place entirely, cocooned from the grimy metropolis. The tributaries of the Lea here wind through a hidden landscape of industrial decay, overgrown with nature that in parts threatens to overrun it. Another train passed by, and this time we were near enough to see the people inside, avoiding eye contact with each other as passengers on the tube do. Behind the red, white and blue train rose the huge cylindrical tanks of the old gas works. The tank of one had collapsed, and the rusting steel framing looked like the rib-cage of a long dead animal. This walk off the beaten track was something of a well-kept secret, a strange little oasis either side of Stratford High Street and bordered by the Blackwater Tunnel Northern Approach road. For some people, it was the threat to this area that provoked their initial resistance to the very idea of the Olympics. Now that idea was to be turned into reality, the people on our walk – many already familiar with the area – took in these surroundings in the knowledge that they would be changed forever, and beyond all recognition on the other side of the High Street where the Olympic Park will be located.

The path curved again, and our party crossed a narrow bridge over the Prescott Channel, part of the waterway that runs between Three Mills Green and Lee Valley Park. The view become more verdant here, with half of the island that sits in the middle of Channelsea River resembling a jungle. I half expected to see Fitzcaraldo's boat float past blaring Caruso from its gramophone. "At least this bit will stay as it is, I imagine," Bob said, as we slowed to a halt and made way for a lone man wheeling his bike in the opposite direction. "I doubt anyone coming to the Olympics will walk down here," he added.

"Hmmm, they would get a bit of a surprise if they ended up on Manor Road heading towards Canning Town," I mused, picturing a tourist in a bright red windcheater with a large camera round their neck, consulting a map in confusion.

The man with the bike had now passed, nodding to several of us on his way in acknowledgement of fellow travellers. We walked on and, for a brief stretch, were protected from the rain by overhanging vegetation. As we made our way up a slight rise the Abbey Mills pumping station could be seen, flickering between tress and bushes to our left. Ahead of us as we reached a clearing was 'The Snail', a large piece of disused pumping machinery shaped like a snail shell. It was covered in graffiti. Nearby, wild flowers, like a burst of fireworks amid all the green, shimmied in the breeze on the river side of the muddy path. On the other side were tall daisies. Beyond was a wire fence and the flat, well kept lawn of the pumping station. Here we left the path and put foot on Abbey Road, walking along the pavement for a short stretch, before doubling back on ourselves where a tall electricity pylon towered above a green metal sign bearing the legend "The Greenway".

The Greenway is a nice name for the cycle and footpath that runs above the Northern Outfall Sewer. When I had first arrived in London fifteen years before, I would often use a short stretch of The Greenway. In the company of friends, I would join it by cutting up the embankment next to the railway bridge on Manor Road, walk along it until the point I had reached with Angry Bob and the rest of the curious on this rainy day, then walk down Abbey Road towards the Adam and Eve public house. Back then we simply referred to it as the sewer pipe. The pub was an oasis of calm in the concrete jungle, and approaching it on a darkening evening you could imagine you were out in the country. The principle reason for us choosing it as a watering hole, apart from saving on a longer walk into Stratford, was the inevitability of a lock-in and a quiet beer garden out back.

The pub was built amid the remains of Langthorne Abbey around 1732, with some of the Abbey's remains incorporated into the building. It was, according to the Essex Naturalist, "a rendezvous for fellows and wenches in the summer". Rebuilt in 1900, it was still described by its 1968 landlord as 'a summer house'. In the 1991 CAMRA guide to East London pubs, a simple one line entry records with mild disgust that no real ales are served. Three years later it was demolished to make way for the Jubilee Line railway depot. The depot now dominates a stretch of landscape that once housed Stratford Market and acted as something of an impromptu playground for local kids, who would get up to various adventures in and around the market stalls, the railway lines, the sewer pipe and the rivers. In a few short years the view was set to change again, with the opening of the Abbey Road DLR station.

As our group climbed the stone steps onto The Greenway, Bob commented on the architectural merits of the two pumping stations before us. One, the original Victorian version, a magnificent and ornate brick building with Moorish style chimneys, built between 1865 and 1868 and nicknamed "The Cathedral of Sewage". The other a bland, silver affair resembling a grain silo. The inside of the former contains a glut of cast-iron glory, testament to the wealth and taste of the Victorian age when form appears to have been held in as high regard as function. "They don't use the old building," a tall and thin man in a green windcheater informed me, just before one of the guides informed the whole group. "Except in emergencies," he added. "Extra pumps," he finished, somewhat elliptically, before getting to his point. "When that one reaches its sell-by-date," he nodded at the new pumping station, "they won't keep it standing will they? Bloody ugly thing." He looked at it with a curious expression and I noticed a raindrop bulbing itself on a curl of his fringe. I wanted to watch it drop off but it was stubbornly suspended and I was worried the man might get nervous at me staring at him like this. A couple of the party took snapshots with their cameras of Bazelgette's marvel, but nobody bothered to take a photograph of the new pumping station.

We continued our walk, spreading out now. Those of us to the rear could barely hear the two guides over the crunch of sandy gravel underfoot. The rain had now become a fine drizzle, but was just as relentless. Occasionally a cyclist or lone walker passed us. The guides ahead had stopped, and our party paused at a marker on the ground that indicated the presence of the Greenwich Meridian Line. It was only a green and yellow compass point logo, but this was enough for more cameras to appear. It is hard to imagine how you might render visible an imaginary line, but there was something bland and disappointing about this little logo. It didn't really do justice to the impact the meridian line has had on mankind's perception of time. As well as symbolising the point where the eastern and western hemispheres of the globe meet, the concept of the meridian line introduced standardised times. Noon wasn't now a vague time that shifted according to when the sun was overhead, but was given a fixed point. It wasn't the only such line in existence; the French, for example, had their own line which passed through Paris. But the Greenwich Meridian Line was the one used most often – by Britain and, significantly, the USA, where in 1884 a conference took place to decide which line was to become the standard. Votes were cast, and the British line won.

Meridian crossed, we continued our walk through the misty drizzle, the depthless white sky feeling like a giant, urban snow globe. Our party had split into different groups, some listening to the two young guides. We were approaching the point where The Greenway is bisected by Stratford High Street, a point Bob and I had passed earlier. On the other side we would be entering the territory of Bob's ire. Our journey until this point, one we had both undertaken many times before, had seen us walk through scenery that is under less threat of drastic change. On the other side of this busy road, the human impact of the Olympics would be somewhat different; the Olympic legacy there would begin with displacement.

Ever since 1749, when the Bow China Works was established on the East Side of the Lea, somewhere between Cook's Road and Marshgate Lane, there has been industry here. Free from the regulations of Metropolitan London and conveniently downwind of the City, dangerous, foul-smelling and polluting industry was attracted to the area in increasing numbers. The residues of the entire industrial revolution have been deposited in these soils, much of it to be uncovered in the excavations for the Olympic Park which, for the sake of a three week circus has brought an era to an end.

The traffic wasn't particularly heavy on the High Street, but sufficient to split our party into three groups as we crossed, the quickest and boldest making it over first. On the other side we walked westwards until we reached City Mill Lock on Blaker Road. Here we walked past the flats at Otter Close towards the Greenway once more, but instead of rejoining it, we descended a staircase that led us down closer to City Mill River. Walking through a low tunnel that took us under the Northern Outfall Sewer, and then under the Docklands Light Railway, we found ourselves in another hidden part of London. Here it was still and quiet. The water didn't move, algae fringing its edges. To our left, on the other side of the waterway, was the back of the Marshgate Lane industrial estate. It was ugly, and in stark contrast to the fecund greenery everywhere before it. This walk wasn't going to win any awards for beauty or gain National Heritage status, but there was something compelling about it. Despite the severe and often decrepit industrial architecture that constituted the human legacy on this once marshy land, the natural world that clung to these ancient waterways was somehow profound. It wasn't a man-made representation of nature within a city, like the great Victorian parks, but the last vestige of the natural history of this piece of land. And it had long been unknown to, and ignored by, the vast majority of this huge city's population.

We suddenly stopped, and as we grouped round our guides, one of them pointed to a huge corrugated shed, long enough to host the 100 metres sprint, on the other side of the river. "That's where the stadium is going to be," he said. We all stared and tried to imagine this view looking any different, but it was impossible. No artist impressions sprang to mind.

Slowly we continued our walk, our path taking us round a corner onto Marshgate Lane, affording a view in the other direction towards Carpenters Road. A guide pointed out which businesses inhabited the various buildings. He was unsure of some detail and consulted with another guide, a young woman. She couldn't shed any light on the matter, but the point was that all these businesses were going to disappear, some the victims of compulsory purchase orders.

Bob shook his head and let out a snort. The subject of relocating the businesses from this area was one that irked him to say the least. It was common knowledge that businesses felt they were being offered a raw deal in monetary compensation, much less than the market rate. Many also feared that relocation destinations would be so far from their customer base as to jeopardise their futures.

"We are all proud to be guardians of this dream," Bob muttered to no-one in particular, but he was looking back towards the area where the stadium would be located. Then he looked at me. "Yup," I agreed. Bob was using then Olympic Minister, Tessa Jowell's much-quoted line about the Olympics, from the re-celebration of winning the bid that had taken place the previous September. He spat on the ground and we moved on.

After following Marshgate Lane, home to many of the businesses that would be relocated by the LDA, we rejoined the narrow waterway path, this time alongside the Lea, and approached Old Ford. This point is where, according to historians, the Romans crossed the Lea. The name of the river comes from the Saxon *lygan* which means fast flowing, and depending on the tides and weather, the stone causeway they built could be a precarious crossing point. Although it was an area of strategic importance, overcoming a major obstacle on the way from London into the surrounding countryside and eventually to Colchester, there was no major settlement here.

It is believed to have been a spot where the practice of 'fulling of cloth' was carried out. This is a cleaning process, a stage of woollen cloth making. It involved walking on, or fulling, the cloth to get rid of dirt and impurities. The process once involved urine, but by medieval times fuller's earth was employed and the work was usually carried out in a water mill called a fulling mill. Wooden hammers took the place of human feet to cleanse the wool. If fulling did take place here, the surrounding area would have seen the wet lengths of cloth that had been cleaned, stretched out and suspended by hooks in frames called tenters. This is supposedly the origin of the phrase 'to be on tenterhooks' – literally being held in suspense.

What isn't in dispute is that the area was visited on at least three occasions by Samuel Pepys, who records the fact in his diaries. On June 2nd 1668 he records visiting Old Ford where he "walked in the fields, very pleasant, and sang: and so back again and drank at the Gun, at Mile End…"

And here, amidst the lush greenery, a strangely familiar house sat on the opposite bank. The scene was somewhat surreal. Less than 400 hundred metres away was one of London's uglier roads. A high-walled, noisy, industrial concrete strip carrying traffic towards the Blackwall Tunnel. Behind us was an area with a history of industry stretching back to the 18th century. All around us, stretching for several miles through all compass points, was the deprived urban heartland of London's industrial past, the East End. And yet here we were by a tranquil stretch of river, with trees and other greenery all around. Up ahead by the lock anglers sat patiently with rods arced like bamboo. And there sat a house with a garden leading to the river's edge.

"That's the Big Breakfast house," I heard one of our guides say to the head of our party.

And so it was. Bob emitted a derisory laugh that perfectly expressed his opinion of the breakfast time television programme that had run for ten years on Channel 4. It had been rumoured that the show's founder, Bob Geldof, was going to blow the house up on the day of the final programme, but this passed on 29th March 2002 without any explosions. The house familiar to TV viewers was built in 1946 to replace a terrace of cottages that were badly damaged by bombing in October 1940. These cottages had accommodated the lock keepers, and historical records offer glimpses of detail like flickers of light on a dark night.

In January 1909, for example, it was recorded that *"A new small wooden lobby for the lock keeper's use was being built to place on the centre pier between the locks, so as to enable the lock keepers to be on the pier day and night; and that the new gas lamps were a great improvement and made the working of the lock much safer"*. There also exists census records of the various lock keepers, walksmen and toll collectors. James Barton is recorded as lock keeper on 17th February 1824, but exactly six months later he is recorded as deceased. On an unspecified date in 1838, William Hare was discharged *"for frequently being absent and also for being drunk"*. Joseph Wybrew, transferred from Tottenham, was earning 28 shillings a week in February 1889 as toll collector and by 1891 was residing in Lock keepers lodge number 1. Five years later he suffered a fit and it was thought he wouldn't survive. However, he recovered and was expected to be back to work soon after. We can only assume he was, but in September of the same year he is recorded as deceased, leaving a 5 shillings a week pension to his widow who died five years later.

J W Lawrence was recorded as a collector in April 1896 and two years later asked the board if he could have a uniform similar to that worn by C N Crace at Limehouse. C Tween, who recorded this information, recommended that the request be granted as Lawrence was a good officer. Two years later his brother Edgar Joseph was appointed collector at 30 shillings a week.

On the 28th May 1912 James Judge saved one W Barrett from drowning. This wasn't the first time Judge had saved someone from such a fate. He was honoured by the Royal Humane Society for his endeavours, receiving 10 shillings and an Honorary Testimonial inscribed on parchment, which the Board framed at their own expense. One imagines this framed recognition of his life saving exploits hanging proudly on a wall in one of the cottages. In 1915 he was awarded a £3 war bonus.

The Great War was two years old when A Judge was appointed Lock keeper at 21 shillings a week. Mrs King, the wife of John King who had resigned for a civilian job with the Army Remount Depot in 1914, was required to vacate the Lock keepers house, presumably to make way for him. Soon after he asked to receive the same wage as his father, who was the other lock keeper at Old Ford. This seems to have been granted as his pay was increased to 25 shillings per week soon after the request in 1917. He earned a £2 war bonus at roughly the same time, but almost immediately is called to the Colours. In November 1919 it is recorded that he had returned to duty from military service, but just two months later his resignation is recorded and he joined the Metropolitan Police force. However, by March Judge was still residing in the cottage, and things appear to have taken a turn for the worse when he refused to leave, incurring the wrath of the Board who instigated legal proceedings. Judge handed over the key to the cottage in May, by which time there were no possessions left, presumably having been surrendered to the bailiffs. By the Autumn Judge had applied for permission for admission to the workhouse for himself and his family, and asked if the Board could provide accommodation. What happened to the job with the police is not recorded and we can only wonder if the sudden downward spiral in the life of Mr Judge had anything to do with his experiences in the war. We only know that his request for accommodation was not granted and by this time a new lock keeper by the name of Smith replaced him. Two years later he was dismissed, apparently after having trouble listening to the instructions of a collector called E J Lawrence. By this time the ex-Army Regular H J Haycroft had been working as lock keeper for two years. He was still in the job 25 years later in 1947, now earning the princely sum of £7.11.

In 2008, Denise Van Outen, one-time Big Breakfast presenter was signed up by Capital Radio to join another old Big Breakfast co-presenter, Johnny Vaughan. The contract was for three years with a reported salary of £1 million. This was still two years in the future as Bob and I gazed at the house on the other bank of the river before moving on, having fallen behind the others.

A pair of patient anglers sat like gnomes on the opposite bank as we walked by the lock. With the tranquil water and lush greenery, trees swaying in the breeze, it was hard to reconcile that this idyllic little scene lay at the geographical point where three of the poorest boroughs of London meet. The two anglers were hoping to catch their fish in Newham, while a few hundred yards to their right was Tower Hamlets, and behind them, Hackney. Poverty, of course, is nothing new to the East End.

In the last gasp of the 19th Century, Charles Booth decided to find out if the levels of poverty in the city were as severe as social reformers claimed. He found that it was actually much worse, and an exhaustive study that ran to 17 volumes and included coloured-coded poverty maps was the result. The eastern edge of one of these maps ends on a line that runs through Old Ford in Bow, bisecting Fairfield Road just where the railway lines pass over it. You can see Fairfield Works, nestled just below a cluster of streets, with Booth's colour-coding indicating it contained households in severe poverty (or 'chronic want' as he termed it), including Spring and Summer Street. The prostitutes living here, according to Booth, would ply their trade on nearby Old Ford and Roman Roads. The area is mentioned as far back as 1630 in a poem by John Taylor called 'At Bow'. Taylor, a waterman on the Thames at a time when London Bridge was the only crossing available to land lubbers, was perhaps more of a wit than a poet. He found the Green Goose Fair, held the Thursday after Pentecost, ideal material.

> *At Bow, the Thursday after Pentecost,*
> *There is a fair of green geese ready rost,*
> *Where, as a goose is ever dog cheap there,*
> *The sauce is over somewhat sharp and deare.*

A green goose was a young goose, but also contemporary slang for a cuckold or 'low woman', and Taylor wasted no time with subtlety in the verse, before going on to describe in unflattering terms the rowdy behaviour of the fair's crowds. Such bawdy licentiousness was eventually banned in the mid-nineteenth century, but it is hardly surprising to learn that prostitution was still a feature of the area, and one written about by Booth who accompanied members of the local constabulary on his walks round the locale. One long-limbed member of the law described the Polish jews as the worst, as they were wont to pester you up and down the street and even grab hold of you. Their 'ponces' were described as mostly foreign, usually Polish jews themselves, and it was a curiosity beyond measure that *"the more these men kick them about the more they like them."*[3] In describing the Jews as central to the problem of prostitution, and responsible for the worst of it, the officer was perhaps voicing the widely held prejudices on Jewish immigration. Bromley and Bow M.P. Captain Colomb was quoted in the East End News in 1888 thus; *"I object to England with its overcrowded population, being made a human ashpit for the refuse population of the world"*.[4] The wife of the main character in Margaret Harkness' contemporary novel *Out of Work*, a carpenter moved to London from the country, voices sentiments typical of the time: *"Why should they come here I'd like to know? London ain't what it used to be; it's just like a foreign city. The food ain't English; the talk ain't English. Why should all them foreigners come here to take our food out of our mouths, and live on victuals we*

---

3 Life and labour of the people in London (Charles Booth)

4 East End News – February 21st 1888

wouldn't give to pigs?"[5] Blaming foreigners has always been a convenient excuse, especially to avoid looking at difficult truths. There was a belief amongst the population of the East End that Jack the Ripper had to be a Jew, for an Englishman couldn't be responsible for such hideous crimes.

Poor as the area was, there was plenty of trade amid all this overcrowding, including many a sailor venturing north. Saturday nights saw an influx of drinkers when the public houses of Stratford closed half an hour earlier than their Bow counterparts, provoking their customers into a mini-pilgrimage down Stratford High Street and over Bow Bridge to continue their revelry.

A further indication that these were mean streets returns us to Fairfield Road and the women who worked at the Bryant & May factory. Inspector Carter, who accompanied Booth on one of his walks on June 1st 1897, tells him that: *"Bryant and May have a rough set of girls. There are 2000 of them when they are busy. Rough and rowdy but not bad morally. They fight with their fists to settle their differences, not in the factory as that is forbidden, but in the streets when they leave work in the evening. A ring is formed, they fight like men and are not interfered with by the police."*[6] Whether Carter had any kind of opinion on the conditions of work for these women is not recorded, but Booth himself refers to the match making industry in one of his volumes. Although

---

5 Out of Work, Margaret Harkness, 1988

6 Life and labour of the people in London (Charles Booth)

he notes that the girls working in the East End are *"more cleanly than they used to be, thus greatly diminishing the danger of necrosis – the terrible 'phossy jaw'"*, he adds that this improvement doesn't offer a clear *"guarantee against the disease where yellow phosphorous is used, and it is used in all except "safety" matches."*

Booth was writing over a decade after the famous Match Girl Strike, a landmark in the history of the trade union movement. The chain of events that led to the strike began with a speech made by Clementina Black, daughter of a solicitor father and successful portrait painting mother. A friendship with Karl Marx's daughter Eleanor led to her joining the Women's Trade Union League. In June 1888 she gave a speech highlighting the conditions of the workers in the Bryant & May factory, where pay was poor and further reduced by draconian fines for insignificant offences such as dropping pieces of matchwood on the floor. In the audience was journalist Annie Besant who, suitably outraged, decided to visit the factory and talk to some of the women who worked there. It was the resulting article in her newspaper, *The Link*, that was to stir up the hornets nest. With the title *White Slavery in London* it is clear what outrage was contained in the article, which concluded with a plea to boycott Bryant & May's matches. With the angry words hitting their target, Bryant & May were stung into action, and tried to force their workers to sign a declaration that they were happy with working conditions. A group of women refused, and the company's response was to sack one of the dissenters.

Outraged, a group of the women threw down their work and the strike had begun. Some of the girls had visited Annie Besant in Fleet Street, and along with Herbert Burrows she dedicated the next two weeks to helping the strikers, raising strike funds, writing articles and holding pubic meetings. A Matchmaker's Union was established and many high profile figures expressed support, though *The Times* was one of the publications who blamed Besant for agitating, conveniently side-stepping any issues of poor pay and conditions, not to mention the scandal of "phossy jaw". Mr. F. Bryant also chose to ignore the health hazard within his factory when interviewed on July 14th by the East London Observer. In an attempt at damage limitation, he appeared to bend the truth considerably when it came to detailing average wages. No mention was made of the system of fines and long hours of work. He also considered himself *"as much a philanthropist, and perhaps more so, than some of those people who write or talk of the rights of the working classes, but do nothing for them."*[7] No mention was made either of the statue that Bryant erected to show his fawning admiration of William Gladstone.

'*In order that his workgirls might have the privilege of contributing, he stopped 1s. each out of their wages, and further deprived them of half-a-day's work by closing the factory, "giving them a holiday"'*. If you can imagine being given a holiday that effectively reduces your wages, and having up to a quarter of your weeks wages docked for the privilege

7 East London Observer no.1602 (Saturday, July 14th, 1988)

of being able to say you contributed to a statue in honour of David all-in-it-together Cameron, then you will probably empathise with the righteous anger that Bryant engendered in his girls by forcing them to honour the then prime minister in such a fashion.

Within four weeks the strike was called off as the strikers were granted what they demanded: sacked workers were reinstated, many of the fines were abolished and pay and conditions were revised for the better. However, it would be another thirteen years before Bryant & May stopped using yellow phosphorous, despite the fact that the Salvation Army had opened a factory at Old Ford in 1891 where only harmless red phosphorous was used, and workers were paid a much better rate.

So, as Booth was to note in 1903, the risk of contracting "phossy jaw" had not been eliminated. The mixers, dippers and boxers in the match factories, exposed to the fumes of phosphorous were most likely to suffer within five years on the job. It was a painful and gruesome affliction, beginning with toothache and leading to disintegration of the jaw and rotting of bone tissue, accompanied by a discharge that smelt particularly rank. Left untreated it could lead to brain damage or death by organ failure. Removal of the jaw was often the only way to save a life if the disease had taken hold.

1888 wasn't a great year for the women of Bow and its western neighbours. As well as exploitation in factories, grinding poverty and mistreatment at the hands of pimps, there was a further reminder of how cheap life was in the shape of the horrific Whitechapel murders. Five are believed to be the work of Jack the Ripper, taking place between August 31st and November 9th 1888. What is less well known is that there were another six murders over little more than a twelve month period in Whitechapel alone.

Though social reformers like Besant and Clementina had been highlighting the conditions in the East End for some time, and others such as Charles Booth and Sylvia Pankhurst would continue to do so, it appears that the murders galvanised public opinion, forcing the Victorian authorities to address the problems that made the Ripper's brutal reign so apparently easy. George Bernard Shaw, scenting a whiff of hypocrisy on behalf of the media who had previously been disdainful of the East End poor, even as lately as the Bryant & May strike, was moved to voice his opinion in The Star newspaper in September 1888. "Private enterprise has succeeded where Socialism failed. Whilst we conventional Social Democrats were wasting our time on education, agitation and organisation, some independent genius has taken the matter in hand, and by simply murdering and disembowelling four women, converted the proprietary press to an inept sort of communism."[8]

The funeral procession of one of the victims, Catharine Eddowes, was to pass through Bow and Stratford to what is now called City of London cemetery in Manor Park, where she was buried in consecrated ground. This detail did not go unnoticed, as it was considered unacceptable for women of her

8 The Star - September 24th 1888

character. The same treatment was not afforded another victim, Elisabeth Stride, who was buried in unconsecrated ground in East London cemetery. A third victim, Mary Ann Nichols was also buried in City of London cemetery, her body being laid to rest in close proximity to that of Eddowes. Both their graves were unmarked until 1996 when authorities erected a bronze plaque serving their memory – but mis-spelling their names, a fault of an original mistake in the 1888 registers.

The last known victim, Mary Jane Kelly, was buried on 19th November 1888, ten days after her murder. The Walthamstow and Leyton Guardian recorded the event.

"The distance from Shoreditch Church to the cemetery at Leytonstone by road is about six miles, and the route traversed was, Hackney-road, Cambridge-heath, Whitechapel-road, and Stratford. In the Whitechapel-road the crowds on each side [of] the roadway were very great, and there was a considerable amount of emotion manifested. The appearance of the roadway throughout the whole journey was remarkable, owing to the hundreds of men and women who escorted the coffin on each side, and who had to keep up a sharp trot in many places. But the crowd rapidly thinned away when, getting into the suburbs, the car and coaches broke into a trot. The cemetery was reached at two o'clock. The Rev. Father Columban, with two acolytes, and a cross bearer, met the body at the door of the little chapel of St. Patrick, and the coffin was carried at once to a grave in the north-eastern corner. Barnett and the poor woman who had accompanied the funeral knelt on the cold clay by the side

of the grave, while the service was read by Father Columban. The coffin was incensed, lowered, and then sprinkled with holy water, and the simple ceremony ended. The floral ornaments were afterwards raised to be placed upon the grave, and the filling-up was completed in a few moments, and was watched by a small crowd of people. There was a very large concourse of people outside the gates, who were refused admission until after the funeral was over."

After the service the mourners, Joseph Barnett, chief among them, went to the Birbeck Tavern which still stands today. The cemetery, Saint Patrick's, can be seen if you journey on the Central Line between Leytonstone and Leyton.

The exact location of Kelly's grave, being unmarked, was a matter for some confusion after some of the cemetery land was reclaimed in 1941. Cemetery super-intendent John Sears was able to clear up the mystery after some research, and also provided a marker using a disused headstone from the 1890s, which he engraved with a simple inscription to her memory. Within hours, however, it had been vandalised, and so even in death, life remains cheapened.

As we walked back along the River Lea, the sky still the colour of dirty dishwater, the shiny new future promised by the London Bid Team seemed a long way off. We passed under the DLR as one of the driverless trains clunked and squealed high above our heads on the way to Canary Wharf, the previous great building project of London. The DLR line to Stratford is symbolic: an umbilical cord from a controversial regeneration project of the past to one in the future. The East End had been in planners' minds for a long time. As early as 1980 this vision, replete with the scent of filthy lucre, had surfaced on celluloid in John Mackenzie's gangster film *The Long Good Friday*, starring Bob Hoskins. Land in this part of London could be had for cheap compared to other parts of the city. With industry dying during the seventies and eighties, it was obvious that this now underused land was ripe for something. In a sense the Olympics was just gatecrashing the party, then practically making out that it was the very reason for the party in the first place.

Our young guides, in their matching burgundy fleeces with Olympic Bid logo, had maintained their chipper attitude throughout our journey, despite the rain, wind and greyness. They had offered tidbits of history and answered questions. But when pressed for their views on the Olympics themselves, their replies had a default, scripted feel. At one point when I asked an awkward question about Stratford City, it was ignored: a line about 'legacy', already the planted buzzword, was given by way of reply. I pressed but to no avail: they had been well trained. They were either worried that somehow any negative thoughts about the Olympics they expressed would be discovered and they would lose their positions, or they didn't have opinions on the subject. It was like walking around a drab, unexciting version of *Westworld*, and the only thing that would liven it up would be for a Yul Brenner *Walk The Olympic Park* robot to malfunction and run amok, chasing us back through the Bow Back Rivers, rifle in hand, destroying the carefully crafted illusion that had been presented.

CHAPTER 3

Dream Machine

This age must have more fools than the last: for certainly fools only are most taken with shows and outsides
                                        Daniel Defoe (1726)

Three teenage boys are walking slowly through Westfield shopping centre's main curving thoroughfare like children who have entered an enchanted forest. Their steps are slow, almost tentative, and they keep looking up and from side to side, eyes wide open with wonder as if they can't quite believe they are here. Can't believe that *it* is here. It is like the mothership in *Close Encounters of the Third Kind*. Huge, shiny and gleaming, it has descended into their manor like Christmas Day appearing unexpectedly in June for a six year old.

It is two weeks after the opening of Europe's largest shopping centre and, with the novelty some way from wearing off, crowds of young people are still rolling up to gawp at the dream machine – the kind of consumer spectacle hitherto reserved for the posher folk up west. It sparkles with light reflected off polished white surfaces and huge glass windows. Video screens flicker overhead. Colour bursts out like fireworks from shop window displays and interiors. Everything is XXL. Everyone is dressed up as if on a first date, as if the shopping centre itself holds them in its gaze, sizing them up, judging them. They are seduced – and they are not the first. This dance has been going on for a hundred years or more.

Not everyone has fallen for the siren song of this consumer behemoth. The dissenting voices may not have been given much publicity, but the complaints are familiar. They include the concerns of retail guru Mary Portas, who published an independent review in December 2011 analysing the very real threat to traditional high streets from mega-malls and online shopping. But the truth is that our relationship with retail has often been an uneasy one. In early modern England the reasons for this uneasiness were threefold, comprising moral anxieties over luxury; economic anxieties concerning overseas trade and the balance of payments; and anxiety about shopkeepers themselves, who were seen with mistrust – particularly when they first made the step away from the market stall, which was open and easy to regulate, and into the closed spaces of shops.[9]

---

9 Nancy Cox, *'Beggary of the Nation': Moral, economic and political attitudes to the retail sector in the early modern period*, contained within, *A Nation of Shopkeepers, Five Centuries of British Retailing* ed. John Benson & Laura Ugolni, I.B. Tauris, 2003. p 26

The idea of luxury as dangerous goes back to Greek times, and with added spin from Christianity it became regarded as sinful, linked to Eve's desires and the consequent fall of man. Thus, luxury as a concept was neatly bound up in the concept of femininity. It is no surprise then that the retail sector targeted women and proceeded to fetishise the shopping experience accordingly. The very things that the Christian moralists were afraid of, things like luxury and seduction, were among the tools used by the arcades and then the department stores of the 19th century. French writer Emile Zola portrays this world vividly in his novel *The Ladies' Paradise*, in which a department store based on the Bon Marché in Paris is used as a metaphor for the capitalist world of late 19th century Europe. 'Mouret's sole passion was the conquest of Woman. He wanted her to be queen in his shop; he had built this temple for her in order to hold her at his mercy. His tactics were to intoxicate her with amorous attention, to trade on her desires'[10]

Brian Nelson, writing in the introduction of the Oxford 1995 edition of the book, refers to the department store as a "precision-made dream machine" and notes that the women in the novel are unwitting victims. When she first arrives in Paris the book's heroine, Denise, sees a window display that uses mirrors to reflect into infinity a row of mannequins that have not heads, but price tags. It is a symbol of women losing their heads in an ecstatic orgy of

---

10 Emile Zola, *The Ladies Paradise*, Oxford University Press, 1995.

consumption. They have surrendered themselves and now exist only as mindless consumers.[11]

What the main protagonist, Mouret, has succeeded in doing is creating desire where none existed. This was what the grand department stores of Europe achieved, establishing in the process the version of consumer society that is familiar to us today. At the time, however, many people were alarmed by the phenomenon.

The Big Bazaar is as yet but an incident, an eccentricity in London, but Paris it wholly possesses and dominates. It rears its brazen head at every other street corner; its multitudinous doors engulf half the retail commerce of the capital. It is in the Paris tradesman's eyes the blight and bug-bear which the Co-operative Stores are to certain London shopkeepers. He wails that the Bazaar is killing the shop in the first city of shops in the world, and if M.Zola be an authority, the "Bonheur des Dames" ought to be conclusive in the matter. Yet the system is hardly fifteen years old. As for the "Bonheur des Dames," it is the Bazaar seen through a kaleidoscope, just as his "Ventre de Paris" is the Central Market transformed into a phantasmagoria. The real "Bonheur des Dames" is a much more humdrum as well as a much mightier business. Its basis is the basis of all evil – the temptation of women. Not the

---

11 Brian Nelson, Introduction to, The Ladies Paradise, Emile Zola, Oxford University Press, 1995. p ix-xx

simple, trite temptation of a window cleverly 'dressed' and cheaply ticketed, but a slow seduction, which operates in this way. The customer enters the Bazaar to buy a pair of three-franc candlesticks, because she really wants them, and because they are really cheap. But before reaching her candlesticks she must pass by fifty counters where precious stuffs, muffs, scented gloves, fans – a myriad things wanted as much as the candlesticks – are being sold "for nothing." Curled dandies, correct in costume as the dandy diplomatist she danced with last night, beg her to look, to inspect; nobody dreams of asking her to buy; and if she is only weak enough to spend thirty sous on a cravat she had no original intention of purchasing, the Bazaar has scored a real victory. She will come to buy a bonnet, and stay to buy a mantle. She will be tempted by a bargain in furs after paying for her summer fan. And she will argue with a semblance of logic that her extravagance is economy. The Monster Bazaar can afford to sell more cheaply than the little shop of old time; even husbands are compelled to recognise the fact. They forget that the modest merchant with his two counters has but a poor show wherewith to seduce his customers; sells fans and only fans; furs alone, not furs, bonnets, gloves, lace, boots, and sleeve links, scents and carpets, under one roof.[12]

The panic that these department stores induced in certain quarters was interestingly still centred on the moral

---

12 *The Standard*, Friday, December 19, 1884.

anxieties about luxury. Quite what well-heeled ladies had to
fret about is something which only the repressed Victorian
mind might find worrying – or rather the minds of Victorian
men, who clearly felt threatened by the newfound freedom
of their womenfolk. The only other concern that was deemed
noteworthy was that of the smaller shopkeepers, though it is
hard to dredge up much sympathy for them. After all, weren't
these the very shopkeepers who had decided that they were
too good for the open-air markets, and retreated to the closed
shops that the working classes rightly mistrusted?

Daniel Defoe, whose take on trade and retail was
full of jingoistic hyperbole, was perhaps one of the first
commentators to describe in writing the art of the con that
unscrupulous shopkeepers engaged in with the unwitting. He
displayed contempt for those taken-in, particularly those who
fell under the spell of lavish retail fittings.

*It is a modern custom, and wholly unknown to our ancestors,
who yet understood trade, in proportion to the trade they
carried on, as well as we do, to have tradesmen lay out two-
thirds of their fortune in fitting up their shops.*

*By fitting up, I do not mean furnishing their shops
with wares and goods to sell – for in that they came up to us
in every particular, and perhaps went beyond us too – but
in painting and gilding, fine shelves, shutters, boxes, glass
doors, sashes, and the like, in which, they tell us now, it is a
small matter to lay out two or three hundred pounds, nay,
five hundred pounds, to fit up a pastry-cook's, or a toy shop.*

The first inference to be drawn from this must necessarily be, that this age must have more fools than the last: for certainly fools only are most taken with shows and outsides.[13]

One wonders what Defoe might have made of Westfield and its highly polished surfaces and flickering video displays enticing the 'fools' nearly three hundred years later. And if they have no money, what else is there to do but admire the view? When Sir Philip Green was quoted as commenting, "There must be a lot of people out of work here," during Westfield's well choreographed opening ceremony, he wasn't just revealing an ignorance about reality outside the bubble of privilege; he also unwittingly drew attention to the achilles heel of the whole enterprise.

Weeks later it was still clear that a large proportion of visitors to Westfield were decidedly time rich and cash poor. To be fair, the point had been made earlier in the year during the London riots. All that summer looting proved that just because a good proportion of the youth had no money or access to credit didn't mean they were going to pass up an opportunity to demonstrate their consumerist instincts.

It was a signifier that hadn't gone missed by Mary Portas. Talking about the fallout from our extended consumer binge, she sees the shift in our values as the key issue, arguing that we no longer value the right things,

---

13 Daniel Defoe, *The Complete English Tradesman*, 1726

such as the place we live and the people who live alongside us.[14] In our hunger to consume, human interaction has become diminished. Though the blame for this can't be laid entirely at the door of our passion for shopping, it is nonetheless in the shops that many of the tools of the digital age that increasingly shape human interaction, such as mobile phones, can be found. In the same report she later comments on the social and economic impact of the dominance of retail giants, highlighting the fact that money spent at a retailer with a localised supply chain has a much greater domestic economic impact than money spent in a supermarket or national chain.[15]

This is an interesting statement from someone who acts as a consultant to the Westfield group. Even a cursory inspection of the stakeholders involved in the project reveals that local ties are virtually non-existent. Westfield, who own half the retail development, are Australian. The remaining 50% is owned by a Dutch, and a Canadian insurance firm. A list of individual businesses in the complex reveals American, Canadian, French, German, Irish, Italian, Japanese, Korean, South African, Swedish, and Swiss ownerships, besides British. Sometimes these individual businesses are owned by bigger organisations, such as the Spanish Inditex group who own Bershka, Pull and Bear and Zara, or The Carlyle Group, the US

---

14 Mary Portas, *The Portas Review: An independent review into the future of our high streets*, December 2011. p13

15 Ibid. p31

private equity group who own Boots and Holland & Barrett amongst others. As Dorothy said, *"I've a feeling we're not in Kansas any more."*

Wherever we are, it is a long way from Defoe's Complete English Tradesman. And yet some of the same underlying rules remain.

The making false lights, sky-lights, trunks, and other contrivances, to make goods look to be what they are not, and to deceive the eye of the buyer, these are all so many brass shillings washed over, in order to deceive the person who is to take them, and cheat him of his money; and so far these false lights are really criminal, they are cheats in trade, and made to deceive the world; to make deformity look like beauty, and to varnish over deficiencies; to make goods which are ordinary in themselves appear fine; to make things which are ill made look well; in a word, they are cheats in themselves, but being legitimated by custom, are become a general practice; the honestest tradesmen have them, and make use of them; the buyer knows of it, and suffers himself to be so imposed upon; and, in a word, if it be a cheat, as no doubt it is, they tell us that yet it is a universal cheat, and nobody trades without it; so custom and usage make it lawful, and there is little to be said but this, Si populus vult decepi, decipiatur—if the people will be cheated, let them be cheated, or they shall be cheated.[16]

---

16 Daniel Defoe, *The Complete English Tradesman*, 1726

It is a few weeks after Westfield has opened its doors for custom before I dare to venture there during the day. Having seen how narrow the main, crescent-shaped parade is, visiting on a Saturday is not even a consideration. Years of struggling from one end of the old Stratford Shopping Centre to the other has seen to that. Early Sunday morning is chosen instead, and I get to see more of the interior.

The demographic is different from the mid-week early evening crowd. The curious are much older and it is obvious that the vast majority are not from Stratford, or even Newham. These are the day trippers, dipping a toe in the water. They walk slowly and stare. Some seem oddly awe-struck, as if they have never before experienced shopping. It is difficult to gauge how much of their excitement is down to the sort of tricks that Defoe identified in the 18th century, and how much was simply down to novelty. The two combined add up to a spectacle that has drawn them here like moths to a flame. Some, who are less interested in the spectacle and more interested in consuming, are sizing up this new beast, making mental comparisons to Bluewater and Lakeside, weighing up whether it will merit further attention in the future.

At various points the walls of shops are broken by areas of seating, with giant picture windows affording teasing views of the Olympic park on one side and what will be the Olympic village on the other. Internally these are the only areas where people can gather, pause from shuffling along the polished floors, pause from spending money. Westfield is no place for the *flâneur*. There is no real escape from the imperative to consume. Sure, you can stop at one of the eating establishments on the lower ground floor and watch this world go by, but the food on offer is fast and doesn't want you to linger, and all there is to look at are the shops opposite and the people shuffling by. Suddenly it feels like a trap. Deviating from the designated route is not an option as the only exits either lead to more shops outside or areas that don't invite curiosity, such as the station and the car park. Outside is better, but not by much. As yet there is, obviously, no lived-in feel, but it's hard to see that there ever will be.

By midday the various floors are becoming busier. Crowds begin to gather round the central balconies that offer views of the floors below. A commotion is occurring outside a card shop, where security guards and a woman in a blue suit are moving with a sense of purpose that the shoppers lack. It is a stage managed event designed to gather a crowd to the shop, which will open its doors with the promise of a special offer that in fact wont be very special at all, but the crowd's gaze is sucked towards the show. It doesn't take much. After all, the shops, for all their dazzle, are static and the shoppers just glide along as if on rails. Any movement that isn't aimless is bound to catch the eye, just as any such movement attracts the eyes of the security guards and cameras. No one runs here – that privilege is reserved for security and those they might chase. Rapid movement represents suspicious activity, wrongness, a flickering distraction that interrupts the dream state and brings people back to the present moment and a level of consciousness that is unwelcome.

George Romero nailed it with his 1978 film, Dawn of the Dead, the bulk of which sees the main protagonists seeking refuge in a shopping mall full of zombies. 'What are they doing? Why do they come here?' asks one character, watching the zombie horde shuffling around on the floor below. Her companion replies, 'Some kind of instinct. Memory of what they used to do. This was an important place in their lives.' The gang of four survivors manage to secure a safe area of the mall in which to hole-up, and it includes access to a department store. Once free from danger, they are able to indulge in a mini orgy of consumption. We see all four wandering around the shops taking what they fancy. They even furnish their accommodation in the store room, but as they realise they are caught in a trap that offers only mindless consumption and no freedom, they make the decision to bust out, with predictable zombie-splattering consequences. Romero paints in broad strokes and it is easy, over three decades later, to point out a lack of subtlety. However, there is no denying the simple power of the message. It is a brilliant metaphor.

The brief distraction outside the card shop is over, and by now Westfield is rapidly filling up. The music being pumped into the atmosphere raises its tempo. At this point, as there aren't any shops my partner or I want or need to visit, there is no reason to remain. Outside the fresh air and lack of walls and ceiling is a welcome relief, but the shops out here just offer an upmarket version of the same essential narrative. Lifestyle is everywhere, but life itself is elsewhere and it is time to return to it.

Our mental image of shopkeepers is as quaint as that we hold of farms (the one with a few happy cows and sheep, a couple of pigs, a scattering of chickens, a red tractor and a barn). At worst our shopkeeper might be curmudgeonly and mean, but he is a British institution, so much so that even Napoleon commented on him as representing our whole nation. The Frenchman's quote, however, was borrowed from Adam Smith. 'To found a great empire for the sole purpose of raising up a people of customers may at first sight appear a project fit only for a nation of shopkeepers. It is, however, a project altogether unfit for a nation of shopkeepers; but extremely fit for a nation whose government is influenced by shopkeepers.' [17]

The shopkeepers, however, seem to have disappeared from view. Only the shopping remains.

Despite a well-greased publicity machine, Westfield's presence in Stratford wasn't entirely free from voices of concern. As the opening day approached, the fate of the old shopping centre on the other side of the Great Eastern Road was a topic of debate that fleetingly made an appearance in the media coverage. Lest anyone get too concerned about Stratford Shopping Centre, it is worth remembering that it was the Westfield of its day, landing like the house in some alternative Wizard of Oz, killing not the Wicked Witch of the

---

17 Adam Smith, *The Wealth of Nations*, 1776

East but a significant part of the original shopping heart of East London – Angel Lane.

This was the lane where Joan Littlewood and the Theatre Workshop regulars used to eat breakfast, where Brendan Behan used to drink and Harry H Corbett used to stroll in the long coat and boots that would later become famous with his character in *Steptoe & Son*. It was the lane where the Beatles rode on horseback, and where the local market was. In the late nineteenth century the pavements outside the small lock-up shops were hemmed in by costermonger barrows. You can see it briefly in Joan Littlewood's film *Sparrows Can't Sing*, in the scene where James Booth skips and dances beside Barbara Windsor as she pushes a pram along the pavement.

In 1893 there were butchers, but no bakers. You could buy tripe at number 8 or eel pie from Edward Varney at 32. A few doors down William Foster could offer you ham and beef. If it was fish you wanted, then there were six establishments serving your needs – fishmongers, fish vendors and fish salesmen. If you didn't fancy your eel in a pie then you could get it stewed at 46, while Herbert Dutton could provide you with a hat at number 60. But then so could Robert Field over the road. Samuel Nash sold leather, Alfred Cavalier dealt in corn and Jas Butcher could sort you out for tobacco and snouts. Thomas Mardon, at number 4, the Broadway end of the lane, would sell you some meat for your cat. He was listed in the directory as a purveyor of horseflesh.[18] A bit further up was the Danish Dairy Company. You could get your hair cut on Angel Lane, stop for coffee or sit in the cocoa rooms at number 14. Herbalists, confectioners, corn and flour merchants, drapers, clothiers, tool-makers, beer retailers, greengrocers, florists, clog makers and watch repairers – all of them were here.

It was still bustling in the 1960s, but by 1974 one whole half of it – the half teeming with commerce and life, with eating, drinking, singing and wisecracking – was gone, along with the streets that fed into it. Only the Theatre Royal remained, defiant and still standing thanks to the determined efforts of

---

18 Henry Mayhew wrote about this, and its relationship with the slaughtering trade in his famous study of London.

"The horse to be slaughtered has his mane clipped as short as possible (on account of the hair, which is valuable). It is then blinded with a piece of old apron smothered in blood, so that it may not see the slaughterman when about to strike. A pole-axe is used, and a cane, to put an immediate end to the animal's sufferings. After the animal is slaughtered, the hide is taken off, and the flesh cut from the bones in large pieces. These pieces are termed, according to the part from which they are cut, hind-quarters, forequarters, cram-bones, throats, necks, briskets, backs, ribs, kidney pieces, hearts, tongues, liver and lights. The bones (called "racks" by the knackers) are chopped up and boiled, in order to extract the fat, which is used for greasing common harness, and the wheels of carts and drags, &c. The bones themselves are sold for manure. The pieces of flesh are thrown into large coppers or pans, about nine feet in diameter and four feet deep. Each of these pans will hold about three good-sized horses. Sometimes two large brewers' horses will fill them, and sometimes as many as four "poor" cab-horses may be put into them. The flesh is boiled about an hour and 20 minutes for a "killed" horse, and from two hours to two hours and 20 minutes for a dead horse (a horse dying from age or disease)." One can imagine that the aroma in the air near a knackers' yard was not pleasant. Henry Mayhew, *London Labour and the London Poor*; 1851, 1861-2

Gerry Raffles. Stratford Shopping Centre stood in its place, shoe-horned into the space that was once so full of life.

But if the Angel Lane shops vanished, the market somehow survived. In a way, you could say that they built the shopping centre around it, though strictly speaking it was no longer occupying the path of the old lane. The pitches were now on the main thoroughfare of the shopping centre, running from just beyond it's central hub towards the Great Eastern Road entrance, in a bent line that cuts roughly past where 'The Shoot' used to be.

Keith Lee, an amiable man whose father was on the market before him, has had his florist stall at one end of this indoor market for 25 years. I spoke to him late one afternoon as the other stalls were closing up around him, and he reckoned that only two pitches of the current market originate from Angel Lane. He didn't think there were that many stalls on Angel Lane, perhaps 12, maybe as many as 20. He rubbed his chin as he tried to remember.

"There were more stalls on the Broadway," he told me, and looking in that direction swept his arm back and forth to indicated the length of the market that no longer exists. "There must have been about 60 stalls. They stretched all the way down to the junction." I told him about a photograph I had seen in the Newham Archives, showing the High Street in the early nineteen hundreds with barrows lining the pavements amid delivery trikes from a shop called Maples.

"They used to wheel the barrows all the way down there," Keith said, hefting an imaginary barrow to indicate the weight, and the effort it must have taken. "They grew the stuff, out in Essex, and it was for Covent Garden. But they would stop overnight in Stratford, and some of them would sell so much here that they never made it to Covent Garden and just went back."

Keith explained that his father had told him about these days and I could sense a bit of wonderment in his eyes, thinking back to a time when the markets were as widespread as the shops are now. There must have been a chaotic bustle on the main thoroughfares of Stratford back then. People would have shared the roads and streets with horse drawn carts and carriages, omnibuses and trams. Market stalls lined up opposite shops with broad awnings and outdoor displays on the already crowded pavements. The barrows would have stretched down the high street towards Burford Road, the public entrance to Stratford fruit and vegetable market, which ran alongside Stratford Market Station and opened in 1879. The Hackney Gazette reported it as consisting of 'light large and lofty warehouses erected in one row; each warehouse being 60 feet in length, making 480 feet in all. The width of each warehouse is 50 feet; half of that width being platformed over. The remaining 25 feet is devoted to two rows of sidings side by side covered with an iron roof 23 feet from the ground for trucks to stand opposite the platform of each warehouse and deal with the expected large traffic in mangold wurtzel, carrot, hay straw, coal, &c.'[19]

Owned by the Great Eastern Railway Company, and situated next to the Borough Theatre, the market was part of a High Street much busier than the dual-carriageway-like incarnation of today. Twenty years later the West Ham Guardian painted a vivid picture of the day-to-day bustle of the market.

On the left of the approach is a factory towering high above the surrounding buildings, while the right is dotted with a miscellaneous collection of shops, packed full of all kinds of fruit and vegetables, crates of oranges predominating. Upon emerging into the market proper, the visitor is confronted with a long covered grove with a platform on either side, backed by spacious dull-looking warehouses loaded, from time to time, with every description of vegetables, and in the summer, with all sorts of fruit. At the rear of either line of sheds, metals run along from the roadway, and here, at an early hour, truck after truck discharges its cargo, soon to be consumed by the inhabitants of Greater London. It is 7.30 a.m., and everywhere bustle and activity reign, no place being found for a loafer. From one end of the covered way to the other, greengrocers' carts and waggons of every conceivable size and shape, are backed against the platforms, and seated at a desk above the salesman

---

19 *Hackney Gazette*, 4th October 1879

is disposing of his wares. Gradually the vehicles grow full, the load including cabbages, cauliflowers, rhubarb, onions, oranges, apples, and tomatoes, and the pile of eatables is tightly corded to the vehicle, to prevent them being thrown off by the swaying of the van. But before the tradesmen quit the market, at least no small proportion of them repair to the coffee stall stationed at the end of the grove. It is no warm job moving about hereon a cold, raw, morning, and the trader is glad to regale himself with a cup of "coffee and two doorsteps". Having thus refreshed himself he will then proceed home with his load, arriving back at about the hour many people are getting their breakfast. The procession of heavily laden carts which leaves the market between eight and nine is a sight well worth seeing, and only the citizen who has witnessed it, and visited the market, can adequately realise the amount of labour entailed in furnishing him with wholesome fruit and vegetables.[20]

There is an honesty about a market that has always appealed to the working classes. Whether there is haggling or not, the exchange between seller and buyer is much less open to trickery and deceit; any persuasion is down to the oratory skill of the stall-holder, or perhaps the artistic ability present in the stalls' display. Quality, value and integrity are what the shopper looks for on the market, and the watchful public can spot any underhand business. It is no surprise that the modern

---

20 *West Ham Guardian*, April 22, 1899

con of selling gullible customers shoddy, or even worthless, goods requires a shop-front.[21]

When it comes to shops, it isn't about where the money goes: it is about who it goes to. When shops were small and independent, the shopkeeper was visible. Shopping was a sociable experience, a local news outlet of gossip and opinion. The hard graft of the owners could be seen and recognised, and the whole exchange happened on a regular basis that only stopped if the shopper, or the shopkeeper, moved on or passed away.

Before the rise of the supermarkets all food shopping involved trips to the greengrocers, who would talk to you as they filled the brown paper bags of fruit, twirled them and twisted the ends. Depending on their mood, a bit extra might find its way into your shopping bag; weights could just be a rough idea, instead of standardised and unshifting, sealed

---

21 This con involves a gang using a temporary residence in a shop, usually on a busy street, such as Oxford Street. A hawker, using a microphone and speakers to project his voice out onto the street is positioned inside the shop at a high counter laden with goods and a crowd gathers on the pavement. Stooges are usually present as well as the necessary muscle to deal with any disgruntlement. Unwitting customers caught up in the promise of a bargain are hustled into paying up front for a growing stack of items that are dispatched to them in bin liners. Once enough people have thus been taken in the shop doors are usually closed and anyone discovering that the items in their goody bag aren't quite what they thought they were when they were parting with their cash have to deal with customer relations in the shape of the burly muscle men. The whole scam of course operates within the small holes that riddle the law like a cheese. It is a variant of the 'Mock Auction' that Dickens' described in his *Dictionary of London* in 1879

in plastic and cling-film. And if the proprietor was tight-fisted, then at least he was *your* tight-fisted greengrocer, part of *your* community. And you would probably have a moan about him to the butcher a few doors down, as he moved his meat cleaver along the side of a joint – *this much? Bit more?* – before raising an arm and bringing it down with a crack, while your children drew faces with their shoes in the sawdust on the floor. Bakers for your bread, fishmongers for Friday's dinner, then maybe popping into the cafe for tea and a bun and a chat with whoever you had bumped into. You didn't have to plan to meet people you knew, it just happened. The only prior planning was writing out your shopping list.

By 1968, with the end in sight for Angel Lane, cat meat was still being sold at Mardon's, though the address was now 4a. Mrs Turners stewed eel shop was now Harold Hitch's eel pie shop. It is strange, in our rapidly changing world today, to think that for over 75 years the same spot at 46 Angel Lane was home to that most cockney of delicacies, the eel. This sense of continuity belongs to another world, one snuffed out by supermarkets and shopping centres. At this tipping point of the sixties – the year students revolted in Paris and daubed Situationist slogans on the walls, the year Martin Luther King and Robert Kennedy were assassinated – Angel Lane was still full of butchers, bakers, greengrocers and ironmongers. There were clothes shops and shoe shops, a milliner and a draper, a dry cleaners and a wallpaper shop. You could buy vinyl records in a shop that still advertised them as gramophone records. You could have something to eat and put some money on the dogs at Hackney, while budding David Baileys could buy at camera at Stratford Photographic Store ltd. at number 71. If you did, then you probably didn't stop to load your film, point the camera anywhere down the lane and click the shutter – after all, this place had been here more or less as it was, narrow and bending slowly, full of shops and barrows and people, for as long as you could remember. And as long as your mother and father could remember, and probably your grandparents too. Why would you take a photograph of something as humdrum as this?

Lots of people were taking photographs of Westfield in September 2011. Once the print media had taken their snaps, lone figures with fat digital SLRs on tripods could be seen wandering the inside and outside of the complex, their results perhaps destined for the increasing mass of stock-images held online for download. People without commercial interests in mind were simply snapping away with their dinky digital compacts or phone cameras. This was only possible because Westfield, bucking a growing trend, had agreed to allow it.

In 2006 I bought a digital SLR myself. Familiar with film cameras, I thought the best way to get used to it was to get out there and start taking pictures – after all, I now had free film for life. I still have the picture files on my computer hard drive – unprinted like, I suspect, the vast majority of pictures taken with a digital camera. There is a picture of a small car park, overlooked by the E15 building at the back of Aldworth Road, and one of the tree on the island opposite the job centre on Tramway Avenue. Another is of one of the office blocks on Stratford High Street, its square bulk wrapped in scaffolding and blue mesh sheeting. One is of the footbridge over the railway lines that leads to Jupp Road, and another shows the yellow and red sign on the wall at the corner of Lett Road advertising the car wash (open 7 days, presumably each week and not in total). Photographs of the humdrum that might one day disappear. But the one that is missing is the one of the inside of Stratford Shopping Centre. That's the one I wasn't allowed to take. When I challenged the security guard who stopped me, he explained that the centre was private property and no photography was allowed without permission.

Soon similar stories were appearing in the newspapers. I was told by one security guard that I couldn't take a photograph of a building even though where I was standing was not private property. Things were getting out of hand. The war on terror was seemingly being waged on the British public, rather than anyone with a desire to actually commit acts of terrorism. *Amateur Photography* magazine threw its weight behind a growing campaign led by the photographic community to highlight the absurdity and draconian nature of this trend, and perhaps this had some influence on Westfield's decision to allow the happy snappers to aim, point and shoot. And so they did, the architecture being of a size, shape and design that made people want to stare and then record it so others could see too.

Jim Pickard was born in 1906, the third child in a family of ten, two years before London hosted the fourth Olympiad.

He lived with his family in the area known locally as The Shoot. This small block of streets, sandwiched between Martin Street and Angel Lane, no longer exists. As Jim points out in his reminisces, it was a very poor area. His father worked in George Fox's fishmongers at 37 Angel Lane, practically within spitting distance of his home. When Jim was older he got a weekend job helping out in the fishmongers

I used to serve the winkles and shrimps and was told that I could eat as many as I wanted, provided that I did not put the empty shells back amongst the full ones. I also used to string the old newspapers together, getting old sheets of clean newspapers and tying a loop of string in the corner so that it could hang and be used for wrapping the fish by the salesman at the front of the shop. At Christmas there was a wonderful display of poultry, Ducks, Turkeys and Chickens by the hundred, these used to hang on a specially prepared trellis from head height up to the top of the eaves of the roof. I learned to pluck and clean the birds and as most people refused the giblets these were taken home and used for many a wonderful meal by my mother and the family. It is most amazing that even to this day people in the East End of London, poor people at that, do not realize the value of poultry giblets and often refuse them when having the poultry cleaned.[22]

At the top of the Lane was Stratford Broadway, with its larger shops and department stores like J.R. Roberts and

---

22 Jim Pickard, *Jim Pickard's Adventures*, Newham Archives

Boardman's, whose window displays young Jim used to stare at in wonder. But grand as these establishments were in comparison to those on Angel Lane, local philanthropy was not uncommon.

A bakers and restaurant in the Broadway named Hayes used to sell cheap bread to the people before opening time and it was common to see children queuing up between 6.30am and 7am in order to get sixpenny-worth of bread. This consisted of between three or four loaves and a couple of pastries thrown in, plus a large slab of bread pudding for the person getting the bread. Naturally this was the inducement for children to get up and queue for the bread. Many a family in the 'Shoot' had cause to remember the generosity of the owner of that restaurant.[23]

If Angel Lane and its market was where the locals shopped, then it was the shops on Stratford High Street and The Broadway that attracted people from elsewhere in the East End and Essex. When the English press wrote about the opening day of Westfield, they did so in unashamedly glowing terms. Criticisms and caution were buried in prose that championed this opportunity for the East End. Statistics were rolled out direct from the Westfield press releases and a certain, *Recession? What Recession?* tone of consumerist triumphalism was the order of the day. This is nothing new,

23 Ibid

and as Defoe made clear all those years ago is in the nation's DNA. Consider how the Essex County Chronicle waxed lyrical about the shopping experience to be had at Stratford in the build up to Christmas 1919.

Stratford Broadway is one of the most noted shopping centres of London; indeed for East London and suburban Essex it is the greatest shopping centre of all, the "hub of the universe" as it were. And this cannot be wondered at. The splendid range of shops of J. R. Roberts' Stores Ltd., the beautiful premises of Messrs. Boardmans, and other leading firms, would alone justify the claims of Stratford Broadway to be to the great districts stretching eastward what Oxford Street and Brompton Road are to Western London. There is hardly anything within the range of human wants – certainly as far as those wants are concerned with draperies and furnishings (and this means a large percentage of wants) – that cannot be supplied from Stratford Broadway.[24]

A year later the newspaper wrote about the Stratford shopping experience again.

In Stratford Broadway the display is really superb. Here is the great shopping centre for East London and Metropolitan Essex, and it is not without good reason that such can be said of it. The great firms of Roberts, Boardmans, Smart Bros,

---

24 *Essex County Chronicle*, Friday, December 12, 1919

Williams and Thomas, and others too numerous to mention, maintain and even enhance the great reputations of former years. Almost every human want can be met at Stratford, certainly in the drapery, furnishing and fancy businesses. The streets are thronged with sightseers gazing on the attractive wares before their eyes in the fine shops that Stratford can boast.[25]

Twelve months later, can you spot the difference?

At the tail end of the nineteenth century J. R. Roberts, which occupied 78–92 Stratford Broadway, described itself as Cash Draper, House Furnisher, Ironmonger &c. In 1888, the year of the Whitechapel murders and the match girls strike, it unveiled its first Santa's grotto, as the idea of Christmas shopping was beginning to emerge. By 1902 it had expanded, now stretching from 74–92 and also occupying 96, and it was a regular advertiser in East End and Essex newspapers. One advert in the Essex Chronicle in 1922 announced the Stratford Shopping Carnival, a one week affair starting on Saturday 14th October, which promised a period of unprecedented opportunities and bargains in every department. It is by far the biggest advert, taking up almost half the page. Roberts was also famous for its Christmas Bazaar's and window displays. One newspaper described the display of 1920.

---

25 *Essex County Chronicle*, Friday, December 10, 1920

The present bazaar embodies scenes and characters from the "Arabian Nights" – quaint, fascinating reproductions that breathe the very mystery and atmosphere of the East – with life-like representations of the characters the children love most. The little ones will see the Genie in his home – the Genie who, wonderfully mysterious, can in a second change poor cottages into palaces of gold filled with untold riches.[26]

There was Aladdin too, with his cave of precious stones, and Ali Baba, but most of the children pressing their noses at the window displays had as much chance of gaining their own riches later in life as they did of finding a genie in a bottle who might grant this very wish. A short article underneath the one describing the J. R. Roberts festive wonderland serves as a reminder of the toughness of the times.

A verdict of Death from natural causes was returned at the inquest on the body of an unknown man who was discovered dying in a ditch on Wanstead Flats. One sentence in a strange letter found on the body read; "Having outlived my means and being 62 years of age, I have resolved to starve it out, rather than go to a workhouse, where I should be always hungry, be looked on like a dog, and be shut up as if in prison.[27]

---

26 *The Essex Chronicle*, Friday, December 3, 1920

27 Ibid

The unfortunate man may well have been haunted by the spectre of the West Ham Union workhouse, situated just over a mile away from Wanstead Flats on Union Road (now Langthorne Road). In 1901 this institution had a total of 2,091 inmates, 333 of which were children. If he had been born ten years later he wouldn't have had to lay down in a ditch to die, as by 1930 the workhouse was a home for the chronic sick, aged and infirm. The world was changing, but for some it just doesn't change fast enough. For others, the cusp of change punctures what might otherwise have been a period of calm and stability.

The retail trade was beginning to change too, and what started as small regional outlets had often grown to large national operations. Marks & Spencer, which had begun life in Leeds, made a radical move of advertising, in their window, free admission. It wasn't that other shops of the time charged, but that upon entering Marks & Spencer you were under no obligation to buy. You could just browse. At your leisure. As successful businesses like Marks & Spencer and Boots expanded, smaller independent shops were soon feeling the pinch.

Shelley Holford was born in October 1887 in the flat above her father's chemist shop.

Powders were sold at a penny a dose to suit the varying ages of children and thousands were sold over the counter. There was no restriction on the sale of drugs, etc. and so opium, laudanum and alcohol were stocked. One regular customer was a cleaner who earned 6/- a week at the leathercloth works. She used to buy six pennyworth of laudanum which lasted a week and must have drained her income as rent had to come out of her earnings as well.

Opening hours were from 8 a.m. to 9 p.m. and 11 a.m. on Saturdays. Early closing started from 4 p.m. on Thursday. The assistants were always in trouble either with drink or drugs and so there were continual changes of them.

Another line in which my father was skilled was dentistry and as small chemists everywhere were being decimated by Boots (previously known as Day's Southern Drug Company), this side of the business became increasingly important. Premises were taken over next door, another surgery was built at the rear and eventually a third was installed on the first floor. He purchased an L.D.S. (Ontario) degree and was one of the earliest to use it.

My father set an hour aside on one or two days of the week when teeth were drawn free of charge for the relief of the suffering poor. Each person was asked to place a penny in the hospital saving box and quite a lot of money was saved this way. Eventually the chemist side of the business was phased out.[28]

Her reminisces, though brief, paint a vivid picture of what Stratford was like in the early part of the 20th century. The Hight Street was then the centre of a thriving neighbourhood.

---

28 Shelley Holford, Local Studies Note No. 27, Newham Archives

Flower girls congregated along the pavements with their heavy laden baskets from Stratford Market. Their stands were opposite to where the hackney carriages stood by the obelisk opposite to Angel Lane and a person could purchase an armful of daffodils for a few pence.[29] She reveals that Maryland Point was a poor trading location in comparison to the High Street and Broadway, and that the only time she went to J. R. Roberts was for the Christmas bazaar, because Boardman's was of a much better standard. Mr. Boardman Senior used to wear his spectacles on his forehead and bore an expression of bewilderment on his face. He had a fine general store which he had built up and put each of his sons into a department.[30] And that brewers, distillers and public houses all did a roaring trade.

At this time Stratford had two theatres and an impressive shopping centre, but this relative oasis was surrounded by industry and all that went with it.

Stratford E. was a place of some importance and merit when I first knew it. Prosperity had come chiefly by the Great Eastern Railway placing their works there, but to a lesser degree the factories played their part for anything could be manufactured on Stratford Marshes that would not have been countenanced elsewhere and smells from Cook's soap works and small sheds where fat was refined abounded. The journey

29 Ibid

30 Ibid

to Liverpool Street Station was always undertaken with a certain amount of misgiving and when the train left Stratford Station handkerchiefs were drawn out, windows closed and ladies giggled and blushed, such was the odour. This was only one of the trials that had to be borne by the people living in the neighbourhood. The land being low-lying, the subsoil water could not be drained and every conceivable device was used to prevent water entering the basements. Rubber balls were fitted in gullies to prevent backwash, boards were put over thresholds, but all to no avail for after a heavy rainfall the mud would pour out of the walls under pressure leaving several feet of unpleasant liquid to be bailed out. I remember my mother with her skirts tied round her waist going after a beer barrel which had floated out of position.[31]

The noxious smells that plagued Stratford for several generations have now gone, and so has the industry responsible for them. Though the railways remain a prominent part of Stratford, they no longer serve the same role in terms of employment. The workers who came to graft on the railways, and were accommodated in the hastily built Stratford New Town, would have thought you mad if you had told them that in the future there would be trains that didn't even require drivers. Perhaps they would have run from these 'ghost' trains, away from Stratford and down to the docks – but the

---

31 Ibid

docks would be deserted of dockers and ships, full instead of shoppers and bankers and luxury houses in the sky.

Westfield Stratford City boasts of over 300 shops. So much choice it would seem, but in reality the choices have already been made for you. Like most things in modern life, choice is illusory. Certainly, no one had a choice about the Olympics or Westfield, but then the locals didn't have much choice about the Stratford Shopping Centre, the now runty-looking ugly sister over the road from the brash new arrival. The entrance to the shopping centre opposite the station, all brick and multi-storey car park, is so ugly they have decided to re-clad it in grey square tiles and further obscure it with a sculpture of what might be metal trees, but apparently is a shoal of fish. The variegated green and yellow 'fish' catch the light and shimmer somewhat on a sunny day, but one wonders what they will look like in ten years time.

Not that it bothers the shoppers safe inside the crescent of Westfield. For the teenagers this is a new hangout. The boys strut and stroll in small groups, wearing their finest. The girls watch the boys while the boys watch the girls. They don't seem to be big shoppers though. Not surprising when unemployment statistics for Newham and neighbouring boroughs are taken into account. Already recognised as among the poorest areas in London, the economic crash of 2008 and the resulting slow-motion impact is fast rendering a generation of young people economically impotent, as credit dries up and educational maintenance allowance is withdrawn.

On the 18th March 2012, the government announced that they were considering suspending the Sunday trading laws for eight weekends leading up to and through the Olympics. If they think that people with no money to spend are suddenly going to find some down the back of the sofa on Sunday afternoon and rush out to save an economy on life support, then I suspect they might be out of luck – though not as much as the poor staff who will have to work the longer hours and further sacrifice family life.

When it come to anti-social working hours, it is hardly surprising that we have been here before. In 1893 George How, chairman of the East London Branch of the Early Closing Association, wrote a letter to the editor of the Daily News on the topic, one which had been an item of debate for a number of years. The movement, he declared, was *in the interests of the shop assistants, whose hours of work are excessively long, and who by their detention until 9.30 and even 10 o'clock at night are deprived of reasonable opportunity for recreation and self improvement.*[32] Interestingly, How, like other parties who had involved themselves with this issue, laid the blame squarely at the shoppers, suggesting that the shopkeepers were forced to cater to their whims.

There used to be a pedestrian subway that took you under the Great Eastern Road directly into Stratford Station, and vice versa. The station entrance, a hundred yards or so away from

---

32 *The Daily News*, Wednesday, January 18, 1893

its present location, was a dingy, bunker-like place. Dark and damp, it led onto long tunnels that eventually took you to the platforms. It was a good option when it was raining, and together with the shopping centre itself meant you could get off your train and travel as far as Stratford Broadway without getting wet. Though the shops closed at normal times, the centre was open through the night as a public thoroughfare; it was mostly the night-time problems of drunks, druggies and muggings that eventually led to the closing down of the subway.

At Christmas the middle of the centre always contains some kind of festive display. One year this included a 20 foot tall talking, animatronic tree. As well as saying phrases such as "Merry Christmas everyone", it would also launch into festive song. After a while it became a comforting part of the journey home, though in the evenings it was often victim to the attentions of local youths who would push it over. In the early hours of one particular December morning I saw it lying on its back, mechanical arms waving, still saying "Merry Christmas everyone", only at half speed, no doubt due to the violence of the kicking it had received. The festive exhortations of joy were now voiced in a deep, slurred tone that suggested the quest for meaning in life had failed and the will to carry on was receding. The next morning on the way to work my partner and I, and the rest of the Stratford commuters, found the tree right as rain again, except for one arm refusing to move. One of the nodding penguins that stood at its feet was missing, though.

If you are heading towards the Broadway exit and reach this central hub, a left turn will take you roughly down the path that Angel Lane used to follow. Passing the indoor market and heading out of the exit doors will see you outside, with Stratford Heights on your left and the Theatre Royal and Stratford Circus just around the corner. If you arrive at the right time you will notice how busy the Theatre bar is.

If you carry on past the central hub, you will exit onto a paved area that leads to the Broadway. This used to be a space thick with street preachers and hawkers of cheap toys that jumped, span, and flashed lights – yours for only a few pounds and the willingness to ignore health and safety considerations. Beyond this gently sloping area stands the Gurney memorial, a 40 foot granite obelisk with two fountains built into its base and flanked by four lamps.

The memorial was erected to commemorate the work of Samuel Gurney, who died in 1856. Known as the "bankers' banker" when he oversaw the spectacular growth of Overand & Gurney (before the catastrophic crash that occurred after his death), Gurney differed from today's Masters of the Universe in that he used his position to follow his philanthropic interests later in his life. These included penal reform (working with, amongst others, Elizabeth Fry who lived in Upton) and anti-slavery. He is the seated figure second from left at the front in the painting *The Anti-Slavery Convention*, by Benjamin Robert Haydon (1840), which hangs in the National Portrait Gallery. His other activities involved education, peace missions and providing the initiative that led to the opening of the Poplar Hospital for Accidents in 1855.

On the day I visited, the monument was surrounded by metal fencing, though the nature of the work being done wasn't clear. Originally it stood prominently in the middle of the wide Broadway on its own island, but now it sits at the far end of a traffic island and some of its impact has been lost. When I lived round the corner from here it was a favourite spot for either Christian preachers or impromptu musical and singing performances, though sometimes the two would be combined. For most people, however, it was just something they passed as they crossed from one side of the Broadway to the other.

I hadn't been here for some time and it was easy to spot the changes. The Black Bull pub had been given a makeover and now it resembled a gastro-pub, rather than the old man's boozer I remember. The Latin ¼ had a new sign, and next to it was Stratford Best Cafe, where I hoped the food was better than the grammar. Next door, as if engaged in some shop-sign arms race, Super Best Kebab House. One of them used to be a kebab shop under a different name, but it wasn't even the best back then, never mind super best. Cafe Rae-Ann, where I had many a Sunday morning fry-up, was still there on the opposite side of the road. I didn't have time to explore in much detail, so set off back to the station. Walking up the paved side of St. John's Church, the shops looked pretty much the same ones that were here for as long as I can recall, though The Fox bar had changed its name to

O12 Bar & Grill, while the car park at the rear, on Eastern Road, was boarded-off. Inside, a lone crane stood tall in the setting sun with an advertising board for Birbeck University hanging from its girth, a clue to the future residents of this small piece of land, that has already been named University Square. The council flats on the other side of the road were now looking cowed by all this growth and the black obelisk of the Stratford Eye apartments towering over them.

The Broadway's days of grandeur were long gone when I first visited Stratford in 1991. Stratford Shopping Centre probably hammered the final nail into that coffin in the mid-1970s. And it is roughly around this time that our high streets and shopping habits started to change, and high streets in every town and city began to look like carbon-copies of each other. But many of these chains began life in humbler circumstances in the late 19th and early 20th centuries, times when the high street was an altogether different animal, and individual shop owners would complain about the market barrows parked outside their shop fronts.

A glance at Kelly's Trade Directory for 1896 reveals the make-up of the Broadway. The most obvious thing to note is that skill and artisanship were part and parcel of the retail experience. There was a tailor, a few drapers and a clothier. Rabbits & Sons Limited would sell you boots, while George Henry Courtney would make them for you. Alfred Wood could make you a watch and Bonallack & Sons could build you a carriage. There were hairdressers, butchers, fishmongers, and tobacconists, but also solicitors, surgeons and dentists.

This was a whole community of people who offered services and goods that people not just wanted, but needed. The only things to survive, apart from St. John's Church and the Gurney Memorial, are pubs – the Old Black Bull and the King Edward (then called the King of Prussia), known locally as The Eddie.

From Great Eastern Road, Westfield now looms high above the people who walk by, like the proverbial castle on the hill. This elevated position might have been ordained by topography, but nevertheless it lends the complex an imposing authority, much like the giant cathedrals of medieval times must have done. But human faith in any concept that provides a reason for *why* we exist will last longer than one merely offering distraction *from* that existence, and in the temples of consumerism the worshipers are required to pay, unlike their religious counterparts.

If one doubts that shopping has become the national duty then a look at the Trading Standards Institute *Young Consumers of the Year* initiative, targeted at schools and colleges, should clear up any doubt. Whereas we were once teenagers, and perhaps motivated to become good citizens, our children are now being labelled as consumers and are in danger of being mass produced as such. It is a project clearly designed to encourage consumption, something so important to a certain brand of Western democracy that in 2001 George Bush appealed to patriotic duty and urged Americans not to let terrorists stop them from shopping. Society is now divided into those who can consume, and those who can't; buying more and more objects becomes necessary if we are to feel as if we belong in this society. To lack the means of consumption is to become an un-citizen. So successful had this conditioning programme been that in the summer of 2011 consuming would take place by any means necessary. The youth who looted were widely and quite viciously condemned in the media, but this reaction seems as useful as criticising Pavlov's dogs for salivating when the bell rings. Here was a generation taught to consume from their earliest years. Some commentators wanted us to believe they were doing what came naturally, but the looting was a logical response to their conditioning.

One of the key aspects of consumerism is the way it fosters a desire for modernity – not just having the latest fashions in clothes, but in every object we buy. No sooner has someone bought the latest hi-tech gadget, than the next incarnation is announced and immediately renders the previous version 'out of date'. The digital age has accelerated and advanced the concept of built-in obsolescence. Mechanical obsolescence can be further complicated by software obsolescence. As we queue to be the first to get our hands on the latest version we never stop to consider that while we know the price of everything, we know the value of nothing. Even when we consume things other than material goods, we are slaves to our need to appear on-trend: holiday destinations become fashionable, then unfashionable overnight. We no longer think solely about what we are buying because we are too busy trying to keep up with the global-Joneses, constructing and maintaining an ideal self that has little to do with our actual self.

Not only do we consume to construct an image of ourselves that we believe is real, but by uploading photographs (images of these constructed images of ourselves) on a social network site like Facebook, we even sign-away the rights to our own constructed image. This photographic image can then be used by a third party in advertising, thus attracting further people to keep consuming and constructing their own image. If, as some cultures believe, a photograph captures our soul, then we are not selling our souls so much as giving them away. As always, the Devil is in the detail.

The shoppers on the Broadway in 1896 didn't have our problems. They had problems of their own, but a crisis of self wasn't one of them. Identity came, for men at least, through work. If work wasn't available, then their main concerns were retaining a sense of pride and avoiding the dreaded workhouse. In the post-industrial era, identity is less about work ethic and more about the consumer ethic. The explosion of easy credit made it, for a while at least, a game everyone could play; fashion, gadgets, cheap flights, exotic holidays, mortgages – even university educations were available. And then we woke up and found out that for most of us, it was just a dream.

Seventy per cent of visitors to the Olympic park will pass through Westfield upon entry. As well as consuming the spectacle (and the food and drink of the official sponsors), they will also be encouraged to consume on the way in and consume on the way out. The government seems desperate for the 2012 Olympic experience to include shopping, as if declaring, "It's not the sport, it's the economy, stupid." But the economy is broken, and for those who still believe in the illusion of unlimited growth, it is broken beyond repair. A January 2012 report by the Resolution Foundation suggested that for low to middle income workers there would be no recovery until 2020, and even then there would not be a return to the income peaks pre-2008.[33] The conclusions are based on the belief that economic recovery will begin in 2017, but nowhere is the issue of peak oil referred to[34]. It may be that we are seeing the end of the dream machine – that Westfield is a representation of the dream we wake from in the morning, the one we desperately try to return to, but even if we do manage to fall back asleep, is never to the same dream. For some, the dream is over.

---

33 *The Essential Guide to Squeezed Britain*, Resolution Foundation, January 2012

34 Peak Oil is a phrase that refers to the peak in oil extraction, after which there is terminal decline. The debate as to whether the global peak has already occurred, or will do so at some point in the near future is a contentious one, but all parties agree that the impact will be profound. Our current way of life is entirely dependent on cheap fossil fuels, and so, the argument goes, unlimited growth is an impossibility if the peak oil theory is correct. For some observers, this peak in oil extraction, and the corresponding downward curve, is at the root of the current global economic crisis. Feel free to research this topic yourself; it is the 'elephant in the room', and learning about it is a very sobering experience.

CHAPTER 4

Land Grabbers

Do not all strive to enjoy the land? The gentry strive for land, the clergy strive for land, the common people strive for land; and buying and selling is an art whereby people endeavour to cheat one another of the land. Now if any can prove from the law of righteousness that the land was made peculiar to him and his successively, shutting others out, he shall enjoy it freely for my part. But I affirm it was made for all; and true religion is to let everyone enjoy it.

(Gerrard Winstanley)

One Friday morning in July 1906 Councillor Ben Cunningham led a band of about 14 unemployed men of West Ham in taking possession of a piece of waste land sandwiched between North Street Passage and St. Mary's Road in Plaistow. The land, once a gravel pit and later used for dust and refuse, was about three acres in extent. By the end of the day 20 men were working upon it with picks and shovels, uprooting the dry grass and turning the soil in preparation for growing vegetables. They named Cunningham The Captain, and appointed a minister of agriculture who decided to divide the ground into four triangles, thus arriving at the name, 'Triangle Camp.' A 'Triangle Hotel' was erected from boards, poles and tarpaulin, and on Sunday night 25 men slept there. A notice inside read 'You are requested not to spit on the floor of this hotel.'

So began the actions of the Plaistow Land Grabbers, a band of unemployed men who, having grown disillusioned with the efforts of the government and local authorities to adequately address their plight, moved into action. The *unemployed question* had been hanging in the air over West Ham for several years, and Cunningham, perhaps taking to heart Keir Hardie's words at a speech in Hyde Park two months earlier, decided that patience on the issue would indeed lead to further neglect by the powers that be. For him and his small band of men, the failure of the Distress committee set up the previous year had led them to only one conclusion. Symbolic or otherwise, they were prepared to make a stand.

One of the men of the camp, named Francis, converted an empty cigar box into a collecting box and contributions collected from curious members of the public were used by the men to buy bread and cheese. Mr G. Blain, Borough road foreman, visited the camp to make an official report on the occupation to the Corporation, but was sympathetic enough to offer a contribution. Messages of support came from the North where an unemployed 'jumpers' camp had already been established in Manchester.

Some of the men had no knowledge of gardening, to the extent that they were downhearted when told that it would be a month or more before the fruits of their labour would be ready for picking. On the Monday this planting began with cabbages, and from various sources around 1,000 plants were obtained, including broccoli, savoy cabbages and celery. By Tuesday most of the planting had been done, and the men busied themselves watering the dry ground. Donations from outside the camp included not just money and plants, but food and items for entertainment. A Mr. Joseph Terrett donated lamb which the men dined on in the hotel, served with peas, a gift from another friend. The same evening some of the men's wives joined them at the camp for tea, bread and butter and watercress. A phonograph and mouth organ contributed to the atmosphere.

Cunningham told the *Express* reporter that the men were anxious to demonstrate to the public that they wanted to work if only given the chance, and that they 'wanted to get the people back to the land.'[34] On the wall at the rear of the plot someone had painted in large white letters, 'What will the harvest be?' This phrase has become synonymous with the Land Grabbers, but less well known is that, according to the Express article, someone had written beneath it 'One month's hard.'[35]

The author of the addition might have been joking, but the threat of punishment was real and it wasn't long before the authorities decided to do something. Councillor Cunningham received a letter from the Mayor saying that, as Chief Magistrate of the county borough, he would act accordingly to deal with the illegal act of this forcible

34 Plaistow "Land Jumpers" – Express, 1906

35 This isn't discernable on the only existing photograph that shows the writing in the distance behind a group of the Land Grabbers so it is possible that this is artistic license on behalf of the reporter

possession of land. Cunningham responded by writing in reply that 'with all respect to your worship's opinion I don't consider that I have acted illegally in taking possession of disused land which rightfully belongs to the people.' And in doing so was referring to a radical belief that had its roots in the period of the English Civil War. It was a bold and clear statement at a time when anti-socialist rhetoric was increasingly being voiced, and committed to paper, by the establishment, who were made nervous by a period of agitation that went back as far as the Match Girls strike and beyond and was currently coming to boiling point with the Suffragette movement. An interesting aside is that this was taking place just two years away from the 1908 Olympic Games which were hosted in London.

Cunningham told a reporter from *The Express* that the council would have to serve a notice on all the men individually to remove them from the land. As such, when knowledge of these notices was received the men would be sent to other ground and new men brought in to replace them. Their intent, which the newspaper displayed in dramatic uppercase was to

SEIZE LAND ALL OVER THE COUNTRY.[36]

The extent of this plan was to find 2,000 men in order to grab 2,000 acres of land. One can imagine a mental soundtrack of kettle drums beating out a drum roll of alarm in the heads of the land-owning class at such subversive talk, but in reality

---

36 Plaistow "Land Jumpers" – Express, July 1906

there was never any chance of success for the land-grabbers. History had already recorded one such failure.

On April 1st 1649, just eight weeks after Charles I had been publicly tried and executed by Cromwell's parliamentarian army, a band of people led by Gerrard Winstanley took to some common land on St. George's Hill in Surrey and started to build makeshift houses and dig the soil for crops. The aims of the group were published by Winstanley in a pamphlet, *True Levellers Standard Advanced*. This was a 'back to the land' movement that sought to right the wrongs committed by the Norman invaders in appropriating the land, as well as the subsequent enclosure acts, which Winstanley believed had condemned the common man to slavery. Calling themselves The Diggers, they saw the old regime as being dominated by 'landlords, teachers and rulers' who were actually 'oppressors, murderers and thieves'. They sought to overthrow them and abolish the idea of property and land ownership. This, however, brought them into direct conflict with the parliamentarians who wanted to establish their own rights to property and who had, as recently as 1643, voted to continue the royalist policy of enclosing the common land, thus further dispossessing the poor.

Winstanley wrote that, 'England is not a free country, until the poor that have no land have a free allowance to dig and labour the commons, and so live as comfortably as the Landlords that live in their inclosures.'[37]

---

37 True Levellers Standard Advanced. 1649

Local landlords reacted to the communes that the Diggers created by sending in thugs to intimidate and physically attack them, and trample their crops, as well as taking them to court for trespass on the common land. The intimidation, attacks and loss of a court case where they were not even able to speak in their own defence, led the Diggers to abandon St. George's Hill in August 1649. Other communes met similar resistance, and by 1651 the movement had been crushed.

Rebellion over land wasn't the Digger's invention, but their direct action echoed through time. Though they failed in their plan, what the Diggers succeeded in was placing an historical marker that future radical thinkers were to return to.

One such thinker was Thomas Spence, a Newcastle born radical and pamphleteer who moved to London in 1792. He was continually harassed by the government and imprisoned on several occasions. His ideas on the rights of women and children were ahead of their time, and on the land question he believed that the natural order of things was that all men held the land in common. Thus control of the land through 'ownership' was a means to control the lives of men who depended on it (to feed themselves and their families). Mankind, Spence believed, could only regain his freedom by reclaiming the land he had lost. Too radical for most free thinkers of his day, Spence nevertheless left a legacy. His ideas of land nationalisation, while dismissed as Utopian at the time, were picked up by the chartists, and one man in particular.

Feargus O'Connor also believed that the root of the problem of poverty was the land enclosures. He thought that if factory workers were unemployed and land was unused, then the two should be brought together. Though discredited for his methods and muddled thinking, his beliefs were heartfelt and his Land Plan, or at least the part that tried to marry the unemployed with the unused land, was essentially the same as that followed by the Plaistow land grabbers some 60 years later. Attempts were made by O'Connor to put his plan into practice by raising capital to purchase land that could be given out via a lottery system to subscribers, who would each receive a parcel of land. Without enough land to go round the plan failed, but the idea of giving away small plots of ground to the common man is one that would return and succeed, albeit only after O'Connor and the land grabbers had failed.

Whilst the authorities were in the process of dealing with this Digger-like insurrection in Plaistow, the land-grabbers themselves busied themselves with the task at hand; soon just over half an acre of land was under cultivation. It was hoped that within a week a further acre would also be under cultivation, and thus half the whole site. Water was proving to be a problem until someone discovered a disused well nearby which was re-employed. The men stuck to their task in a fittingly puritanical fashion, save one who was expelled from the camp for allowing his thirst to tempt him into drinking, as the *Express* reporter described it, 'somewhat liberally'. No doubt Gerrard Winstanley would have approved of the discipline of the remainder.

Money was coming into the camp slowly, but other types of donation led to a store of fish, mutton, potatoes, loaves of bread, a pound of tobacco, two parcels of clothing and even a gramophone with 25 records. A new 'hotel' was being erected using railway sleepers dug up from the dust shoot. A lady sent a Union Jack which the men intended to dye red and put up to replace the old flag which had become worn and tattered. It is tempting to conjure up an image of the men in the camp one hot evening, tired from their toil but content with a simple meal inside them, listening to music on the gramophone, some smoking tobacco, the dream of reclaiming the land still breathing for luxurious moments. Or perhaps they were anxious. Money, after all, was low and though the generosity of the public meant that food was still being donated (a local butcher had offered another 16lb of mutton, while a fishmonger promised 100 pieces of fish with a supply of potatoes), doubts as to how long they could remain were surely circling.

Cunningham too must have been under some strain. Being a local councillor and clearly in charge, he perhaps had the most to lose from intervention by the authorities. Letters promising action were addressed to him, as were others from anonymous observers. One such, dated 18th July 1906, read:

Dear Sir – Have forwarded copy of "the new Education Bill" hoping you will read the contents of it to the inmates of Triangle Asylum every morning before they commence work. I am, sir, hoping to meet you in the Padded Room very soon. I am yours up the stick through overwork. C. H.

The enclosed 'Education Bill' was in actuality a copy of a novel called *Work, work, work!*

On the afternoon of Wednesday 18th July, the same day C.H. had penned his strange missive, the camp was visited by Jack Williams from Manchester. He damned it with faint praise, saying it was all right in its way but that progress was too slow. He suggested that similar energy put into capturing the food stuffs, as opposed to growing them, would do much more good. *The Express* quote him as saying, 'The fact is we've got a class to convince who will not be convinced till something outrageous is done. The only way to get recognition is by striking terror.' This would appear to be a reference to the 1886 Trafalgar Square riot in which Williams, together with fellow Socialists John Burns and Henry Myers Hyndman, was implicated. This had involved the looting of shops and carriages and the stoning of exclusive clubs such as The Reform and The Carlton, where a member had appeared at the window holding his nose and servants threw crusts of bread and matchboxes. It had done more to frighten the upper classes than anything else, and the establishment reacted accordingly.[38]

Harking back to the riot at Trafalgar Square 20 years before may have been a measure of Williams' frustration at the lack of progress at Triangle Camp, or with the movement as a whole. He had, after all, been in charge of the July 11th seizure of a plot of church land in Levenshulme, Manchester,

---

38 City of Cities: The Birth of Modern London – Stephen Inwood, 2005

where 13 unemployed men stated that their action was but the beginning of a widespread movement for the compulsory seizure of uncultivated land. But it was Hyndman himself, a more important figure, who had written in 1881 about the land issue.

Possession of the land is a matter of such supreme importance to the liberty and well-being of Englishmen, that the only marvel is not that there should be a growing agitation on the subject to-day, but that the nation should ever have been content to bear patiently the monopoly which has been created during the past 300 years. It affords indeed a strange commentary upon the history of human progress, that we have to look back more than 400 years to the period when the mass of the people of these islands were in their most prosperous and wholesome condition. In those middle ages which our school-books still speak of as days of darkness and ignorance, the great body of Englishmen were far better off in every way than they are now. The men who fought in the French wars, and held their own against every Continental army, were sober, hard-working yeomen and life-holders, who were ready to pay for their victories out of their own pockets, instead of saddling their descendants with a perpetual mortgage in the shape of a huge national debt. They owned the soil and lived out of it, and having secured for themselves power at home and freedom by their own firesides, they kept them.[39]

---

39 England For All. Chapter 1; H.M. Hyndman 1881

The Plaistow Land Grabbers remained on their plot. At the time of Triangle Camp, although Plaistow was well on its way to complete urbanisation, there were still open areas of land nearby. Just 40 years previously it had been a large, growing village in the middle of rural land, and the older men of the camp would have lived through the urban transformation. For them, the enclosure acts may have meant that the common man was no longer part of the common land, but now the very land itself was being obliterated by industry and the houses of the people who worked in these industries – including many who had come to the city precisely because the land now offered no means of survival.

On July 26th the local authorities made their first move to eject the men from the camp, with a large force of police stationed in the vicinity, as well as several thousand curious onlookers, many of whom were themselves unemployed. With funds low, the opportunity to raise money from such a large audience in attendance was taken, and collections boosted their coffers. At around midday Mr G. Blain, road foreman, formally demanded possession of the ground. Cunningham replied that he and his men were unable to comply with the Mayor's request, whereupon Blain withdrew. A reporter for the *Western Times* reported that 'there was no disorder, and the utmost good feeling prevailed.' Good feeling wasn't forthcoming from the Corporation, however, who promised to instigate civil proceedings to reclaim the land.[40]

---

40 The Western Times – July 27 1906

On Saturday 4ᵗʰ of August West Ham Corporation officers returned with the police and cleared the camp. Cunningham refused to leave and was carried away, after which the men of the camp left. The 'Triangle Hotel' was pulled down, and along with the men's bedding put in an adjoining field where the men also collected. A second band of men then reoccupied the land, but leaderless they decided to flee when the police returned at night. But Cunningham and his men were not finished and a month later a final attempt was made to seize the land once more.

Triangle Camp, Plaistow, the whilom colony of unemployed, is making more history. It was the scene of great excitement from two o'clock on Saturday afternoon until midnight, and during the whole of that time about 120 policemen were on duty.

Since the dispersal three weeks ago of the original "land grabbers," or "squatters," Councillor Cunningham has found the operations of his movements to meetings in a mineral water maker's yard close by.

Mr. Cunningham having publicly announced that he would again go upon the ground on Saturday, Triangle Camp, from 8 o'clock in the morning was patrolled by a specially selected force of police, and at 2 o'clock there were under the direction of Sub-Divisional Inspectors Fowles and Sly, 120 men, ten of whom were mounted, while on the gravel field the West Ham Corporation posted about 30 employees.

Addressing a gathering outside Upton Park Station, Councillor Cunningham was interrupted by Inspector Howlett, who touched him and said, "Mr. Cunningham, what occurs to-day we hold you responsible for."

As soon as the Councillor set off in the direction of Triangle Camp a crowd of several hundreds went after him. Joined by two or three other men, Cunningham went in a house in Northern road, and in the garden there were eight or nine of the other squatters.

There intentions were to climb the garden fence and jump on to Triangle Camp, but the force of Corporation employees evidently alarmed all but four of the party. With three others, Cunningham got on the land, and at once all was excitement.

Efforts being made to prevent the intruders' entrance, one or two of the Corporation employees were carried to the ground; and Mr. Blain, the Corporation road foreman, received a blow on the face, and then defended himself with a stick he carried.

Meanwhile, Cunningham was set upon by three men and borne to the ground, being placed face downwards. He struggled violently, saying he was being hurt, and when he showed signs of submission he was allowed to rise. Then, held by the neck and arms, he was hustled off the land, his complaints of ill-usage being met by a statement that if he went quietly he would not be hurt.

Two men were arrested.

The dense crowd was in a state of great excitement, but the police kept the people on the move, and the strong force effectually spoiled the possibility of an attempt to break down the fencing.

By and by Mr. Cunningham arrived in safety at his "headquarters," and, the crowd following into the mineral water yard, a meeting was held. While he was recovering from his "rough and tumble" the Councillor was served with a writ for being on the land on August 28.

Addressing the meeting, Councillor Cunningham said he would not be surprised if he were sent to gaol, but what he had done he had done with an honest heart.

No untoward incident occurred at the Triangle on Sunday. The plants set out by the campers about two months ago have taken root, and are now in a very flourishing condition.[41]

On September 3rd one of the men of the camp appeared in West Ham Police Court.

Mr G. Pollard, a 35 year old gardener from Plaistow, was charged with striking George Blain, the Corporation official, in the face on the previous Saturday. Presumably no mention was made of what damage Blain might have inflicted upon anyone when defending himself with his 'stick'. Pollard received a sentence of six weeks imprisonment, two weeks more than the *one months hard* that had been predicted by the camp graffitist.[42]

Cunningham was sent to prison for contempt of court and served a five week sentence. Meanwhile the vegetables he

---

41 The Herald, Saturday, September 8, 1906

42 Western Times, Tuesday September 4th 1906

had helped to plant grew quietly in the soil from which he and his men had been evicted. No one knows who, if anyone, tended them, and if they did who reaped the harvest. At the municipal elections in November Cunningham stood as an Independent Labour candidate but, disowned by his own party, came bottom of the poll, and was never to regain his seat. As if to underline the hopelessness of the men's cause, the following year over 1,000 local residents emigrated to Australia and Canada on government advice to solve the unemployment problem.

It is striking to think just how heavy handed the authorities' response was to this minute insurrection. The plot of land is insignificant in size and was not being put to any constructive use. But the powers that be viewed the Socialist movement as a menace. Though Cunningham was probably thinking foremost about helping out his band of unemployed men – most likely dock workers – the political edge to the act of taking the land is what created fear. Hyndman himself had written about the land issue a quarter of a century earlier in righteous prose that no doubt conjured up the ghosts of Spence and Winstanley.

No man, not a landlord, can read through the records of this disgraceful pillage even now without a feeling of furious bitterness. Nothing more shameful is told in the long tale of class greed than this of the seizure of the common lands by the upper and middle classes of Great Britain. To deprive the people of their last vestige of independent holding, and thus to force all to become mere hand-to-mouth wage earners at the mercy of the growing capitalist class, such was the practical effect of these private enactments, conceived in iniquity, and executed in injustice. For up to so recent a date as 1854 these enclosures were done by private bill, and of course exclusively in private interest. There was no public discussion whatever; and rich men who coveted a few thousand acres of common which belonged to their poorer neighbours, simply laid hands upon them and added them to their estate. Fierce protests were often made in the neighbourhood, but they were invariably unavailing. In the course of 150 years, between 1700 and 1845, no fewer than 7,000,000 acres of public land, and probably a great deal more, were enclosed by the landowners of England in Parliament assembled, without one halfpenny of real compensation ever having been made to the public whose rights were thus ridden over.[43]

It wasn't what the Plaistow men did with the land, it was the seizing of it that inspired the reaction. Certainly, as far back as 1838 the benefits to the working man of land on which to grow food was acknowledged by, among others, Samuel Gurney. He provided plots of land for labourers and, interested in how they were working this land, decided to lower the rent and award prizes for those who cultivated it in the most profitable and systematic way. S. Catton, writing about some of these labourers who had shown some of their vegetables at the South Essex Horticultural Society exhibitions commented:

---

43 H. M. Hyndman, *England For All*, (Chapter 1 – The Land), 1881

The occupants are sensible of the benefits derived to their families from holding these allotments as was proved by a question put by the proprietor at the July meeting; viz that if there were any who wished to give up their land he was willing to accept of their resignation. The simultaneous answer was, "No, no sir. We now know the benefit of possessing these allotments and should be sorry to be deprived of them."[44]

The proprietor in the above quote was Gurney, who had provided the men with bread, beef and good porter at the meeting to discuss the prizes on offer. The communication from S. Catton appeared in *Labourer's Friend Magazine*. This was published by the Labourer's Friend Society which had been established by Benjamin Wills, a London surgeon, who wanted to increase the living standards of the poor after the end of the Napoleonic wars. The Society included many people of high standing, such as Sir Thomas Baring, founder of Barings Bank. Allotments were seen as one way for working class men to gain some self-worth and independence. Established in 1815, their goal from the outset was to bring about the provision of land suitable for small allotments. The society believed that separation from the land as a result of enclosures was to blame for the miserable condition of labourers.[45]

44 *Labourer's Friend Magazine*, January 1838

45 Jeremy Burchardt, The Allotment Movement in England, 1793-1873, The Boydell Press (2002)

It is surely no coincidence that the Swing Riots of 1830 occurred in those parts of the South and East of England that had suffered the most from enclosures. Though the rioters were dealt with in a brutal fashion – with execution, imprisonment and deportation the fate of many of those arrested – the riots had an impact on subsequent reforms, including the Poor Law Amendment Act of 1834, though this merely transferred the relief system into the dreaded workhouse. It also, possibly, had an effect on the efforts of the Benjamin Wills to encourage provision of land for allotments. It is believed that up until 1830 this had been a completely unsuccessful enterprise, but after this date progress was forthcoming, albeit mostly in rural areas.

Another article appearing in the Labourer's Friend Magazine referred to a general meeting of the labourers who had allotments on Samuel Gurney's estate. It took place in the National School room, Plaistow, on Thursday 9th August 1838.

He [Gurney] repeated, that it gave him much pleasure to find that they considered their pieces of land really beneficial to them, and hoped that it might contribute in some degree, through their industry and economy, to enable them to maintain that independence, comfort, and respectability, which it was so desirable that the important class of the community, to which they belonged, should be able to maintain; for a day labourer, who conducted himself properly, and supported his family without any charitable relief from his neighbours, was as independent as it regarded society at large, and as much entitled to respect as those who rode in their carriages...And he thought it must be far more gratifying to their own feelings to know that they could, by their own honest efforts, support their families, than to place their reliance upon any "Union" or "Board of Guardians" whatever. And if the land that they possessed helped them in any measure to accomplish this, his object was gained. He thought, too, that there was a pleasure connected with raising vegetables for their own use; and he believed, that a basket of potatoes, taken fresh from their own ground (for it was their own while they paid their rent), must taste sweeter than those purchased from the market gardener, or farmer. "Yes, Sir," said one; "and what is better, it don't touch the pocket."[46]

One wonders how Gurney would have reacted to the plight of the land grabbers had he been alive when they cultivated the plot of land at Triangle Camp.

The efforts of Cunningham and his men may not have been in vain, however. Perhaps mindful of a repeat of their act, local councils subsequently seemed less resistant to providing land for allotments. Certainly their appearance became more regular. In 1909 six acres of land in Manor Park were made available for cultivation rent free, the only stipulation made by the owners being that the seventy allotment holders contribute a penny a week for the upkeep of fences and other expenses.[47] At the end of the previous year, ten acres of land were let out in small allotments near Church Road, East Ham, for a rental

---

46   *Labourer's Friend Magazine*, November 1838

47 The Devon and Exeter Gazette, Monday, August 16, 1909

of a penny a week.[48] By 1916 activity in East Ham and West Ham had increased significantly.

East Ham Allotment Holders' Association with the assistance of John Bethell M.P., the president, have secured possession of the remainder of Manor Farm, East Ham, a piece of land comprising over twenty acres. This addition brings the area of allotments held by the association up to sixty acres. The association has a membership of 600, all working men.[49]

The sudden upswing in land available was in large part due to necessity, brought about by the war. In 1916 the Board of Agriculture and Fisheries wrote to local councils to inform them that a Regulation – the Cultivation of Lands Order – had been made by Order in Council, with the object of increasing food supply by extending the existing powers of providing land for cultivation.

The matter is urgent, as, if land is to be in the best condition for putting in Spring crops it is desirable that it should be broken up before the Winter is over. The President realises that Local Authorities are already seriously overburdened with work, but the urgency of increasing the food supply by

---

48 The Manchester Courier, Wednesday, December 23, 1908

49 Lichfield Mercury, Friday, December 15, 1916

all possible means is such that he feels sure he can rely on the active co-operation and assistance of your Council.[50]

With the help of the Vacant Land Cultivation Society, local residents of East Ham and West Ham and their respective councils took advantage of these new powers and ensured a proliferation in the number of allotments in the war years. In 1918 even West Ham Park was the site of 500 allotments of five rods each. By now both areas had become urbanised, so these small plots of land were in many ways symbolic of a way of life long since lost, and an indicator of the impoverishment of industrialisation. Now that the working class men of East and West Ham had won this victory – no matter how small – in the battle for rights to the land, they were keen to make it permanent, as the inter-war years saw many plots being reclaimed.

In 1939 the government launched the *Dig for Victory* campaign. Allotments had proven useful in combating food shortages during the blockades of the first world war, so the same tactic was employed again on a much grander scale. In 1942 the West Ham Allotment Society Limited (WHAS) managed allotments on at least seven sites, including Millmeads (120 plots), Wanstead Flats (430 plots), West Ham Park (240 plots), Temple Mills (46 plots), St Mary's Road (28 plots), Union Cottage (11 plots) and Clare Road (2 plots). This provided an impressive 877 plots, all managed by one Society on 54 acres of land.[51]

---

50 National Archives

51 West Ham Allotment Society Limited, February 28, 2007

Once again, however, councils reclaimed much of this land (in this case West Ham Council), and by 1951 the WHAS land was reduced by more than half. In 1957 they were forced to quit the Wanstead Flats, and in 1967 the land at Mill Meads, due the construction of the new Abbey Mills pumping station. By 1969 the Society was managing just 34 plots, at Millmeads. In 2007, the lock and water control system in the Prescott Channel was ready for construction, which meant that ten of the remaining plots were reclaimed by British Waterways. However, negotiations were made on their behalf with Thames Water and land adjacent to the surviving plots was secured.[52]

Not so lucky were the plot holders at Manor Garden Allotments, who had the misfortune to be located on the edge of the Olympic park. Established in 1900 by Major Arthur Villiers, director of Barings Bank, the land provided 80 individual plots that were worked for 107 years, until the Olympic Delivery Authority evicted the holders. The plight of the allotments attracted a lot of media attention – more so, in fact, than the plight of the residents of Clay's Lane who lost their homes and the gypsies who lost their camp at Temple Mills.

The plot holders were an eclectic and diverse mix. They included Samuel and Samantha Clarke, the couple behind the Moro restaurant in Clerkenwell, who based their third cookery book around the allotments. The site, though close to industry and busy roads, was sheltered in such a way as to feel part of a rural rather than urban world. Not that this

52 Ibid

mattered to the Olympic planners who, despite claims to be the greenest games on record, deemed that this naturally idyllic and peaceful spot that had been cultivated by local people for over 100 years was worth destroying for the sake of a path and some landscaping that is needed for three weeks. Despite a campaign to save the site, the bulldozers moved in and took it apart. When promises were made with the London Olympic bid for the most sustainable games ever, no one saw fit to explain specifically what that meant. It was just a bit of newspeak, like *legacy*. A report by the Soil Association that focused on food provision, and how it should be local, organic and ethical[53], would seem to have been ignored by the ODA – after all, how much more local could they get than Manor Garden Allotments? They could have literally thrown the vegetables onto the Olympic site, perhaps inventing a new Olympic sport of tossing the cucumber in the process.

A temporary site for the evicted plot holders, of no beauty and poor access, was found. The promise that the destruction of the Manor Gardens site was just a temporary measure led to the additional promise of relocation. The trouble is that the relocation is not to the original site but split into two sites nearby. To add insult to injury, the whole area has quite possibly been contaminated; it was reported by numerous sources that work on a nearby section of the Olympic park disturbed radioactive waste. Dust from this disturbance was carried by the wind, not

---

53 Robin Webster, Feeding the Olympics, How and why the food for London 2012 should be local, organic and ethical, The Soil Association. (2007)

only over the Manor Garden allotments as they campaigned for a stay of execution, but also over the residents of Clay's Lane, as well as the men working on the Olympic site. The land, it appears, is not ours once more. The Olympic games, it seems, is just a Trojan Horse for yet another land-grab.

Until the 19th century this area was still largely rural, and wasn't considered part of London. The Eastern edge of the city remained the River Lea, and over this border the land was a mixture of marsh and arable. Small hamlets existed at West Ham, Plaistow and Stratford, but life for the people who lived here was clearly different to those who lived in the city. History, for them, was running at a different speed.

The idea of marking land to signify ownership (hence, landmarks) appears to go back to Biblical times. The Romans introduced a form of land registration when they settled in England and Wales, which was linked to a land tax (tribute) called tributum soli. The Anglo-Saxons also had to pay tribute, this time to the Danish invaders. The Rudyard Kipling poem, *Dane-Geld A.D. 980-1016* neatly describes this arrangement.

It is always a temptation to an armed and agile nation
To call upon a neighbour and to say: --
"We invaded you last night--we are quite prepared to fight,
Unless you pay us cash to go away."

And that is called asking for Dane-geld,
And the people who ask it explain
That you've only to pay 'em the Dane-geld
And then you'll get rid of the Dane!

A system was needed to record land ownership in order to collect this tribute. But the inevitable happened when this recording process converged with the diminishing threat of Viking invasion. The temptation to collect the tax was too great to relinquish, and so we find that the nationality of 'Dane' is transferable. Though Kipling probably didn't intend it to be interpreted this way, he nevertheless points out in his poem the dilemma of paying the *dane-geld* in the first place.

It is always a temptation for a rich and lazy nation,
To puff and look important and to say: --
"Though we know we should defeat you, we have not the
time to meet you. We will therefore pay you cash to go away."

And that is called paying the Dane-geld;
But we've proved it again and again,
That if once you have paid him the Dane-geld
You never get rid of the Dane.[54]

William the Conquerer played the 'Dane' to devastating effect. Armed with the Domesday book of 1086 he was able to levy tax in a more systematic way than had ever previously been achieved. William declared that he was the owner of all the land in England, and as such it was he who leased it out. No surprise then that the land was predominantly parcelled out to his loyal Norman followers. The clergy too were targeted, with Normans replacing Anglo-Saxons.

---

54 Rudyard Kipling, *Dane-Geld* A.D. 980-1016

By the time of William's death in 1087, the manor of Ham was owned by Robert Gernon and Ranulph Peverel. This land covered 8 hides and 30 acres, and probably comprised most of West Ham.[55] There were 60 acres of meadow, woodland for 100 swine and 8 mills (the largest number in Essex).[56] The value of the land when Gernon Peverel had received it was £12 but it had doubled in value within 20 years. In the same time the population rose from 50 to 130. This is a significant rise for such a small community at this time, even over a 20 year period. It is suspected that the new arrivals came for a reason, which was forest clearance, an early form of intensive farming that was being practised by Gernon.[57] Though this level of growth in population was unusual during the early Norman occupation, and thus was significant in comparison to neighbouring areas, our knowledge of subsequent history renders our view not unlike that of looking the wrong way through a telescope. It isn't so much the passage of time that makes this small cluster of people and animals surrounded by meadow, marsh and woodland, seem so far away, as it is the obliterating impact of the changes upon this land. This was true, even when Katharine Fry wrote about it in the mid-19th century.

---

55 A hide was between 60 and 120 acres

56 'West Ham: Agriculture', A History of the County of Essex: Volume 6 (1973),

57 Ibid

...how great is the difference compared with the present state of the district! How small were the flocks and herds that grazed upon the widespread pastures, extending from the river Lea to the river Roding! Four farm horses then sufficed for the tillage of the district, while now (1850) we see long strings of loaded waggons nightly pursue their way to the London markets.[58]

But Fry would have been astonished if she had known that the population of West Ham in 1850 (circa 18,000, according to the 1851 census) would by 1901 have exploded to 267,000, and was still climbing.

Gernon was succeeded by William de Montfichet, who in 1135 founded the Cistercian Abbey of Stratford Langthorne and endowed it with his demesne land. The site of the Abbey was east of the Channelsea River and west of Manor Road, previously known as Marsh Lane, which gives us some clue to the nature of some of the land nearby. Monks from the Abbey of Savigny in Normandy were brought to Stratford.

The Cistercian monks were much devoted to agriculture and horticulture, which seem to have flourished under their care. Their selection of a site, although it might be solitary, was generally found in a fertile valley or well-watered plain; orchards and gardens abounded within the precincts of their

---

58 Kathryn Fry, G. Pagenstecher, History of the parishes of East and West Ham

abbeys, and it is very probable that some of the fruits now known in this country were originally introduced by them.[59]

As well as being keen on agriculture, the Cistercian monks had a reputation for avarice. Katharine Fry indicates that the 'brethren at West Ham formed no exception to this rule, for they never rested until they had obtained from the heirs of William de Montfichet the whole of the lordship of Ham, so far as it was in their power to bestow'.[60]The Abbey, in fact, became one of the richest in England and, because of its proximity to London, one of some importance.

The Abbey and its grounds would have been an impressive and perhaps imposing sight to anyone approaching London from the east. Inside, the monks lived an ascetic life, sleeping on beds of straw, wearing simple clothes and refraining from eating fish or animal products.[61]But this was to change over time as indulgence crept in. The Abbey's demesne lands stretched over a large area by the middle of the 13th century, and Fry implies that the spoils of this land were now being enjoyed by the monks.

The pleasures of the chase as well as a supply of game for the table were thus secured to the monks of Stratford, and fish they could obtain from their own waters, since they had a fishing-

59 Ibid, p92

60 Ibid, p99

61 Jim Lewis, East Ham & West Ham Past, Historical Publications. (2004)

house and piscatories on the river Lea. It would appear as if the churchmen of that age had widely parted from the simplicity and self-denial of their ancient founders. An old writer says of them "Bacon, cheese, eggs, and even fish itself can no more please their nice palates; they only relish the flesh-pots of Egypt, pieces of boiled and roast pork, good fat veal, otters and hares, the best geese and pullets, and in a word, all sorts of flesh and fowl do now cover the tables of holy monks..."[62]

One can imagine that the peasants weren't quite so lucky, though they got their revenge during the Peasant Revolts in 1381 when they invaded the Abbey, burnt its charters and stole its goods.

The grounds of the Abbey are thought to have been surrounded by a moat, and within it lay a slaughter house, barn, dove-house, stables, fish ponds, gardens and orchards. On one edge, on an island in the Channelsea, was the Abbey mill, which had once belonged to Queen Maud. The monks looking out over the open land in the opposite direction would have been able to see in the distance the tower of All Saints Church. A road led between the Abbey and this church. Its path is most probably followed today by Abbey Road, from Bakers Row, where the Abbey gatehouse is supposed to have stood.

Though the Abbey had at various times been host to the Kings of England, everything was to change when Henry

62 Kathryn Fry, G. Pagenstecher, History of the parishes of East and West Ham

VIII was in power. Inflation and costly wars against France and Scotland had drained the royal coffers and Henry looked for solutions. Casting a covetous eye at the riches of the church, the King used anti-Papal sentiments to push forward with the Dissolution of the Monasteries, and in 1538 the Abbey of Stratford Langthorne was resigned into the hands of King Henry VIII. The Abbot William Huddleston, the Prior William Parsons, the Chanter John Meryst, the Sacrist John Ryddsall and eleven monks were forced to sign a deed of surrender. One of the monks, John Wyght, had to sign with the mark of a cross as he was illiterate. These men, who had lived a sheltered and comfortable live – who had worked on the Abbey farm, tended its gardens, fished its waters and enjoyed its luxuries – were now cast out as needy men.[63]

King Henry VIII then granted the Abbey to Sir Peter Meautas, who let it fall into ruin. In 1784, when Thomas Holbrook bought land adjacent to the Adam and Eve public house which had been built within the Abbey grounds, he proceeded to dig up much of the remaining derelict buildings and foundations and use them or sell them for building materials. By this time West Ham was estimated to contain about 2,000 acres of arable land, a quarter of which was potato crop, and 2,500 acres of meadow and marshland. In 1853 just over 1,000 acres were under cultivation with potatoes, wheat, turnips, oats and rye being grown. By 1905 there remained only 127 acres of arable land and 51 acres of permanent grass. Of

---

63 Ibid

course, in that time the population had grown from around 19,000 to nearly 270,000 people. Factories had been built and the the Northern Outfall Sewer completed. These factors, added to the construction of the North Woolwich Railway through Abbey lands in 1840, meant that the decimation of the Abbey was complete. Not for West Ham, glorious arched ruins of Abbey walls to catch the light of the falling sun and attract tourists. The only evidence of the existence of its Abbey resided in All Saints Church, and for a time was built into the walls of the original Adam and Eve public house.

Excavations took place in 1994, when the Jubilee line extension was under construction. Part of what must have been the Abbey graveyard was uncovered and 500 bodies were removed. A further 80 burials were found at a different site, and excavations near Abbey Road bridge uncovered foundations of the Abbey, including pillar bases of the nave and a chapel wall. A picture is now beginning to emerge of the footprint of the Abbey and its grounds. West Ham Depot, for example, stands on ground that is believed to have been the gardens and agricultural land that the monks would have cultivated.

The Adam and Eve had a slab in its kitchen with brass studs for affixing religious icons.[64] It is unlikely that it was still there in 1991 when I last drank in this pub with friends. Sitting in the beer gardens on balmy summer evenings, or chilly winter ones, none of us had any idea that we were

---

64 WA Heritage, *Bridge Row Depot, Bakers Row, Stratford, London, E15; Archeological Desk-based Assessment* (2008)

drinking on the old Abbey grounds. The Adam and Eve was demolished in 1994 to make way for the Jubilee line.

Each time I walked from Aldworth Road to pick up a parcel from the Post Office on Abbey Lane I would pass the top of Bakers Row, by the Depot, and each time would see the overgrown patch of land opposite the row of small terraced cottages. Some of the residents in these cottages looked upon this piece of ground with despair, as it became a magnet for fly-tipping. Vowing to do something about this eyesore, they contacted the council to find out who owned the land, with a plan in mind to do some planting on it. They learnt that it was owned by the parks department and protected by English Heritage, as it was on the site of the Abbey. This protection was limited to commercial development, so Dasha French and Andreas Long, along with others, formed a community group called Friends of Abbey Gardens (FOAG) in December 2006, in order to raise funding for their project to transform the plot of land.

I visited the gardens on the first Saturday in December, 2011. The Saturday before my partner and I had taken our daughter and baby son to the Abbey Gardens Winter Chill, an event designed to bring some warmth and light to the darkness of a late winter afternoon. There I had been introduced to Erwan Guillo-Lohan, the chair of Friends of Abbey Gardens, and arranged to visit during one of the daytime gardening sessions to learn a bit about the history of the group and its work. It was a bright, crisp morning, and after being shown round the garden by Erwan and garden club leader Hamish Liddle, we retired to the cabin to talk, over a mug of tea and rock buns.

The project began initially with the idea of creating a public communal space. Having been covered in weeds and rubbish, and fenced-off for so long, the liberation of the small plot of land gave the nascent group a blank slate. After securing a grant from *UnLtd Awards* they created a website to generate public interest. The Docklands Light Railway extension was in progress at this time and a station was planned at the bottom of Bakers Row, adjacent to the far edge of the garden. On learning of the DLR's Public Art Strategy, FOAG wondered whether their own project could in some way link in with this initiative, and a tender was put out to this effect.

Erwan recalls that one suggestion was for a paved area with a fountain, while another was to pave the street all the way to the station, so it is hardly a surprise that they chose to run with the greener ideas of *Somewhere*, a creative company run by artists Nina Pope and Karen Guthrie. The pair secured funding from the Arts Council, while FOAG generated funds from Newham Council, who Erwan describes as being helpful and supportive, though he realises that it is a two-sided relationship when he says "We're a bit of a poster child for Newham."

Outside, Erwan had pointed out where the excavation team had uncovered remains of the Abbey in 2007, including part of the gatehouse which was situated roughly halfway down what is now Bakers Row. The brick foundations still visible in one section of the garden are those of the row of terraced houses that used to face the existing ones; they were demolished in the 1970s. He also explained that an environmental health inspection of the ground revealed contamination present in the soil, in the shape of arsenic, lead and benzo(a)pyrene, a legacy of the area's industrial past. This necessitated a costly solution involving the laying of a membrane that allows water to seep down, but prevents contamination heading in the other direction. Further protection was offered by planting in raised beds with enough top soil to ensure safety.

The first growing season was 2009 and included a Harvest Festival, where Sam Clarke of Moro cooked fresh garden produce for the 150 strong crowd. Regular gardening club sessions were held on Saturday's, led by Chris Cavalier.

"Chris was brought in by Somewhere," Erwan told me in the course of a potted history. "He wasn't actually a gardener before this, but he was very enthusiastic and good at engaging people. He was instrumental in getting people involved in the first year."

These gardening sessions, now led by Hamish Liddle, are perhaps the focal point of the whole operation. Liddle, who runs a gardening business, is paid on a contract, but everyone else contributes on a voluntary basis.

"People come with little knowledge," he explains, "and learn a lot, but importantly they learn how to look after *this* garden." Not only does this work for the collective ethos, but on an individual level each volunteer realises that it is their garden, as much as they want it to be, and around twenty people have keys to the cabin.

This isn't an allotment. As the plot is a heritage site, it is open to the public. While FOAG do all the gardening work, the council are in charge of maintaining the grass. From dawn till dusk it is open to anyone. I asked if there had been any vandalism, and Erwan and Hamish look at each other, trying to remember.

"People nick stuff sometimes, but it's not been so bad as to get people down too much." Erwan finally says. Hamish adds, "When people plant things they have to recognise that anyone can theoretically take them – it is a collective and open space." He pauses, as if trying to remember any details of negative reaction, but they appear to be few and far between, then Erwan recalls the time a note appeared, tied to the railings.

"It was from a local teenager who had come here with his girlfriend, and wanted to say thanks, because it was a nice quiet spot for them to get away for a while."

"Why else do you think people come here," I ask, meaning those who volunteer.

"All sorts of reasons," Erwan offers. "Nobody owns anything. There is the freedom to contribute as much or as little as you want. There's also the novelty aspect, the fact that we grow a wide variety of vegetables you don't find in the supermarkets."

"People bring things that you couldn't normally buy," adds Hamish. "For example, we have had people from Bangladesh bringing seeds of vegetables to grow here because they can't buy the food in the shops."

We talk for about half an hour about the history of the group, and the problems of funding that centre on the fact that there is money available to start projects, but much less to run them and sustain them. It is soon time for Erwan and Hamish to get to work. Back outside volunteers are working, including Lydia, the provider of the buns, and Charlie, who was born in Bethnal Green but, like many in the East End's migratory tide, ended up further east. He sits legs crossed on a bench outside the cabin, rolling a cigarette with the nimble fingers of a man who has got it down to a fine art. A fur-trimmed hat protects his head from the chill breeze. Behind him stands Bill Cunningham, flanked by two policeman. The photograph of the land grabbers has been blown up and stuck on the front of the cabin. The writing on the wall behind Cunningham has been reproduced, this time in orange plastic letters cut to mimic the hand painted style of the original graffiti, and proudly appears on the back wall of the Abbey Gardens plot. Both were the idea of Nina Pope and Karen Guthrie, who had come across the story of the Plaistow men when researching their commission. And so the words *What Will The Harvest Be?* appear on the wall of some public ground, a mile away from the wall where they originally appeared. A hundred and more years later the fate of the gardeners is somewhat different.

But Cunningham and his men didn't have the luxury of having permission to do what they did, and if the plot of land at Bakers Row wasn't protected by English Heritage, it is tempting to think that FOAG wouldn't have got very far either; they probably wouldn't have got the chance, as private development would have been on to the site like a rash.

With the common man long since deprived of the land, it is now in urban and suburban spaces that modern enclosure takes place. When I first arrived in London in 1991 a couple of friends took me on a drive down to the Docklands, to see up close the tower that stood alone, luminous against the black night sky viewed from the window of a flat on Manor Road, West Ham. We span round roundabouts and glided along deserted roads before parking somewhere in the heart of the development. Walking around the artificial streets on a winter's night, a few things struck me. Who would want to live here where the 'streets' were deserted? And everywhere we walked we were followed by the artificial eyes of security cameras. This was the dawn of a new era, when CCTV was still something of a novelty and 'leverage' was something most likely gained with the aid of a stout stick.

There was something *bad* about Docklands at this time. Canary Wharf tower stood alone back then, its pyramid top shining blue at night, a tiny red light blinking out a warning signal – but was it for the aircraft or for us? It was like some strange obelisk, a portent of doom perhaps. In John Mackenzie's 1980 film *The Long Good Friday*, Bob Hoskins plays the head of a London firm which is hoping to cash in on the proposed siting of a 1988 London Olympics on the disused docklands. It all goes wrong when his American mafia partners get cold feet due to an alarming number of killings in a short space of time – bloodletting that involves the IRA. The famous last scene sees Hoskins climb into his chauffeur driven car, only to see his wife being driven away by another car. An IRA man in the passenger seat (the then unknown Pierce Brosnan) turns to point a gun at his head. The camera focuses on the face of Hoskins, which reveals the flood of emotions that comes with a realisation of how he has arrived at this point, and what his fate is.

It is also the face of a man who knows his time is up, not just on this mortal coil, but in history. Though released in 1980, the film was made and completed in 1979, the year that Margaret Thatcher came to power. Year zero. It heralded the privatisation of the public, and new planning laws that enabled public-sector land in urban and suburban areas to be seized by a mix of stealth and economic force; modern day enclosure. The Docklands was the first big testing ground, and it was a resounding success for the private businesses involved. For the inhabitants of the rest of Tower Hamlets, however, it was ultimately just a brutal display of wealth that literally towered over what remained one of the poorest boroughs in the country. In some respects it was a blue print.

The same principles are used in gated communities, private developments designed to prevent all but the residents from entering. They have a history that stretches back much further than people might realise. One of the oldest was built by W.G. Tarrant in the 1920s, in the countryside around Weybridge. It is called St Georges Hill, the very same hill upon which Gerald Winstanley and the Diggers made their camp in 1649.

CHAPTER 5

Plaistow Past Tense

"London, when it came, came with a rush, and swamped the old village of Plaistow"

John Spencer Curwen

We were going to see something that wasn't even there. Admittedly this was a hard sell and I was surprised that my partner agreed. If she had been in any way familiar with Plaistow, she wouldn't have left the house. Those local to this part of E13 would hardly be inclined to go for a midday walk round the residential streets of anywhere else, so why would an outsider feel the need to walk round theirs? After all, there is nothing to see. Life exists mostly behind closed doors, or inside cars going from one place to another. Even the pubs are being sucked dry of their sap, blinking out of existence one after another like victims of some strange plague. Gone. Probably forever. Likewise, the places I was interested in, on the whole, no longer exist. There are barely even traces. Even the memories of them belong with the dead, the bones of some of whom, I expect, lie buried in the earth of East London Cemetery.

So, on a warm Monday in August 2009 we took the Jubilee line one stop to West Ham, changed to the District Line and got off one stop later in Plaistow. We took our seven month old daughter with us, wheeling her in her buggy. Normally an inquisitive traveller, she wasn't taken with the charms this part of the East End had to offer. She slept for much of our journey, which was primarily to locate the original site of the Land Grabbers' Triangle Camp.

As you exit the tube station and head down the gradually diminishing slope of the High Street, you can't help but be underwhelmed with the sheer drabness before you. The colours are greys, muddy browns and dirty white. Buildings look unloved. The green facade of the Costcutter supermarket on the junction of High Street and Upper Road adds some colour, but its hue fails to lift the spirits. Today, even the clouds in the sky are uninspiring, a bland carpet of ill-defined cumulus obscuring the blue, and moving monotonously over the urban sprawl that sees one part of Newham blend seamlessly into another. A stranger driving through wouldn't notice or care where one place suddenly becomes another. Only local pride cares about that. And historians. And cartographers.

One particular cartographer, John Roque, spent ten years working on a map of London that was published in 1747. At the time it was the most detailed map of the city. On it we see Plaistow as a small village hugging what are now named North Street, Richmond Street, High Street, Balaam

Street and Greengate Street. According to John Spencer Curwen, the latter ended at an eponymous gate that prevented cattle from straying off the marshes to the south[65]. To the north Roque indicates cultivated fields, while gardens and orchards are depicted within the village itself.

When Curwen wrote about Old Plaistow, over 150 years after Roque published his map, much of the "Old" was still there, in terms of architecture at least. Though the village had by this time grown into a town, Curwen believed it had lost none of its former interest. He wrote that with the art of observation and reflection, even the dullest places can become intellectually stimulating. Today, however, these skills alone are not enough. Much of what was interesting has disappeared, and it now requires imagination to see what once was, and the ghosts of those who once breathed the air.

Ghosts like Emily Harriet Coombes, who was murdered by her own son one night in Cave Road in 1895, and lay on the bed upstairs decomposing in her own dried blood, only the rats for company, nibbling at her flesh, eating her brain away. She was a very excitable woman, Emily. Cried and laughed at the same time, but that's no reason to drive a dagger through her heart. It seems young Robert can't have been right in the head to do such a shocking thing as kill his own mother.

Ghosts like Florence Billing, who was shot dead by her husband because she was a drunken and intemperate woman who drank away the rent money, so he had to pawn all the

---

65 Old Plaistow – John Spencer Curwen: 1905 4th ed.

sheets and blankets in the house. He shot her dead, kissed his youngest daughter, said goodbye and walked away along Shepherd Street. Underneath the skin of the twentieth century with its uniform urban logic lies this fascinating period of change and upheaval, containing stories of displacement and despair. Underneath these pavements isn't the beach, but marshes and once fertile land. Where unremarkable buildings now exist, grand ones once stood, and all that remains of the people are the bones in the cemeteries. This is a different Plaistow that exists in the lost land between memory and imagination.

There are two theories as to how Plaistow derived its name. One is that it comes form the word *playstow*, meaning play place, and was sometimes used to describe a village green. The other theory is that it comes from Hugh de Plaiz, once Lord of the Manor, thus stow, or village of de Plaiz. Whichever you are inclined to believe is probably less important than acknowledging the local pronunciation, which is *Plarstow*. As we will see, the early inhabitants were a rural mix of the noteworthy and those who worked the land, or kept the livestock that fed on it.

The old village stopped where the firm ground ended, and the marsh was used as grazing ground for cattle and sheep. Oxen were used for ploughing, but also for pulling wagons through the streets, which were lined with great elms.[66] They were also employed in the mill where chaff was cut, or water pumped for washing potatoes and other vegetables.[67] In 1720

---

66 Ibid. p19

67 Ibid. p56

an ox reared on Plaistow marshes became the largest ever sold in England, weighing some 236 stone.

The Rev. R. W. B. Marsh, who lived in Plaistow for 42 years from 1842, described it as a very primitive village when his father first arrived in 1799: 'out of the world it led nowhere; it was what Lancashire people call a poke (or pocket) – a way in, no way out'.[68] He was, of course, talking in geographical terms and referring to barriers such as the marshes and the river, but as Plaistow grew into a poor industrial area swamped by urban sprawl, there are many who may have found that there was indeed no easy way out of their poverty trap.

Above the village the farm land was for the most part devoted to potato growing. Elsewhere market gardens and orchards provided an abundance of delights, a roll call of which is immortalised in *Plaistow, A Poem*, published in the January 1734 edition of *London Magazine*.

> *Does curious fruit your palate please?*
> *Profusion wantons on our trees.*
> *The pippin, and the Windsor-pear*
> *Grow ripe in their perfection here.*
> *Our orchards hit each taste that comes,*
> *With grapes, nuts, berries, medlars, plumbs.*
> *Walk thro' this garden, view this wall,*
> *How plump this peach ! nor is it small,*
> *These apricocks, ripe to decay,*

68 Ibid. p45

Wou'd in your mouth dissolve away.
What flavour ! what delicious juice,
These nect'rines to the tongue produce!
And what more lovely can you see,
Than those red cherries on the tree?
Come here ; for what I need not tell,
Ambrosial sweets will meet your smell,
Pinks, roses, lillies, to your eyes
At once in gay confusion rise.
Wild variegated scenes appear,
And mingles sweets perfume the air.[69]

The poet also makes reference to hunting game and hares with hounds, nets and guns, an activity which Curwen also remembers from his youth almost a hundred years later.

The marsh itself was in winter the haunt of swarms of wild fowl, and as the shooting was practically free, and nearly every working man had a gun, there was plenty of sport. Herons fished in the ditches, and an east wind brought thousands of plover, duck, teal, widgeon, and snipe. The best way was to go out by night, lie low, and wait for the dawn. It was cold work, but I am told it was capital sport. I can testify too that the ditches were fine places for skating. You could go, as in Holland, straight on for miles.[70]

---

69 Plaistow. A Poem – London Magazine, January 1734

70 Old Plaistow – John Spencer Curwen p.19

This arcadian vision contrasts strongly with the incoming tide of heavy industrialisation. Rev. Marsh, in the appendix to Curwen's book, laments the loss of the trees and gardens that were to make way for a 'colony of streets', but like Curwen he falls short of romanticising rural England in the way that painters like Constable did. Curwen himself, as well as opining that Plaistow was still a place of interest, also made some observations on the problems that industrialisation brought in terms of population, which increased eightfold between 1861 and 1891: namely, that an influx of people with no attachment to an area leads to mistrust. To see the darker side of this mistrust, we have to look to the newspapers of the day.

Richard Harvey, a ship's apprentice, was out hunting one Tuesday in November 1864 with Josiah Garter and other parties, when he was sent into the reeds to drive up birds for the men to shoot at. It was here that he discovered a decapitated body. In the Stratford Police court Garter described the corpse as having had the flesh from its hands gnawed away by rats. The headless corpse was that of John Fuhurhop, a German national. The long arm of the law moved swiftly enough, without the aid of modern surveillance, to have arrested two suspects by the following day, namely Ferdinand Edward Karl Kohl, a native of Holland, and his wife of just five weeks Hannah, an English woman. On the same day, inspector G. N. Goode found the victims head in the hole of a water rat.

Local interest in the case was great. The Daily Post recorded the inquest room as being crowded to suffocation and also reported that the crime scene had been visited by thousands.[71] Another newspaper reported that four thousand people from Silvertown had gone to see the body. The inquest was held at the Bell and Anchor Tavern, Victoria Dock, and *The Daily News* reported the grisly details.

On the skin of the neck, and on the vertebrae of the neck, were the only evidence of murderous violence that were to be found on the body. The skin on the front of the neck presented the distinct marks of attempted cuts made with a knife that had lost its edge. The bone was chopped much as a piece of wood would be by a chopper. The flesh was absent from different parts of the arms and trunk, but this was owing to the gnawing of rats. The head, however, was terribly injured: right over the nose was a severe injury from a blow, and over the left eye and temple the skull was indented by another blow. At the back of the head, near the base, was a punctured hole, which had penetrated to the brain, and through which a finger could easily be inserted. In Mr. Morris's opinion this wound had caused death instantaneously, and that then the other blows were inflicted merely to make certain of the death. The brain had exuded through the wound at the back of the head.[72]

Khol had met Fuhurhop on a steamer from Germany to England. Noticing that Fuhurhop was well-to-do in comparison to himself, Khol didn't take long to ingratiate himself. Fuhurhop,

---

71 Daily News Thursday 11 November 1864

72 The Daily News – 11 November 1864

who spoke no English and was intending to travel on to America, lodged on his arrival with a Mrs. Warren. After a short while, however, he moved in with Khol, who was no doubt waiting for the opportunity to divest him of his money and belongings. These included gold sovereigns and other valuables, which he took to a variety of pawn shops after the murder .

Khol chose a remote spot for the murder, down a narrow path through a reed bed near a mangold-wurzel field. Wide enough only to travel in single-file, Khol made sure that Fuhurhop stepped onto the path first. Thus his fate was sealed. The path was submerged at high-tide and was a place that very few people would ever consider going to. If it hadn't been for Josiah Garter and the hunting party, Khol may have gotten away with his foul deed. His complete lack of care afterwards, though, made his arrest inevitable.

Although the scene of the crime no longer exists – or is now buried beneath the streets and dual carriageways that cover the part of East London where Canning Town meets Silvertown – the murder and its press coverage shed light on the issues that industrial growth brought. Poverty is an obvious one, along with the sudden influx of strangers. Both were clearly factors in this case involving two foreigners. As my partner and I walked down the high street, stopping off to buy a bottle of water at the colourful Costcutter supermarket, thoughts of murderous deeds from long past were not on our minds. A sign above the supermarket revealed, however, that although the physical geography of the area may have changed beyond all recognition over 145 years, one thing remained constant; the displaced are still placed, or placing themselves, in the area. It read: *Large selection of Russian, Lithuanian, Polish & German delicatessens, beers, wines and spirits available here.*

Upper Road, on the top corner of which the supermarket sits, runs south from the High Street towards Grange Road. It bends just over halfway down where it runs over the Northern Outfall Sewer, now rebranded the Greenway. On the south side of this construction lies East London Cemetery, and it is on this stretch of road that 120 years earlier the brief saga of the Plaistow Ghost took place, recorded for posterity by Reynolds Newspaper on Sunday 2nd June 1889.

George Orchard, 16, a brass-moulder, of 77, Grange Road, Plaistow, was charged, at West Ham, with disorderly conduct and with wilfully extinguishing a public street-lamp at Upper road, Plaistow.

Prisoner, when asked to plead, said that he had got up the lamp-post and turned the gas down, as the people wanted to see "the ghost." (Laughter.)

Mr. Baggallay: The what? A ghost?

Prisoner: Yes; and I was asked to put the lamp out

Constable Dubery, 144 K, said that about half-past ten o'clock the other night he was on duty in Upper-road, Plaistow, when his attention was attracted by a crowd of about 200 people who were "waiting to see the ghost," and they had an idea that if the lamps were turned down they could see it better. Witnesses saw the prisoner go up a lamp post and turn the light out, and he added that every night for

*the last month there had been a large disorderly crowd about
that road waiting to see "the ghost."*

Mr. Baggallay: Has anyone seen it?

Witness: I have been on duty there for a month.

Mr. Baggallay: And you've not seen it?

Witness: No. The crowd is always very disorderly.

*Mr. Fowler (the clerk): They have found out now what
"the ghost" is, haven't they?*

*Witness: It has been discovered that it was a granite
tombstone. When the light caught it at a certain angle, it gave
it the appearance of a ghost.*

Mr. Baggallay: This road is close to the cemetery is it not?

Witness: Yes, it is very lonely.

Mr. Baggallay: Not lonely if there were 200 there.

*Witness: It is a long road, and there are no houses.
The crowds are very disorderly; they push people off the path,
and skylarking generally goes on.*

*Mr. Baggallay: It must be stopped somehow, of course;
but how far this can be done by dealing with this little boy I
don't know.*

*Prisoner: The cemetery-keeper, a grave-digger, and
another man went into the cemetery and they hollored out,
"Turn out the light." I did so, and just at that moment the
constable took me.*

*Witness: The cemetery-keeper has been out several
nights with a gun to keep the roughs away.*

*Mr. Fowler (the clerk): There is some suspicion of
body-snatching?*

Witness: I've never heard of it.

Mr. Baggallay: I read of it this morning. Perhaps the press were before the police for once. (To Prisoner): Well, you'd better not put the lamps out again: and I think the police had better see that some extra constables are put on the spot for duty.

Inspector Bishop: All right, your worship. The lad is a good boy.

Mr. Baggallay: He did as he was told. (To Orchard): You may go.

Prisoner was then released.[73]

Aside from finding amusement in the hapless Constable Dubery, it is interesting to note the subject of body snatching being raised. It is a topic that Curwen also alludes to in his book some 16 years later. In the earlier half of the century a gang of body snatchers had operated from Barking, 'and whenever a burial took place at East Ham Church the grave had to be watched all night till nature had rendered the corpse valueless for sale.'[74]

We walked down the High Street towards the Broadway, a short stretch of road leading to Greengate Street, passing The Black Lion on the way. This pub, one of the oldest in the area and with its coach yard still in existence, is said to have been

---

73 Reynolds Newspaper, Sunday, June 2, 1889

74 Archer Philip Crouch, Silvertown and Neighbourhood (including East Ham and West Ham): A Retrospect, 1900

a watering hole for Dick Turpin. It is likely that he frequented it as he worked for a time on Richmond Street, at the bottom corner of which the pub stands. Turpin worked as servant to Farmer Giles at a house in Richmond Street and after stealing two of his employer's fat oxen, his criminal career began. When the skins were sold at Waltham Abbey they were recognised, and Turpin only avoided arrest by leaping from a window to escape the officers. He next settled in Epping Forest, stealing deer and house breaking, before turning to the robbery that forged his legend. He married a woman from East Ham who would often stay with him in his cave hideout in the then little frequented forest. Eventually he would move north, and it was here that his lawless life came to an end. He was tried in Yorkshire for horse stealing and executed on April 7th 1739.

More recent customers of note have come in the shape of footballers from West Ham United, including Bobby Moore and Harry Redknapp. Redknapp recalls that nobody would bother them while they drank, a situation unimaginable in today's celebrity-drenched era. Graham Paddon, a member of the West Ham team who won the 1975 F.A. Cup, remembers the victory parade passing the pub the day after the match. The streets were packed to bursting with men, women, children and even dogs sporting claret and blue. The thirsty players requested a crate of beer from the landlord, but the victorious team were told they would have to pay for it.

Other sporting connections with the pub include the Black Lion Monarchs, the cycle speedway team who used the track built by Harry Eyre over tennis courts on the ground at the rear of the pub. Popular locally until the 1960s, the best boys hoped to graduate to speedway proper and perhaps race at the West Ham Speedway circuit at Custom House.

Though the days of cycle speedway are long gone, the famous West Ham Boys boxing club remains. Formed in 1922, their alumni includes Terry Spinks, who won Olympic gold in 1956 when he was just 18; Nigel Benn, who won the ABAs as a West Ham Boy in 1986; Jimmy Tibbs; and Mark Kaylor. The club had just had a stay of execution from a planned sell-off by the landlord of the pub to developers who wanted to build a block of flats. A week-long campaign by locals persuaded him to change his mind.

By now it was approaching midday and the sun was nearly overhead. I pulled the hood of the buggy down over my sleeping daughter and looked up at the sky. The cloud cover had thinned out, but they looked like cumulus. I wouldn't have bet on it, however, as since learning about the different types of clouds at school I had, like most people, let the knowledge drift away, out of my memory banks like a wispy stratus formation. Clouds are just clouds. Some are fat, some are thin. They change shape. When they are dark it tends to rain. If there are too many up there obliterating the blue then my mood gets pushed down by their presence.

Luke Howard saw clouds a bit differently. In 1783 violent volcanic eruptions in Iceland and Japan had sent massive amounts of volcanic ash and dust into the atmosphere, causing hazy skies in the Northern Hemisphere between May and August. In Norfolk the sunsets were copper-coloured. On the 18th of August a further event occurred that added to the dramas of the sky.

About Nine o'Clock at Night, a Body of Fire, or some other luminous Matter, took a horizontal Direction from North to South, across the Firmament, and its Transit emitted Light nearly as vivid as the Rays of the Sun at Noon-Day; it was not circular, but of an irregular Form, and had a Tail something resembling a Kite, with variegated Colours; the Reflection was so powerful, that it affected some People's Eyes like a Flash of Lightening. Such a sudden and uncommon Phenomenon created much Astonishment in all that saw it, and had a powerful Effect on the Minds of the vulgar; they (as is generally the Case when any Thing preternatural happens) portending that some terrible Calamity would happen to the Country.[75]

Howard was just ten years old when he witnessed these events. The astonishment they created in him was never to leave, and a lifelong fascination with the skies ensued. Some twenty years after the dramas he observed, Howard presented a paper to the Askesian Society called, *On the Modification of Clouds.* This paper proposed that clouds could be classified. Howard posited that all clouds could be put into three distinct categories; cumulus, stratus and cirrus. He added a fourth, nimbus, to describe clouds in the process of turning to rain, hail or snow. Although he wasn't the first person to do so (a Frenchman

---

75 Northampton Mercury – Monday 25th August 1783

Lamarck had done so a year earlier), by using Latin names he transcended national and language barriers. Consequently it is his nomenclature, not Lamarck's, that remains today and was used in the wonderfully named *International Cloud Atlas*, first published in 1896. Howard's genius was to, in the words of Goethe; 'hold fast conceptually the airy and always changing form of clouds, to limit and fasten down the indefinite, the intangible and unattainable and give them appropriate names.' As well as poets like Goethe and Shelley, his work was also praised by the painters Turner and Constable, the former famous for depicting skies that look aflame, perhaps like the ones Howard observed as a boy during the *Great Fogge*.

As well as naming clouds, Howard wrote about the atmosphere, rain and London climate; he discovered that the urban centre was warmer at night than the surrounding countryside, attributing the difference to the extensive use of fuel in towns and cities. But as impressive as his meteorological work was, his main trade was a chemist. It was in this capacity that he moved with his family to Plaistow to set up a chemical laboratory, living in Chesterton House, Balaam Street. This grand house and gardens became a clinic of the Plaistow Maternity Hospital in 1915, before being demolished in 1960. His second son, John, was born in Plaistow in 1807 and would in later life receive great acclaim for his work relating to the use of quinine in the treatment of malaria and fever. Quinine and aspirin were two of the pharmaceutical chemicals that Howards & Sons were best known for. The laboratory moved to Stratford Mills in 1805, but the family remained in Plaistow until 1812, when they moved to Tottenham. They bequeathed to Plaistow a valuable water pump in Chesterton Road at a time when wells were few and far between. The family name lives on in the form of Howards Road.

The top of Balaam Street comes out at the beginning of the Broadway. On the corner, where the roads meet, stands the Coach and Horses, its windows blacked out to the world and another name to add to the long list of disappearing pubs of England. Dick Turpin supposedly frequented the pub to gamble. Continuing in this vein of notoriety, it is on this corner, just before the pub, that Dr. Dodd lived. He is listed in the National Portrait Gallery online archives thus;

William Dodd (1729-1777), Parson and forger. Sitter in 6 portraits. The son of a clergyman, he was noted in his youth not just for academic excellence but also for his elegance of dress and, like a moth to the flame, an attraction to the gay amusements of his day, that was to prove ruinous. Once describing himself as "a zealous votary of the god of Dancing", he quit University for the bright lights of London seeking fame as an author, but only succeeding in marrying the daughter of one of the domestics of Sir John Dolben, then residing in Frith Street in Soho. Now economically impotent he was rescued by his father and in 1751, the ink on his marriage certificate barely dry he was ordained a deacon by the Bishop of Ely, at Caius College, Cambridge. He dedicated himself to studying the duties of his new profession with such attention, and apparent sincerity, that in 1752 he was elected to succeed the Rev. Mr Wyatt, vicar of West Ham, whom he had been working with.

During his 14 years in West Ham he became a popular preacher and an active promoter of Magdalen House charitable hospital, as well as the Society for the Relief of Poor Debtors and the Humane Society. In 1763 he was chaplain to the King and was recommended to the Earl of Chesterfield as a tutor to his nephew, the Hon. Philip Stanhope, who was being groomed as the Earl's successor.

Resigning his lectureship in 1766 he left West Ham and the house in Balaam Street for London, where his penchant for the extravagant life returned with a vengeance; it wasn't long before he was living beyond his means. The beginning of the sorry end for Dodd came in 1774 when, as a result of an insulting letter to Lady Apsley involving a bribe, he was struck off as a chaplain, which led to abuse and ridicule in the press. On the 4th of February 1777 he forged a bond for £4,200, in the name of his former pupil, now Lord Chesterfield. When Chesterfield expressed innocence as to the signature on the bond, Dodd was arrested. Though he returned at once the bulk of the money, and his former pupil wished the matter to be hushed up, the Lord Mayor denied him such clemency and he was sent to trial.

At the trial the jury returned a verdict of 'guilty', but presented a petition recommending the doctor to royal mercy. On the last day of the sessions Dodd was asked by the clerk what he had to say in his defence. Dodd proceeded to speak, and in doing so bared his soul. 'Many motives impel me to beg earnestly for life. I feel the natural horror of a violent death, the universal dread of untimely dissolution. I am desirous to recompense the injury I have done to the clergy, to the world, and to religion, and to efface the scandal of my crime, by example of my repentance; but, above all, I wish to die with thoughts more composed, and calmer preparation.'[76]

He then begged for mercy before collapsing. For a man used to the idea of the Lord's forgiveness, it must have seemed as if God had suddenly been sucked out of the Universe as the cold, dread words left the lips of the Recorder and the sentence of the law was passed: 'I am obliged to pronounce the sentence of the law, which is – That you, Doctor William Dodd, be carried from hence to the place from whence you came; that from thence you be carried to the place of execution, and that there you be hanged by the neck until you are dead.'[77]

Aside from the name, these are the very same words that Ferdinand Edward Karl Kohl would hear nearly a hundred years later, along with many others, some of whose stories appear in this book. But unlike Kohl, Dodd was tormented by hopes of a pardon as great efforts were made to save him by individuals of all ranks. Newspapers were filled with letters of support. A petition of nearly 30,000 signatures was presented to the king, at a time when the population of Plaistow numbered somewhat less than 2,000. All to no avail.

---

76 The Newgate Calendar

77 Ibid

On the 27th of June Dodd was taken by mourning coach from Newgate to Tyburn, crowds thronging the streets, until he reached his hanging place. Here he was put in the cart alongside a man called John Harris, whom he spoke to before praying for them both, and also his wife. Another man had been sentenced to death at the same time, but had received a last minute reprieve. Details of who this lucky man was, and the length of his good fortune, have disappeared into the historical mist however, like the fine details of a dream after waking. Lost.

The house by the Coach and Horses where Dodd had lived was pulled down in 1890. Now housing corporation flats stand in the spot, next to the dead pub on the Broadway. It is believed that bull-baiting used to take place in the Broadway, at a time when only two or three houses stood and beyond lay open fields. Curwen recalls the inhabitant of one of these houses, a Mr. Hall, who would fire his gun every night at 10 o'clock in his back garden, surmising that it was either to tell his neighbours it was time to retire, or warn prospective burglars of the fate that would await them should they be foolish enough to enter his abode. Also on Broadway, on the south side, stood the grandest house in Plaistow, lived in by the Marten family. William Wilberforce was a frequent visitor to this three storey abode, but the building was pulled down in 1882, some thirty years after the Marten family left for Blackheath. Robert Humphrey Marten had bought the house in 1806 and it wasn't long before he upset the less financially blessed inhabitants of the village, who tended to take solace for their poverty in ale, and at fairs like the rowdy, bawdy ones at Bow and Barking.

Attempts at establishing a similar fair at Plaistow at the turn of the 19th century were scuppered after three years when, in 1808, the magistrates put it down, with the help of special constables who were drafted in to quell the riot that resulted from this act of suppression. But if the locals couldn't have the 'World Turned Upside Down', then they were determined to hang on to their right to indulge in less carnivalesque pursuits, such as Easter sports days opposite the Greengate Inn and feast day held at the Black Lion, which involved much drunken revelry and rambunctiousness.

In 1809 Marten decided to put a stop to the 'rural sports' that had been taking place on Whit Monday since three years previously and, calling a meeting of a few of the more 'respectable inhabitants of the village', posted a bill proclaiming any such games or fair illegal. In response another bill was posted, reputedly by the hands of John Cochrane, encouraging people to assemble, enjoy the games and races, and be ready for the donkey race at 3 o'clock.

Suspicious that the gathering of 'people of the lowest description" were going "to commit the most offensive acts, and to claim a universal license to play the fool, and to establish a fair at Plaistow,'[78] Marten and his high-minded companions raised the issue with Mr. Manby, the local magistrate. On the day, constables and peace officers from Woodford, Barking and

---

78 The Sporting Magazine. Vol 36. 1810

West Ham arrived to put a stop to proceedings. The offensive acts, apart from the donkey racing, were sack racing, gurning competitions and 'giving a bounty to those who shall eat hasty pudding with the greatest voracity.'

Not missing a chance for mischief on the day, the crowd, led by young William Grewer, decided to call on the estimable Marten for a tip – half a crown – for the sports. When he refused, tempers frayed. When the farmer James Adams arrived in his carriage with Richard Gregory, he was met by Timothy West, the butcher who had served his family for twenty years. West, presumably not concerned about losing a customer, but incensed that a customer of his would try to stop the fun, stood before Adams' carriage and cursed. "Damn your eyes, Jem Adams, I thought you knew better," then addressing the crowd added, "turn him over the rascal, turn him over." But though they might have given his carriage a good rocking, they did not turn it over and Adams was eventually able to drive on, noticing as he did the hallooing crowd carrying somebody dressed in ribbons, an apparently disturbing sight to the eyes that had only just been damned.

The special constables, meanwhile, were busy stopping every attempt to run the donkey race. Revellers were dashing about amid the donkeys, running away from special constables. Fifes and drums were being played and Archer, dressed in his ribbons, was standing in a cart bawling and ridiculing every person that passed, until the peace-officers took him into custody in the watch house. The constables, sticking to their task to the letter, then prevented Cochran and Birch from contesting a running race by blocking the road. Cochran ran into them and, upset that they were denying his progress down the King's highway, called them black-guards and directed a stream of foul and vulgar abuse in their general direction. When the same constables yet again prevented a donkey race (this time a solo-affair), Cochran called them a parcel of rascals.

The rascally parcel also had to prevent Thomas Bowman racing Archer's donkey, and then a more formidable obstacle of several asses being run from the Greyhound public-house. Bowman and Archer, meanwhile, were put into the watch house: Archer first, and then Bowman, who had come to rescue him.

The whole affair led to "The King v. John Cochran and others," with the charge of conspiracy and riot. The prosecution included such local notables as Mr. Gurney (counsel), Mr. Ward, and of course Farmer Adams and Robert Humphrey Marten. For the defence stood Sergeant Best. When various constables were questioned as to the use of their long staves to strike men, boys and women, and of pushing people off donkeys, blanket denial was the order of the day. However, in summing up the judge, Justice Heath, expressed his opinion that there was no evidence of any attempt to establish a fair, and that donkey races, women racing for shifts and other such larking about did not constitute a riot. Sergeant Best, by declaring that the "Methodists" wanted everyone to be as glum as themselves, was playing to a gallery that would have been very aware of the significance of the carnival. If those who had gathered for fun on the Broadway hadn't managed to turn the world upside down, they certainly gave it a wobble.

The Broadway now is nondescript. A handful of shops, houses and a constant stream of traffic make it a place where you have no reason to linger. Life is elsewhere, and most of the grand houses of old Plaistow have long since been ground to dust.

We turned onto North Street, my partner drinking from the bottle of water as the sun got hotter, and Luke Howard's clouds became ever more lonely up in the blue sky. Over the road was the Prince Regent pub and, on the corner where we stood, a three storey block of purpose-built flats. In the 1970s a couple of shops, Vickers and J J Perry, stood in the same spot, their roofs a ramshackle patchwork of corrugated iron panels. Health and safety in those days were two words that had yet to make each other's acquaintance. Many of that generation still had memories of the war, and playing as children on old bomb-sites, so buildings with far more angles than might be considered structurally sound were a common site and of little concern. In 1984, sometime after a fire in what was then an electrical suppliers shop, the whole corner was demolished. The only trace of the previous occupancy are the memories of locals and a handful of black and white photographs in the Newham Archives.

We walked up North Street, pushing our daughter in the buggy before us, still sound asleep.

"So, what exactly are we looking for again?" my partner asked. We had paused outside Eleanor Smith School, a primary for pupils excluded from other schools. Being summer it was closed, bright red metal shutters pulled down tight over all the windows. I checked an A-Z, still not sure which was the best route to take after St. Mary's Road, which lay just ahead.

"Something that probably isn't there anymore," I said. She threw me a look. I shrugged. "Somewhere around here," I added and pointed with my finger at the map.

"And where are we now? On the map?" I pointed at North Street on paper, then pointed up at the actual street in the direction we were heading.

Between Glasgow Road and the end of the street there lies a cluster of bland houses, the type that you can find in any town and city in England, built in the eighties of dark red brick with small windows and a small footprint. In another time, another Plaistow, this is where the Curwen print works once stood. An illustration of the works from 1896 depicts something far grander than today's impoverished architecture. The works was established by the Rev. John Curwen, who had been appointed pastor of the Independent Chapel. It was in the chapel and the school he established next to it that Curwen first started his press, after deciding to print his adaption of Sarah Glover's 'tonic sol-fa' notation for music.

Curwen realised that this method of notation was a simpler way of achieving musical literacy, with the potential to reach the wider audience of the working classes. He also saw the benefits of having a form of notation that didn't require any of the special characters or printing processes that traditional staff notation did. The standard printing press characters would do the job just fine. Upon his death in 1880, Curwen was succeeded by his sons, John Spencer and Joseph Spedding, and the future of J.Curwen and Sons as a printer of growing repute was established. Noting the advanced techniques being used in Germany, the Curwens acquired the lithographic equipment that enabled them to carry out all their work at the Plaistow base. Spedding's son, Harold, who when only fourteen had accompanied him on fact finding missions to Leipzig, joined the company in 1908. A few years later Harold was to link up with two significant figures. The first was journalist Joseph Thorp, who began to act as his agent and, more importantly, suggested using artists as a way of forging an identity for the Press. The second, Claud Lovat Fraser, was one such artist.

Key to the success of the business was diversifying into more commercial avenues. As well as books, Curwen became known for the quality and attention to aesthetics in all its products, ranging from booklets, display cards, business cards and other advertising materials to Christmas cards and wrapping paper. A leaflet advertising the company in 1920, designed by Lovat Fraser, reveals the prevailing ethos: *Get the Spirit of Joy into your printed things. The world's dead tired of drab dullness in Business Life.*

There was precious little joy to be seen as we wheeled the buggy along. And precious little life on the deserted midday summer streets. We reached the top of North Street where several roads converge; North Street running north west onto Pelley Road, while Richmond Street joins St. Mary's Road in a dog-leg that crosses North Street. If you stand in the middle of this crooked crossroads, where once stood a gas lamp standard, and look South, East or West, you are confronted with joyless modern housing where attention to detail is totally absent. Richmond Street, in particular, when compared to historical photographs and written accounts seems to have suffered cruelly at the hands of post war town planners, with only the Black Lion pub at it's end providing any sense of history.

A painting of the view to the south of this crossroads, by A. Viney Rust, depicts the scene sometime in the 19th Century. Where a row of houses and school playground now exist at the top of Richmond Street, there used to be Smith's Timber Yard and, next to it, Pinnock Place, a short row of houses occupied by immigrant Irish potato workers. One of the houses had an overhanging first floor, and was described by Curwen in 1891 as the oldest house standing in Plaistow. Perhaps these workers were related to the Irish contingent blamed by Robert Humphrey Martin as making up the majority of the unruly mob who caused chaos on the High Street back in 1806.

The God-fearing amongst Pinnock Place wouldn't have had far to go to confess their mortal sins: a stone's-throw distant was the Church of St. Mary, built in 1830. Though not particularly large, it was an impressive site, standing on the outside corner of North Street and St. Mary's Road. Curwen chose the site on the opposite corner to build his print works. Both buildings are now gone. The church was rebuilt on a much grander scale in 1894, but by the late 1970's its size became its downfall as dwindling attendance rendered it somewhat impotent. A tiny church, by comparison, now stands in its place, lost in a children's playground and looking more like a scout hut. This can't even be seen when looking at this corner. Both the church and the print works have been replaced by housing of an uninspiring design. What remains, however, provides a rare monument to Old Plaistow: the building housing the Given-Wilson Institute, named after Thomas Given-Wilson, who succeeded R.W.B. Marsh as vicar of St. Mary's in 1884. It was during his incumbency, which ended upon his death in 1914, that the first church was demolished and the second, much larger church was built. Forming part of the original church buildings, the institute is now an open charity providing its space for local people.

The Rev. Marsh had lived in one of two houses that resulted from the conversion of Dr. Dodd's residence on Balaam Street, and a few pages of his recollections of Plaistow appear in the appendix of the fourth edition of Curwen's book. Given-Wilson also appears in this edition of the book, but only in the preface, where Curwen laments somewhat his well meant attempts to draw attention to the growing poverty in Plaistow. Curwen feels that Given-Wilson is exaggerating the extent of this poverty, but his attempt to deny the encroaching reality of the future now seems absurd, as he likens the more well-heeled members of the local population to those in places like Belgravia and Mayfair. They may well have been, but their ancestors clearly didn't hang around to see Given-Wilson's concerns seem more like a prophecy.

Data collected by the St. Mary's Church Community Audit in 2010 revealed that only 58.2% of the ward were economically active, with youth unemployment at 20%. Only 35.9% of people owned their own homes, and 8.8% received Employment and Support Allowance or Incapacity Benefit. One hundred and five years after Curwen wrote the preface to the last edition of his book, the area he described has been swept from memory like leaves in a storm.

Even in Curwen's day, however, the history of this small area of land had been mostly erased, living on only in fragments of written word. The church as Curwen, Rev. Marsh and Given-Wilson remember it stood on the site of the original manor of Hugh de Plaiz, whose "stow" – meaning place or seat – this was in the thirteenth century. A map that appears in Katharine Fry's *History of the parishes of East and West Ham* shows the manor house depicted as the manor House of Bretts, called "Bretts Bower". Although no definite idea of what it actually looked like can be derived from this, it is clear that the manor house was surrounded by a moat. Centuries later the moat remained only in part, as a pond which would frequently flood Palsy Lane, as St. Mary's Road was previously known. Rev. Marsh remembers one day picking 25 different types of wild flower in Palsy Lane.

There were no wild flowers in the summer of 2009 as we walked down the road. The only clue that a church once loomed high here are the short grave stones that poke out of the grass in the park, like a set of crooked teeth. The present day church is obscured from this vantage point, but the children's playground can be seen in the distance. Closer to the road are park benches, one of which was host to three men who looked old enough to have grown up in Eastern

Europe when the communist regime was still in place. Now they were here, oblivious to Plaistow's history, victims of a history elsewhere. They were drunk and argued over a bottle. Whatever they hoped for when they left their homelands clearly never came to pass, and here they landed, like seeds blown in on a wind that promised much, but delivered little.

The 2001 census revealed that over 50 languages were spoken in the ward, and since then a migration of people from Eastern Europe and Africa has no doubt added more to this linguistic stew. Thus, many of the present population of Plaistow have memories of a life elsewhere, histories scattered across the globe. The photographer, Larry Towell, has written that, 'land makes people into who they are. Of that I'm sure. If they lose it, they forfeit their solvency and a little bit of their souls, which they will spend the rest of their lives trying to regain.'[79] He was writing about the truly landless – Menonites, Kurds and Palestinians – but the principle still applies. As much as you might want a new start, the past will always sit on your shoulder like a ghost.

The three men in the park and a couple of children playing in the playground were the only people we had seen since turning into North Street; the only thing missing from St. Mary's Road was some tumble weed blowing past. The sun was bursting like a ripe melon overhead, and I pulled the hood of the buggy over my daughter who had woken and was staring out

---

79 Larry Towell, The World From My Front Porch, Archive of Modern Conflict (2008)

with wide eyes. She wouldn't remember any of the journey, at least not in a way that can be unlocked by language. It would lie buried in her memory banks, to all intents and purposes lost.

Opposite the Eastern-most edge of the park is a building squashed between two terraced houses, the bottom half of which is a wooden garage-style door, a smaller door set within it, painted dark blue. A painting and decorating firm called Multapply have their sign above the door on the day we pass. Here at 32a St. Mary's Road is where The Curwen Studio existed between 1958 and 1964, in a converted stable.

The studio was established as a separate space from the main Curwen works. Here, the artists could work on prints without being concerned about the industry-standard mechanics required to turn their original art works into a print-run of identical items. These were the beatnik days of art, literature and jazz, a brief period before The Beatles ignited the pop explosion and kickstarted the version of the sixties that has become the de facto standard of the nostalgia industry.

With Robert Erskine in charge of commissioning and Stanley Jones at the helm, the studio was an outlet for numerous artists, including Henry Moore, Graham Sutherland, John Piper, Ceri Richards, and Alan Davie, whose bold colourful prints echoed the work of artists like Klee and Picasso but also captured perfectly the free spirit of the times. The artistic spirit of Paris and St.Ives had found an unlikely home in East London until, six years after opening, the studio moved to Midford Place in Central London, where artists of the calibre of Barbara Hepworth worked on prints.

Throughout this time the ethos of Curwen remained broadly the same. An executive was quoted in a New Society article by Benedict Nightingale as saying; 'We don't believe in high prices at all. Our basic philosophy is that original prints should be available to quite ordinary people.' The Rev. John Curwen, who had set up the press to do the same with the Tonic Sol-Fa notation, would have been proud that one hundred years later, unlike Plaistow itself, nothing had changed.

We continued our walk down St. Mary's Road, past the Lord Stanley pub, done up boldly in the claret and blue of West Ham United, and turned just after the Lister Community School onto Eastern Road. We still hadn't encountered a living soul, aside from the drunken men in the park. As it was the summer holiday, the playground of Plaistow Primary School was as empty and silent as the streets surrounding it. The school looks brand new, but in the stark light of the overhead sun the thick, double gates and tall metal fencing around its perimeter lend it the air of something more unsettling. Without the noise and chaotic activity of children, the grassless playground is just a barren expanse of clean lines and right angles.

This view is from North Street Passage, a long path that runs between Eastern Road and Western Road. It is the sort of alleyway you wouldn't relish walking through late at night, perhaps, but today it offered some respite from the sun. It is also a deceptively long passage. After pausing to stare through the web of metal gates and wire fences that stand between us and the primary school, wondering if this was, after all, the site of the Land Grabbers stand one hundred and three years ago, we saw that we were merely halfway down North Street Passage, which bends slightly in the middle.

We wheeled the buggy quietly on. Then on our left, like a magician unexpectedly pulling a bunch of colourful paper flowers from his sleeve on a black stage, there was an eruption of lush green vegetation, flecked with yellow, orange, purple, red and other colours. Not only had we found the site of the Triangle Camp but, as if to vindicate the efforts of the men of 1906, the very ground they set out to cultivate was now allotments.

A wide pathway runs through the middle of all the greenery, but we can see that the entrance is at the opposite end, on Queens Road. We peered through the green metal railings, and beyond it a mesh fence, further reinforced by the thick fingers of a wild blackberry bush that cling to it. The blackberries were still mostly green, only a few beginning the first blush towards ripeness. Many of the plots were growing sunflowers, while the usual array of wooden fencing, ramshackle sheds made from old doors, scraps of wood and corrugated tin, and planters fashioned from anything from plastic barrels to old tin baths, stamped each with the individuality and resourcefulness of their owners. A yellow sign on the fence warned of Anti-Intruder Devices.

Such is the lushness of the growth (beans, peas, sweet corn, nasturtium, leaks, cabbages, and courgettes are just a few of the things we could discern), that at first the allotments looked as deserted as the streets. But then we saw a head bob up from behind some tall stalks and disappear again, perhaps stooping to weed or dig into the soil. It is the only sign of life, aside from that of the abundant plants. We couldn't make out the far corners of the plot of land, but perhaps there still existed the wall on which the men daubed their slogan in white paint: *What will the harvest bring?*

It is fitting that a century on from Bill Cunningham's land grab, the very same land is being lovingly cultivated by the local people. After the land grabbers were removed from their camp and Cunningham was sentenced, the fate of these men disappears into the darkness of lost history. And what of the things they planted? Did anyone tend them? Did they flourish and, if so, did the people living around St. Mary's Road benefit from this modest harvest? We'll never know.

Curiosity satisfied, we continued our journey, deciding to head for Upton Park station via a winding loop that saw us walk down Samson Street, past the derelict looking Plaistow Hospital. We are a stone's throw from Cave Road. This is where Emily Coombs was stabbed through the heart by her own thirteen your old son, Robert, and left on her bed with only the rats for company while her murderer and his younger brother went on a spending spree, breaking open a cash box with a hatchet and using half-witted family acquaintance John Fox to pawn items of value.

...all over the house were found half consumed jam tarts and sausage rolls; new clothes have been brought and both in the few days had led a somewhat "fast" life in the West end, riding about in cabs and going to theatres.[80]

---

80 Lloyd's Weekly Newspaper, Sunday, July 21, 1895

The two boys had a reputation in the neighbourhood, and the general opinion was that poor Emily was too lenient. Robert had been a continual source of trouble at school – when he bothered to turn up – and some were of the opinion that he wasn't 'right in the head'. His father, who was at sea at the time of the matricide, reported that Robert had marks on his temples caused by instruments used at birth, and that he suffered from headaches. He also said that his wife had been an excitable woman who cried and laughed at the same time. In retrospect it seems easy to see why. The newspapers had other targets for blame;

Both Robert and Nathaniel have been greedy devourers of sensational literature; indeed, there have been found in the house all kinds of penny 'dreadfuls' and blood-curdling narratives...The demoralising influence of pernicious reading had began to tell on the boys for some months, particularly on the elder, who a few years ago was treated by a now deceased doctor at Bow for a brain affection.[81]

The story is shocking, but little seems to change. On Christmas Day 2010, Kristy Bamu was murdered in a flat in Manor Park after days of torture by his sister Magalie and her partner Eric Bikubi. Both were said to be obsessed with witchcraft, and claimed they believed Kristy to be a witch. The roll-call of the brutalised and murdered in the East End is a long one. Perhaps

---

81 Ibid

there should be a monument to honour them, seeing as none chose their fate. And as for the murderers, theirs is a list of the maddened and deranged, jilted lovers and abusive partners, child killers and parent killers, killers of prostitutes and the down and outs, and those who never meant to kill in the first place, or had one moment of madness when they just couldn't take it any more. How do we separate the darkness of their hearts from the dark soul of the environment they lived in?

In February 1888, the year that Jack the Ripper later savaged his female victims in Whitechapel, Emma Elizabeth Aston was found guilty of killing her two children, two year old Bertie and twelve month old Frank. Emma, 39, took a lodging in Whitfield Road, Upton Park, with a weekly rent of 3s. 9d. A man, supposedly the father of Bertie and Frank, would send money, but the payments became irregular. Then in February, he sent 1s. with a letter to say there would be no more. That night Emily went to bed with her children at eleven o'clock. The next morning Mrs. Jones, the landlady, was surprised to find her alone in the parlour, fully dressed and crying. Mrs. Jones asked her what was wrong.

She said she had murdered her two children, and that she felt a weight on her head and was compelled to kill the children; she was also told to commit suicide, but a voice called out, "Don't, don't." When she was asked by the doctor what made her do what she had done, she replied "Want," and added

that she was in debt and the father of the children would not
send her any money to support them.[82]

And on and on through time it goes. Like a drop of ink on
blotting paper the East End grew and grew, and with such
a high density of poverty came a steady stream of what the
newspapers of the day liked to call *tragedies.*

We were on the Barking Road now, our daughter
kicking her legs in the buggy, cooing at the traffic which flashed
the sun back off its windscreens as it passed. A billboard
high on the side of a shop displayed the holy trio of West
Ham United FC: Bobby Moore, Geoff Hurst and Martin
Peters. *See West Ham Win the World Cup* was the bold
offer in claret and blue letters, a reference to the captain and
goalscorers of England's triumphant team of 1966. The poster
was advertising the online archive of a tabloid newspaper.
The club's ground was not far away.

Barking Road was built between 1807 and 1810,
designed to take traffic between the Iron Bridge at Poplar and
Barking. Before this the journey had entailed a convoluted
route via Stratford, and then Ilford. This straight, Roman-
like road was a bold statement, suggesting that the low-lying
marshes could not halt progress. It seems, however, that the
people weren't in a hurry to hitch a ride to the future. For years
the tollman on the Iron Bridge didn't take enough to pay his
wages, and some days there wasn't a soul to be seen along it.

---

82 London Standard. Wednesday 21 March, 1888

There were only six houses along its entire length as late as the middle of the nineteenth century. The marsh contributed to the road's weak foundations, and at this time it must have seemed as if it was going to halt progress in its tracks.

The driver of the Barking coach, which ran over the Iron Bridge, had to run his vehicle along the path, for which he was duly summoned and fined. Along the sides of the road were ditches with willows growing in them, where the satin moth hovered, and the reed-warbler built its bottle-shaped nest... The marsh itself was in winter the haunt of swarms of wild fowl, and as the shooting was practically free, and nearly every workingman had a gun, there was plenty of sport. Herons fished in the ditches, and an east wind brought thousands of plover, duck, teal, widgeon, and snipe. The best way was to go out by night, lie low, and wait for the dawn.[83]

Now any birdsong is drowned out by the urban hum. Ahead of us on the wide sweep of pavement where Barking Road is met by Central Park Road, there is a statue of the same three men we saw on the billboard, together with Ray Wilson. Bobby Moore is being held aloft, and in his raised hand is the World Cup. 1966 seems another lifetime ago, like looking through the wrong end of a pair of binoculars. Our heroes look up Green Street, in the direction of West Ham's ground. Ray Wilson, who played for Everton, seems decidedly out of place

---

83 John Spencer Curwen. *Old Plaistow* (1905)

here. I wondered to myself why this statue wasn't outside the ground. Perhaps this is as near as Ray wanted to go.

The Newham Bookshop, one of the few independent bookshops left, was disappointingly closed, it being a Monday, so we pushed on down to the corner and turned up Green Street. We were no longer in Plaistow now. This was East Ham, which is confusingly the home of West Ham United, whose ground is on a street leading to Upton Park tube station. The Boleyn Ground got its name from Boleyn Castle, the grounds of which the club rented from 1912. It was rumoured that Anne Boleyn had stayed, or even been imprisoned there, but there is no evidence. In an area fast and free with names, it was also known as Green Street House. Most people, however, call the ground Upton Park, because that is the name of the nearest tube station.

The club itself was formed in 1895 by Arnold Hills and David Taylor, respectively the owner and foreman of the Thames Ironworks and Shipbuilding Company. Playing their games at the Hermit Road ground in Canning Town, they were initially known as Thames Ironworks FC. They drew their first ever match 1-1 with Royal Ordinance. On December 16th that same year they pioneered floodlit football, with a pitch surrounded by light bulbs attached to poles and a ball dipped in whitewash to make it more visible. The following September, in a game presumably played at night, they beat a team called Vampires in the London League, First Division. Four years later they changed their name to West Ham United, retaining a link to their former incarnation with the still used nickname of

"Irons". After playing at a number of grounds over a period of twelve years, they finally settled at the bottom of Green Street.

West Ham played in the famous *White Horse Final* at Wembley in 1923, when 200,000 people turned up. The huge crowd spilled over the terraces and onto the pitch; only the intervention of mounted policeman, including one on a white horse, was able to clear the playing area so the game could begin. West Ham lost to Bolton, and had to wait 41 years before they reached the FA Cup Final again. This time they emerged victorious, beating Preston North End 3-2. The team, managed by Ron Greenwood (who would later manage England), included Bobby Moore and Geoff Hurst. The following year they won the European Cup Winners Cup, defeating German side TSV Munich in the final with two goals from Alan Sealey. By now Martin Peters was in the side, and thus the famous World Cup winning trio, immortalised in the statue on Barking Road, were together.

In 1975 West Ham beat Fulham in the final, and the victory parade brought parts of Newham to a complete standstill. Six years later they defeated Arsenal courtesy of a rare headed goal by Trevor Brooking. Then, after a 25 year wait, West Ham reached the final of the FA Cup again, facing Liverpool in 2006. I watched the first half of the game in the Princess of Wales, around the corner from where I lived. The pub was packed with men and boys, and turned predictably rowdy when Jamie Carragher put the ball into his own net to give the Hammers the lead. When they got a second goal seven minutes later, beer was flying through the air and grown men were bouncing off the walls. A Liverpool goal six minutes later brought with it a nervous atmosphere; West Ham had been punching above their weight to get this far, and Liverpool were strong favourites.

At half time I went outside to get some air, and decided to check out the mood in the nearby Queens Head on Tramway Avenue. Here the crowd was more mixed, and also more nervous. When Gerrard equalised for Liverpool, groans were audible and a sense of doom began to descend. Most of the people seemed to think it was all over, so when West Ham scored yet again with 25 minutes to go, the atmosphere turned into a strange mix of joy and fear. Nobody could quite entertain the idea that they might hang on to their lead, but the minutes ticked by and soon the game was into its final moments. The faces of men, women, boys and girls all around me were contorted with suspense, finally beginning to think that this was the year, at last beginning to ready themselves for an explosion of joy at the final whistle.

A ball was lofted into the West Ham box, and cleared up-field. As it fell into the path of Liverpool captain Steven Gerrard, my heart sank. Not being a West Ham fan, my disappointment wasn't going to be as great as the people who surrounded me, but the betting slip with a fiver on West Ham to win the F.A. Cup at sixteen-to-one that had been snug in my wallet since the fifth round was halfway to being crumpled up and tossed onto the pub floor. Gerrard duly struck: 3-3. There was still extra time to play, but somehow defeat was now inevitable, and the fact that the final blow came via a penalty shoot out seemed additionally cruel. It was like the Cinderella story without the happy ending.

And it hasn't been much better for West Ham United since. As we strolled past the ground three years after the defeat to Liverpool, my partner asked why it resembled a giant plastic castle. I shrugged.

"Something to do with the badge, I think."

"It looks...." she struggled to find the right word.

"Quite," I said, looking at it and wondering if anyone at the club had been too afraid to admit that it looked awful; after all it must have cost a few quid. Not enough to buy a decent player perhaps, but still...what was wrong with it before?

We carried on up Green Street past Queens Market, which had not long before been saved from developers who had initially been given the green light to build a 31 storey block of high-priced flats and reduce the market in size by 25%. A local campaign had attracted the attention of Boris Johnson, who directed Newham Council to refuse planning permission. The developer, St. Mowden, refer to themselves on their website as regeneration specialists who understand local needs and are conscious of the impact to communities of their developments. So quite how they failed to understand that the local community - who formed a campaign group to get their message across loud and clear - simply didn't want luxury flats that would have forced change upon their market is a matter that only a communications expert might be able to explain – unless of course the words on the company's website are, in reality, empty of all meaning.

I suspect the vultures will be back and circling over Upton Park before long. They were spotted over the Boleyn Ground for a spell, when it looked as though West Ham would be moving into the Olympic Stadium some time after the games. This messy affair that involved, in no particular order, spies, Tottenham Hotspur Football Club, Leyton Orient, broken legacy promises and the whiff of filthy lucre, eventually led to an embarrassing about-face. So for now Green Street's twin attractions remain, but as long as they represent examples of prime real-estate, then a sense of permanence can never be established. This is the East End after all.

CHAPTER 6

Agit-Prop to Pop - The Entertainers

On a wet Sunday in February 1953, Joan Littlewood and seven others crammed into an old Alvis car and drove to what they called Stratford-atte-Bowe. After a cold and wet drive of eight hours they arrived at the side entrance of the Theatre Royal on Angel Lane, which they were going to rent for the sum of £20 a week. Gerry Raffles, Joan Littlewood's lifelong companion and fellow traveller, perhaps took time to survey the front of the building, which had opened 69 years previously in 1884 and certainly seen better days, unaware that in the future the ground he stood on would be named after him. The terraced houses next to the theatre, and Salway Road itself, would be long gone by then. Barry Clayton, recalling the day of his audition in the summer of 1954, remembered how different Stratford looked back then compared to now.

Rows of grimy houses crowded the mucky station, while the air was thick with a terrible smell from the Yardley's soap factory down the High Street.[84]

The old theatre had fallen into state of neglect. It was dirty and smelly, but the grace of its former glory remained beneath the decay and grime. The stage was covered in grease, the stalls in paper and orange peel, and the boiler didn't work, but it was their new home, and they spent their first cold night sleeping in its various quarters. By the second day they had put up a poster advertising their first performance – Shakespeare's *Twelfth Night*. After receiving a donation of cash, toilet rolls and bottles of disinfectant from Harry Ibbotson, friend of Sam Wanamaker, they were ready to roll. Unfortunately the rain had washed away the flour and water paste that had been used to stick up the poster, so at the last moment Harry Greene had to dash off to rustle up an audience, armed only with a smaller version of the sodden poster. Thus their debut performance was witnessed by hardly anyone, but at least the few present applauded, and the applause echoed considerably in the draughty, empty space. From this inauspicious beginning did the small wonders of the Theatre Workshop's tenure at Stratford grow.

The Theatre Workshop was born in 1945, when Raffles, Littlewood and her then husband Jimmie Miller (later to become known as Ewan MacColl) decided that the time was ripe for experimental theatre in England. Influenced by Bertoldt Brecht, Erwin Piscator and Rudolf Laban, their manifesto stated, *'Theatre Workshop is an organisation of artists, technicians and actors who are experimenting in stagecraft. Its purpose is to create a flexible theatre-art, as swift moving and plastic as the cinema, by applying recent technical advances in light and sound, and introducing much of the "dance theatre" style of production.'*

Committed to left-wing ideology, the Company devised and commissioned plays by and for the working classes and performed in Northern England, Scotland and the Continent. After seven such years they reached a turning point when Miller decided to leave. Jimmie, Ewan – call him what you will – was already established as a folk singer of some repute, the composer of *Dirty Old Town*. He made the decision to follow the world of Hootennay's rather than the world of theatre, and would pass the songwriting torch onto his daughter, the late Kirsty MacColl.

Though written about Manchester, *Dirty Old Town* could just have easily described London, the Big Smoke, in the 1950s. Britain was only just emerging from its austerity years and the prevailing atmosphere was still gloomy. When Joan and her partners in crime arrived in Stratford to drag the theatre kicking and screaming into the modern age, Queen Elizabeth had only just started her reign following the death of her father the year before, and was still a few months away from her coronation. David Bentley had been hanged in January, and sweet rationing had just ended, much to the delight of the nation's children who stocked up on toffee apples, nougat and liquorice sticks. Luckily for them, the four year old NHS had introduced flat rate charges of £1 for ordinary dental treatment. But grey and austere as the times seemed, Britain was edging towards the cusp of change; a modern era was just around the corner. As if pointing the way, Crick and Watson published their discovery of DNA.

But for now the incurable optimists of Salway Road, E15 had to endure a silent box office and each night at curtain call Avis Bunnage would implore what amounted to an audience to 'Tell your friends.' Little did they know that not only were they in the poorest London borough, but that nobody had ever made the theatre pay. It didn't help when the woman they took on in the box office kept dipping her fingers in the till. After she was given the heave-ho, she went to authorities to report the goings on in the theatre; people were sleeping in there when they shouldn't be, like a bunch of gypsies blown in from up North. The sanitary inspector turned up for a nosey around, and when he saw the beds in the dressing rooms, perhaps licked the end of his pencil in eager anticipation of being able to write in his notepad – gotcha! But Gerry gave him some flannel about an actor needing to be fully relaxed before going on stage, to be lying down in zen-like mental preparation for entering their role, as it were. The inspector didn't notice the gas rings and food that had been stashed away in dim corners.[85]

---

85 British Library Theatre Archive Project. 2007

Still, they did have the goodwill of shopkeepers and stall holders on Angel Lane to boost their spirits, like Bill Pohl the butcher, Dai the fishmonger, and Bert and May at the Cafe L'Ange. If Les Back at the vegetable stall gave them the bird every time they passed and Mrs. Egg who sold them bacon advised them to get a proper job, then they were just illustrating, with a biting cockney humour, the local mistrust of any arty-farty business going on in this historically poor network of streets. A modern world may have been over the horizon, but the order of the day, in the East End at least, was one of conservatism.

Jean Gaffin, who grew up in West Ham and worked at the theatre, remembers the lack of interest from the locals in the early days. Stratford and the surrounding areas were distinctly working and lower middle class. The loyal following they developed was both small and from outside, people making a journey along the Central Line into, what was for them, the unknown: to this compact little theatre nestled amongst the two-up-two-downs a short walk from the grubby old station.[86]

The truth of the matter was that the theatre had led a somewhat troubled existence from birth. 'Charles Dillon has applied for a licence to build a permanent theatre in Angel Lane,' said the local vicar in 1884. 'No doubt his only object is to gain an honest livelihood, but the very position of the proposed theatre will necessitate a low kind of drama;

---

86 British Library Theatre Archive Project. 2007

the place will become the resort of the worst characters of the neighbourhood.' Various local figures, from clergy to schoolteachers, were of the same opinion and petitioned against the granting of a license. Dillon won however and on Wednesday 17th December 1884 the theatre opened with a performance of Lord Lytton's Richelieu.

The gallery that first night cracked nuts throughout the early scenes, and Dillon, playing the lead role, had to appear before the curtain to ask them to refrain. Despite this he won much applause. One newspaper reported on the opening: 'On Wednesday evening last a new theatre was opened in Selway-road, Angel-lane, Stratford, giving promise of abundant amusement to dwellers in the far East. The outside of the building we must describe as ugly in the extreme, but the interior presents a very pretty and attractive appearance.'[87]

After describing in some detail the interior, even as far as informing its readers that the theatre seats had been coated with a fireproof cyanite solution recommended by a Captain Shaw, the report finally gets round to the performance of its principals. Blanche Elliot, whose performance as Julie de Mortemar was to be complimented, made for a very attractive presence, so much so that a local police sergeant who sat next to the reporter remarked that 'if that 'ed of 'air's all 'er hown, sir, it's a very fine one, and she ought to be proud on it.'[88]

---

87 ERA – December 20th 1884

88 Ibid

The suggestion that the police sergeant was perhaps more impressed with Miss Elliot's hair than he was with the dramatics on show was hardly subtle. Though he was able to silence the nut crackers on this first night, they appear to have gained their revenge by staying away in numbers significant enough for Dillon, who was unwilling to lower the tone of his dramatic aspirations, to throw the towel in. After two seasons he sold the theatre to local coal-merchant, Albert Fredericks. Fredericks had already been helping with the finance of the theatre, and it stayed in his family for nearly fifty years.

In this time they bought a block of terraced houses in order to convert them into a workshop and dressing rooms. In 1891, deciding the stage wasn't big enough they purchased the fishmongers behind the theatre on Angel Lane so it could be expanded, creating one of the deepest stages in London at 38 foot. Of course all this expense would have been foolhardy without the theatre repertoire receiving an overhaul too, and Dillon's semi-classical diet was replaced with a more varied programme that included popular melodrama. The only significant change to the theatre under the tenure of the Fredericks family during the next thirty or so years was the addition of electricity in 1902, together with a refit that led to it being described as one of 'the handsomest and cosiest of suburban theatres.'

In the mid-1920s the East End was suffering particularly from the post-war depression. Despite reducing prices and playing twice nightly, the Theatre Royal couldn't retain its audiences who were turning instead to the glossy glamour provided by the cinema. By the time the Fredericks family closed the company in 1933, the repertoire consisted of revues and variety. A string of managers tried and failed to inject life back into the theatre, in terms of box-office takings, but all failed and it closed during the Second World War. In 1946 David Horne took over and together with his wife, Ann Farrer, re-opened the theatre and kept it going with a run of straight drama. But by 1950, they too gave up. The next manager turned to risque revues, but titillation proved as unsuccessful as serious drama. So just when the theatre seemed to have reached its nadir, a company who had appeared under the Horne tenure with a Christmas show a few years before crammed as many of their members as was physically possible into a draughty old Alvis and drove down to Stratford-atte-Bowe, one wet Sunday in February.

The Theatre Workshop's existence as a touring troupe (in the North, Wales and on the Continent) had been somewhat precarious, which led to the fateful decision to try their hand at establishing a permanent base at the then unloved, down-at-heel Royal. And if the locals didn't seem to love the Royal in numbers that would ensure its survival, then money from elsewhere was crucial. Gerry Raffles wrote to the Town Clerk of West Ham on 14th April 1953, requesting that the Borough Council consider the necessary funding to make the Royal a Civic Theatre. He pointed out that the company were doing their best save this beautiful old building from a lowly existence as host to variety shows and striptease, to give it – the only theatre in the whole borough – the kiss of life.

Perhaps sensing that the million or so people in this particular catchment area weren't going to flock to its doors, or merely just sharing their indifference to the dramatic arts, the Council replied that they weren't prepared to sacrifice any ratepayers money. Undeterred by the lack of enthusiasm – let alone cash – Littlewood, Raffles and the rest of the Company dug in for the duration, incurable optimists that they were. This optimism proved invaluable as the neighbouring boroughs of Barking, Bethnal Green, East Ham, Ilford, Leyton, Poplar, Romford, Shoreditch, Stepney, Stoke Newington, Walthamstow, Wanstead and Woodford all turned down Gerry's entreaty.

As well as a new play every fortnight, they gave classes in a local school, put on a children's theatre on Saturdays and organised jazz, calypso, skiffle, blues and folk concerts on Sunday evenings. The locals still didn't stir, preferring to sit on their doorsteps and listen to the music wafting out into the air for free, while local kids blackmailed owners of flash cars parked along the Salway Road to hand over protection money – a few bob to stop any dodgy sorts scratching the lovely paintwork.

Such was the state of their financial problems in 1955. It was quite possible that the ever-resourceful street kids were making more money protecting cars than the Company was in producing plays. When the Arts Council withdrew an offer of £100 in financing, and Martin's bank in Manchester stopped the account of Theatre Workshop Limited due to a winding up order, things were looking decidedly bad. Gerry did manage to prevent the theatre falling into the hands of the Official Receiver, but financial calamity was followed by loss of personnel as both Harry Corbett (whose Richard II forged a dramatic reputation that viewers of his later role in television's Steptoe and Son were mostly unaware of) and George Cooper were tempted away by better offers elsewhere. At this moment, even Joan's optimism must have seemed more like denial.

As if to prove, however, that it is darkest just before dawn, the following year saw a beer-stained, badly typed manuscript land on Joan's desk. The title of the work was *The Quare Fellow*, the author a shy, hard-drinking Irishman by the name of Brendan Behan. Behan was born into a working class family in Dublin in 1923, and was blessed with a father who saw fit to read classic literature such as Zola and Maupassant to the children at bedtime. At 16, and already writing prose and poetry, he joined the IRA. In an episode that illustrates his wayward temperament, he undertook an unauthorised solo mission to England to blow up the docks in Liverpool. Arrested in possession of explosives, he was sentenced to three years in a borstal (one wonders what would have been his fate had he embarked on such a caper today), an experience which informed the title of his autobiography, *Borstal Boy*. In 1942, and back in Ireland, he was sentenced to 16 years imprisonment for the attempted murder of two detectives of the Garda Siochana, only to be released four years later under a general amnesty for IRA prisoners and internees. A year later, at the age of 24, his terrorist exploits were over and he settled instead on a career as a writer and drinker, in both of which he was much more accomplished.

By the time the tatty script of *The Quare Fellow* landed on Joan Littlewood's desk, the play had run successfully for six months at the Pike Theatre in Dublin. About an unseen protagonist – the quare fellow – whose execution is the following day, the writing and subject matter appealed greatly to Joan's left-wing outlook. Having been under MI5 surveillance (from 1939 until the 1950s) for her communist sympathies, she would have been un-phased by Behan's political past. Having just performed a critically acclaimed *Mother Courage* at the Royal (Brecht himself insisting that she play the lead), The Theatre Workshop was establishing a political stance that would culminate in *Oh, What a Lovely War!* eight years later.

Gerry twice sent Behan the fare to England, and twice he drank it. The third time he sent him a ticket and a map, and applied for a dispensation from the Home Office so he could stay for the duration of his play. Digs were found in a small house by the railway sidings in Stratford for Behan and his wife, Beatrice. For some reason the accommodation lacked electricity. Joan polished up the script, trimming it of Catholic schmaltz, and one Monday morning gave Behan and assorted others a preview at the theatre. At the end a journalist who wanted to interview him appeared at the dress-circle door with his two pet poodles.

'I see you laugh at your own jokes, Brendan,' he said.
'Yes, but I don't fuck me own dogs,' B.B. Replied[89]

---

89 Joan Littlewood, Joan's Book, Methuen, 2004 – p 470

The first night was a success, so much so that Malcolm Muggeridge wanted a television interview the following day. As well as a short scene from the play, what BBC viewers saw was a clearly drunk Brendan Behan, muttering whatever came into his head. What they didn't see was Joan Littlewood, hiding crouched behind his chair lest he fall off it, such was his state of inebriation. The interview made Behan a bit of an anti-hero to the man on the street, and the publicity certainly did the prospects of the play no harm. Whether it was his gift with words or with drunkenness, it was the start of his celebrity and went a long way to raising the profile of the Theatre. After a critically lauded run of *The Good Soldier Schwejk*, which also wowed Paris, the attention garnered by Behan's play (which later transferred to the West End with a young fellow Irishmen by the name of Richard Harris) had nudged the efforts in E15 across a line where reluctant acceptance from the theatrical establishment gave way, increasingly, to acclaim. Prestige may have finally decided to descend upon the East End theatrical enclave, but one thing that stubbornly refused to change was the boiler. Despite everyone's best efforts it still wouldn't work, so in the winter months the excitement of recognition came without warmth for the Company and their audiences.

If things were beginning to change for the better, it didn't mean that difficulties were a thing of the past. Lack of funding was a perennial problem, and the Company frequently relied on the good will of others when it came to basic things such as food and a warm place to sleep. But the struggle was part and parcel of the life for the group, most of whom resisted the lure of the traditional, more lucrative West End for the freedom to remain at the cultural vanguard. As such, the changing times were becoming more in step with their pioneering spirit.

The world in 1957 was a different beast from that of four years previously when the Theatre Workshop arrived in E15. Bleak Britain had thawed and colour was being blown into its grey cheeks. When Russia launched Sputnik 1 into orbit the promise of a new frontier must have seemed tangible. Progress was propelling Britain rapidly away from the years of post-war trauma and austerity, and the future seemed enticing and attainable rather than menacing and inevitable. New frontiers were everywhere. Jack Keruoac's On The Road set the template for restless teenage explorers everywhere, and fellow American Robert Frank had just finished photographing it. Miles Davis released Birth of the Cool, heralding a new jazz era, while Elvis Presley released Jailhouse Rock and Jerry Lee Lewis shook the older generation even further with his Great Balls of Fire. Lennon and McCartney first met at a church fete in Liverpool, where a club called The Cavern had opened in January. In the world of literature John Braine published Room at the Top, while Ayn Rand sowed dangerous seeds with her book Atlas Shrugged. Britain dropped its first H-Bomb in May, the same month that petrol rationing finally ended and a report was published suggesting that homosexuality should no longer be a crime. Everything seemed to herald change, from the French New Wave cinema to the Angry Young Men of British writing. Although the Lady Chatterley trial and the promise of new sexual freedoms was still three years away, it was easy for a generation used to going without to believe the Conservative prime minister Harold MacMillan when he said that Britons had never had it so good.

But of course change doesn't arrive all at once and the establishment, in all its guises, had most to lose from the new winds blowing in. In the context of the times it is worth reminding ourselves just how radical the Theatre Workshop was in comparison to the prevailing ethos, typified by the West End. Not only were they left-wing, but they looked towards the Continent as much as anywhere else. Adopting the ideas of the then relatively unknown (in Britain) Bertolt Brecht made the Theatre Workshop seem like dangerous upstarts. The very idea of ignoring the proscenium arch, and of actors breaking all the rules by turning their backs to the audience, were just two of the things that put them beyond the pale as far as theatrical establishment were concerned. The fact that Joan Littlewood and Gerry Raffles had been under MI5 and Special Branch surveillance because of their Communist leanings lent the group a political as well as artistically subversive air. When they decided to put a building site on stage, complete with cement mixer and building site language, it was all too much for some, most noticeably the Lord Chamberlain.

The play in question, *You Won't Always Be on Top*, was being analysed by various members of the Workshop in January 1957 when plain-clothes detectives entered the theatre to serve a summons on Gerry Raffles, Richard Harris and John Bury. Henry Chapman, building labourer and writer of the play, was also served a summons. On 16th April 1957, members of the Company crossed Stratford Broadway towards the Court House to take part in one more small battle against the censorship laws. Luckily for Littlewood and her fellow thespians, it turned out that the magistrate had been in the building trade all his life, and a few rum words were not enough to convince him of any need to punish the protagonists. They were let off, free to celebrate in the theatre bar and read all about their victory in the evening paper. It was a turning point of sorts, as what followed was a string of hits – *A Taste of Honey, The Hostage, and Fings Ain't Wot They Used T'Be* – that all transferred to the West End and beyond.

A Taste of Honey was written by Shelagh Delaney, a 19 year old Salford lass. Littlewood adapted the script to smooth its rough edges. A new actor, Murray Melvin (who was on a grant from Guildhall School to study drama) was propelled from tea-making duties to the role of Geoff, one of the two leading roles, the other being the pregnant Jo. Touching on underage pregnancy, abortion, inter-racial sex and homosexuality in the pre-permissive age was guaranteed to attract attention, and the 'grim-up-North' gritty realism would later be translated to film with Rita Tushingham playing the lead. The play was a critical success, and flushed with the financial gains Shelagh Delaney left her lodgings in the home of Littlewood and Raffles in Blackheath and moved into a flat with Una Collins. Brendan and Beatrice Behan moved

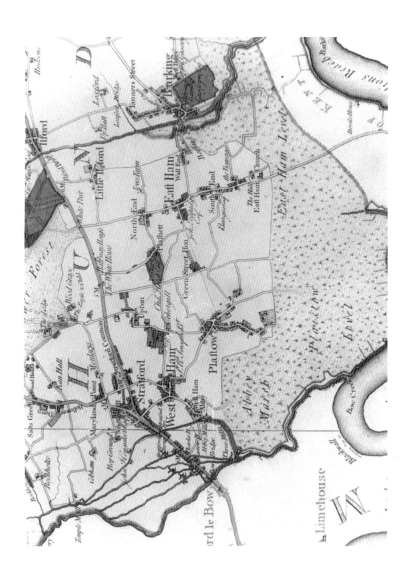

Chapman and Andre map, 1777
(Newham Heritage & Archives)

Old Bow Bridge, 1804
(Newham Heritage & Archives)

Three Mills
(Neil Fraser)

Broadway, Stratford, 1927. The Angel Pub is shown at centre,
on the corner of Broadway and Angel Lane

(Newham Heritage & Archives)

Inside Westfield

(Neil Fraser)

Councillor
Cunningham.

**Types of Unemployed Men at
Triangle Camp,
5 a.m., July 24, 1906.**

Organiser
King.

The Plaistow Land Grabbers, 1906
(Newham Heritage & Archives)

Richmond Street, Plaistow, 1935
(Newham Heritage & Archives)

The Theatre Royal, Stratford
(Neil Fraser)

Abbey Mills Pumping Station
(Neil Fraser)

Angel Lane, 1964
(Newham Heritage & Archives)

Angel Lane development site, 1971
(Newham Heritage & Archives)

Abbey Mill, late 18th century
(Newham Heritage & Archives)

Little Tommy Lee Sewer, Pretoria Road, Canning Town, 1888
(Newham Heritage & Archives)

Street vendors, Martin Street, 1912
(Newham Heritage & Archives)

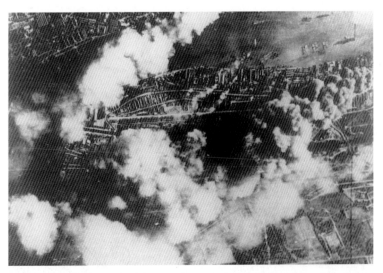

Silvertown, photographed from a German Bomber, September 7th 1940
(Newham Heritage & Archives)

Stratford Railway Works –
Engine Repairing Shop
(Newham Heritage & Archives)

Stratford railway lands, 1970. The
former Railway Works are in the
foreground
(Newham Heritage & Archives)

C.J. Mare & Co. Shipbuilding Works, 1854
(Newham Heritage & Archives)

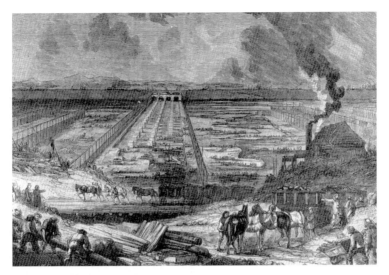

Victoria Docks construction
(Newham Heritage & Archives)

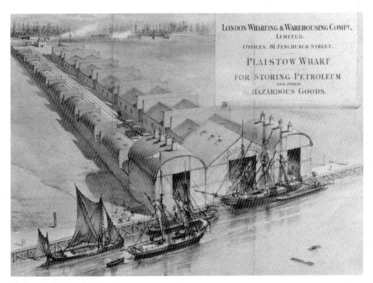

Plaistow Wharf
(Newham Heritage & Archives)

Call on at the docks. Sometimes only a handful of men would get work for the day unloading ships
(Newham Heritage & Archives)

The Royal Docks, circa 1935
(Newham Heritage & Archives)

Millenium Mills
(Neil Fraser)

Beckton Gas Works, 1950s
(Newham Heritage & Archives)

Tate & Lyle, Plaistow Wharf
(Neil Fraser)

City Airport, with the Tate & Lyle factory in the background
(Neil Fraser)

Thames Barrier
(Neil Fraser)

Old Council Offices
(Newham Heritage & Archives)

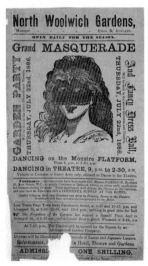

Poster for North Woolwich Gardens
(Newham Heritage & Archives)

Anish Kapoor's Orbit Tower and
the Olympic stadium, 2012
(Neil Fraser)

Stratford Station 2006
(Neil Fraser)

Stratford Station and Westfield, 2012
(Neil Fraser)

Olympic Village
(Neil Fraser)

Olympic Stadium
(Neil Fraser)

Railway land, Stratford, 2012
(Neil Fraser)

New Skyline
(Neil Fraser)

into the Blackheath house, no doubt glad of more salubrious surroundings than their original digs by the railway.

The Hostage was Behan's work, inspired by a story of a soldier taken hostage in Cyprus, in the days when such an act was rare enough to demand attention. Behan also drew on his own experiences of looking after a hostage while with the IRA. He took pity on his captive, taking him on a tour of the pubs of Dublin before drawing a circle around him and daring him to step out if it, actions indicative of Behan's typical state of inebriation. Work on the script itself proceeded at the usual, deathly slow Behan pace; Gerry had to threaten him with a pistol before any real progress was made, though the Saturday before the opening night still saw a complete lack of the Third Act.

It proved to be, of course, all right on the night. Harold Robson of The Times, in a review headed Triumph at Stratford East, wrote a review full of praise for the play and the 'inspired, chuckle-headed, aggravating, devoted and magnificently alive' company of Theatre Workshop. Other critics, including Kenneth Tynan in the Observer, were equally impressed, but to Behan the play was still a work in progress. He would change lines or add wisecracks he had heard while hanging about on Angel Lane next to the theatre, joking with the shopkeepers, stall-holders and flower sellers.

At the beginning of 1959 David Booth enquired as to the contents of a bulky package that Littlewood hadn't got round to opening. It contained the script of a musical written by Frank Norman, Fings Ain't Wot They Used T'Be, and

Booth, later to gain celluloid fame as Private Henry Hook in *Zulu*, was going to get the plum role of *Tosher*, the pimp. Lionel Bart was drafted in to work on the songs and his tunes drifted out of the theatre and into Angel Lane, where the locals took the theme tune and added their own words. Though Gerry and Joan had always talked about theatre for the masses, in reality the masses didn't care too much for the dishes that were being served up. But Frank Norman's work, with its cockney vernacular, promised the real deal at last. Night after night the theatre was crammed with locals who, like the play's author, had never before set foot inside a theatre.

Sticking more or less with the *Fings...* setting, Theatre Workshop followed it up with *Sparrers Can't Sing*, a gentle look at amiable working class culture which Littlewood also directed as a film a few years later. By then the East End life it depicted, of sing-songs round the 'old joanna' in the local pub, was fast disappearing. Filmed in Stepney, Angel Lane, Stratford and various other locations, it starred a whole host of Theatre Workshop regulars including Booth, Barbara Windsor, Roy Kinnear, Victor Spinetti, Murray Melvin, Brian Murphy, Yootha Joyce, Harry Corbett, Arthur Mullard and Avis Bunnage. It was also notable for the appearance of The Krays at the launch party, an entrance that apparently saw the rapid exit of Ronnie Knight, who had turned up with a few unsavoury friends. Some of the villains in the Kray entourage made it into the scene in Angel Lane where David Booth goofs around beside Barbara Windsor pushing a pram, and the Kray's club appears in the film's ending when a mass brawl erupts. During filming, Big Scotch Pat and Scar-faced Willy were posted on the door to keep out the curious. The barmaid in the club scene is Queenie Watts, who was also the subject of the Michael Orrom documentary film *Portrait of Queenie*. She was the real-life barmaid of the Ironbridge Tavern on the Isle of Dogs, and according to a Times reviewer the best blues singer in London. So good, in fact, that she was invited to sing in America – but so attached was she to her pub that she declined.

The film's premier was at the ABC in Stepney, and it seemed as if the whole area had turned out onto Mile End Road, apparently with a bit of encouragement from Ronnie and Reggie. The guest of honour was no less than Princess Margaret, while the East End's own princess, Barbara Windsor, was the star turn. As it happened the Royalty didn't show, but after-show festivities at the Kray's Kentucky club across the road, and later on Esmerelda's in the West End, carried on regardless.

Littlewood had tired of the film by then, perhaps not realising at the outset just how much work would be involved. She had still been working on the last reel when Gerry heard a BBC radio programme, *The Long, Long Trail* written by Charles Chilton, and sensed it could be adapted for stage. The resulting play, *Oh! What a Lovely War* was to prove Theatre Workshop's biggest hit, and marked the peak of their fame at E15.

The anti-war satire that threw it's spotlight on the human cost of World War I is perhaps the clearest example of how Theatre Workshop managed to embody the zeitgeist in their middle period at Stratford. Having captured the growing confidence of a working class whose opportunities were growing, they now tapped into the increasing reluctance of Britons to accept the jingoistic view of war, as epitomised by Rupert Brooke. In doing so they played a significant role in shaping, and ultimately popularising, a new attitude to war and its human cost.

With a cast dressed mostly as Pierrot dolls (Joan's idea), a selection of songs from the period (including those sung and adapted by the soldiers) and projected visuals that detailed historical detail and grim statistics of the death toll, it was a powerful piece of agit-prop theatre. Yet the songs also gave it a sense of nostalgia, particularly for those old enough to have lived through the war, and this broadened its appeal considerably.

But at this high-water mark in Theatre Workshop's reputation, Joan Littlewood seemed to tire of the stage itself. Already disillusioned with her one film-making experience, she now turned her attentions to a project called Fun Palace, in collaboration with architect Cedric Price. He had taken disdainful remarks she made about 'quaint old theatres' when the pair met in 1961, and used them as inspiration for a radical design for a fun palace. Too radical for various local councils to accept, as it turned out: The initial idea of siting this at Glengall Wharf on the Isle of Dogs was rejected by Poplar council, and so Littlewood and Price shifted their attention to a small plot of land called Mill Meads, nestled between Three Mills and the Abbey Mills pumping station. The proposal was that the Fun Palace would form part of the Lea Valley Development Plan, which had been inspired by the efforts of Hackney mayor Lou Sherman.

By now the duo had attracted a lot of attention and a following of enthusiastic supporters, many of whom were becoming involved in the project. Cybernetics and Situationism were both increasingly influential in the growing melting pot of ideas being generated, and though notes of caution were aired the optimism (this was the sixties after all) was still high amongst the collaborators. The arriving 'Leisure Age' was becoming something of an obsession with the intelligentsia of the day and there was even talk within government of establishing a Ministry of Leisure with the idea of formally overcoming the entrenched puritanical tradition of the English psyche. Joan meanwhile talked of the need to "cheer London up".

Price had come up with a modular design involving a framework of steel lattice girders and towers complete with a crane to be employed in rearranging the interior 'walls' of the building to change its shape and function at any given time. Studios, auditoria, walkways, escalators, galleries, screens and lifts would create an evolving space designed to let visitors explore their creative desires, or simply be entertained in a creative fashion. A 1964 pamphlet designed for the conference on the Lea Development Plan announced, amongst other things: *Joan Littlewood, with architects, designers, engineers*

cyberneticians, cooks, topologists, toy-makers, flowmasters,
think clowns, offers you the occasion to enjoy, 25 hours a day,
space, light, movement, air, sun, water, in a new dimension.[90]

Publicity was arriving at a rate of knots, with extensive coverage in The Architects Journal, a planned televised segment in BBC's *Time Out* programme and press as varied as *The Tribune, Sunday Telegraph* and *New York Herald.* As exciting as developments were, changes at council level were beginning to cloud the optimism. The LCC had been a progressive and heavily Labour-influenced organisation who had been supportive of the project. The creation of the Greater London Council however, not only weakened this left-wing control but relegated decision-making on parks and open spaces to local borough level – in this case the newly created Newham, a merger of the previous East and West Ham boroughs.

The application procedure and decision making process was a drawn out affair and as hopes for success receded Littlewood's rhetoric became more radical, which in turn further isolated their position. In the event, Mill Meads was rejected as a site by the council who wanted to use it for storm water retention, but they suggested that Distillery Island might be used instead. Price wavered on the offer of the smaller, alternative site and by the end of the year this too was not an option. In January 1966 the plug was finally pulled on the project as far as the Lea Valley was concerned.

---

90 Fun Palace brochure draft, Cedric Price Archives

In retrospect it is easy to see why the Fun Palace was rejected. For all the radical enthusiasms of certain figures in the sixties, there was a more mundane reality for the majority and this was conservative and somewhat puritanical. The work-ethic was too strongly ingrained in the culture to view Littlewood's ideas with anything other than suspicion. This wasn't a simple entertainment venue like William Besant's *People's Palace* which had offered the working classes of the East End a swimming pool, library, gymnasium and winter garden, when it opened in 1887 on the Mile End Road. The Fun Palace represented a moveable feast, both physically as a building and ideologically, offering a radical alternative to cultural norms and prevailing pedagogy, so it is hard to see how the local population would have taken to something as unconventional as this when they had already shown a distinct lack of interest in the more avant garde trimmings of a traditional theatre. For all Littlewood's desire and efforts to radicalise the masses the fact remained that most were not interested.

George Cooper remembered only too well the failure of Theatre Workshop to attract the working class audience that Joan had so wanted. Those who came and witnessed his performance as Malvolio in Twelfth Night threw pennies and toffees on stage, and mocked his hat. They hadn't, as Joan liked to think, been robbed of their theatre as they never considered it theirs in the first place. It belonged to the theatre intellectuals from up West and elsewhere.[91] It was, quite frankly, in the wrong bleedin' place.

If the adults of East 15 failed to appreciate the efforts of Theatre Workshop, and the establishment recoiled from the Fun Palace, then efforts to engage the younger inhabitants of Stratford proved more fruitful. In an attempt to stop the local youth from vandalising the theatre and harassing the actors on their way home, Joan decided to create a space for them, which she dubbed the Playbarn, where they were encouraged to explore acting and would ultimately become involved in a film. At this time the area around the theatre was slowly being demolished. Salway Road, Angel Lane and neighbouring streets were being flattened to make way for a shopping centre and the extension of Great Eastern Road. The amount of land once occupied by terraced houses that had been tuned to rubble was increasing, and Joan's beloved Café L'Ange was under threat. The debris of tin cans, old prams, mattresses and assorted junk was beginning to lend the area around them a Blitz-like air.

The council were planning to include the theatre in this demolition project, but Gerry rose to the challenge of saving it, making sure that the wrecking balls didn't accidentally-on-purpose stray off target. Eventually, and in the nick of time, he secured listed building status for the theatre and waved the paperwork in front of the demolition crews who were itching to swing their wrecking ball. As the rubble of the demolition

---

91 British Library Theatre Archive Project. 2007

piled up around them, Joan decided one day to start clearing it up and before long was joined by some local children. With additional help, from local students and others, the area around the theatre was cleared and chess-board paving put in its place. As the houses on Salway Road were pulled down and demolition carried on apace, Littlewood and her cohorts took over the derelict space and encouraged the local youth to have constructive fun. Between six and eight on Friday evenings a band of them self-dubbed 'The Nutters' were allowed the stage at the theatre to do as they wished. Young children were taught how to make maps of Stratford, solve algebraic problems with coloured cubes and play volleyball. They also created and ran their own Easter Fair. Lionel Bart joined in, taking a circle of budding songwriters through their paces in the playground of a deserted school. Jimmy Winston of The Small Faces busied himself in a variety of ways and The Who played an impromptu concert, donating £1,000 for 'The Invisible Fun Palace'.[92] The Theatre itself stood alone amongst the rubble of old Stratford Streets.

She was interviewed by The Guardian in early 1973 and Angel Lane was gone. A new "piazza" was going to be built within ten feet of the theatre's emergency exit. Productions like "Costa Packet" (which looked at the perceived rip-off of package holidays) and "Is Your Doctor Really Necessary?" (a look at the NHS) may have been catering to the local audience but the critical acclaim of the sixties work was absent. By 1975

---

92 Joan's Book – Methuen, 1994. pg 762

the "piazza" had been built, named, in a rush of inspiration, Stratford Shopping Centre. This was the year that Gerry finally obtained enough funding for a season of plays with a nucleus of old company members on proper salaries. Also, for the first time there wasn't the need to transfer plays to the West End, which in the past had depleted their stock and hampered operations considerably. But just at the moment when security had seemingly been established, Gerry died suddenly of diabetes on April 11th 1975, aged 51. Joan never recovered; four years later she left E15 and moved to France, never to return or direct again.

In 1978 Claire Venables became Artistic Director, staying at the theatre for two years. In 1979 Philip Hedley took over the role. Having worked under Littlewood, Hedley was keen to see a return to the glory days and to rekindle the idea of providing theatre for the locals. He succeeded where Joan hadn't, by bringing the locals through the theatre doors in sufficient numbers. Instead of avant-garde drama, Hedley focused on catering to what the local residents wanted and adapted to the changing demographic of Newham. As well as providing music hall-style variety shows for the old-time East Enders, increasingly he looked to cater for Newham's Black and Asian community. By 1990 half the productions were of Black or Asian origin, reflecting the ethnic balance of the community. Popular shows using the full gamut of theatre trap doors and transformations included *Phantom of the Opera*, *The Invisible Man*, and *Curse of the Werewolf*. Continuing the Theatre Workshop ethos, political work was also included in the repertoire, dealing with issues such as the NHS and the Poll Tax. The British premiere of Federico Garcia Lorca's *The Public* defied the Government's Section 28, which banned the promotion of homosexuality. In 1990, musical performance *Five Guys Name Moe* became a critical and commercial success. It transferred to the West End, a sign perhaps that Hedley had succeeded in what he set out to achieve – recapturing the glory years of critical acclaim and also catering successfully for the local audience. The late 1990s saw the start of the Musical Theatre Writing Workshops, which were led by lecturers in musical theatre writing from the Tisch School of the Arts in New York. There was also still a place for traditional pantomime at Christmas, and they established a reputation as the best in London.

In 2006 Kerry Michaels took over from Hedley and continued with the ethos. His first play was *The Battle of Green Lanes*, written by Cosh Omar and set amongst London's Cypriot community. Other performances included *Come Dancing*, written by Kinks singer Ray Davis who performed in it at Stratford. In 2009 Michaels launched *Open Stage*, a groundbreaking initiative that gave locals complete control over the programme of events for the first six months of 2012.

The area around the theatre today, called the Cultural Corner, is a far cry from the rubble-strewn landscape of the late sixties. Regeneration in the mid-90's saw a cinema, pizza restaurant and arts centre built. If this isn't quite as radical as Joan Littlewood would have proposed, it has proved to be a big hit with the local residents, particularly the young, of which Newham has a higher percentage than any other London borough.

Though the most renown by far, Theatre Royal wasn't alone in providing a home for the dramatic arts. An article in The Era reported the following 11 years after the opening of the theatre on Angel Lane.

A very interesting function took place on Monday at Stratford, the laying of the foundation stone of a new playhouse, which is to be called the Borough Theatre, and is conveniently situated in the High-street, Stratford, next door to Stratford Market Station, and five minutes walk from Stratford Main Station. It speaks much for the interest this event excited, and the respect and esteem in which Mr Albert Fredericks – for whom the new theatre is being erected, and who is also the popular proprietor of the comfortable little Theatre Royal in Angel-lane – is held by the inhabitants of this densely-populated district, that quite an hour before the time appointed for the ceremony a large crowd had assembled in front of the site awaiting the arrival of the Mayor of West Ham, Alderman G.Hay, who had been invited to lay the stone.[93]

The theatre, originally called the Borough Theatre and Opera House and designed by Frank Matcham, opened the following year in August 1896, with a performance of *Henry IV* by Mr Beerbohm Tree and his Company. Seating 3,500, it was

---

93 The ERA. November 2, 1895

decorated in gold and ivory with deep red seats and carpets, and staged drama with a pantomime at Christmas. Stratford High Street was a much more bustling affair at the turn of the century, with many shops as well as the theatre extending down from The Broadway to the station and beyond. In 1933 the theatre was turned into a cinema. Matcham's auditorium was removed and replaced by an art deco auditorium, alterations that also saw a refacing of the corner entrance. It was now christened The Rex, and came complete with its own wurlitzer organ and seating for 1,899. It's life as a cinema lasted until 1969 when it was converted for use as a bingo hall. This came to an end in 1974, and after a brief existence as a cinema showing Asian films, the building was closed down, remaining empty and derelict for 21 years.

In 1996, with the help of a local Government regeneration fund, businessman Malcolm Campbell re-opened the building and restored much of its former interior grandeur. In this guise it served as a concert venue and nightclub, called simply Stratford Rex. It played host to mainly reggae and rap artists, including the 2008 concert when Lil Wayne stormed off stage after a drink was thrown at him from the crowd. As well as club nights playing drum and bass, R'n'B and speed garage, the venue also played a role in the Grime scene, holding a special place in the heart of Bow-born Dizzee Rascal who played there as a virtual unknown. All this clubbing activity came to an end in 2010 when the council repossessed the venue, claiming that the tenants had neglected it and owed a year's rent of £40,000 and two years of business rates amounting to a further £130,000.[94]

Three years after Borough Theatre had opened, Stratford saw the opening of yet another establishment, this one built on the sight of Rokeby House.

The new building is situated in the Broadway, and considering that there exists no other hall of varieties in Stratford – a district as thickly populated as any around central London, the promoters of the undertaking have every reason to feel sanguine as to the success of the New Empire Palace of Varieties.

It will be conducted on the two houses a-night principle – that is to say, two performances each evening will be given, the same artists appearing at both, the first beginning at half-past six and finishing at half-past eight, and the second opening at nine and concluding at eleven. The hall will be made as attractive and comfortable as those palaces of pleasure situated at the West-end of London, and on the nightly programme will be found the names of leading artists in the variety profession. In fact, everything will be done by the management to make the New Empire worthy of its name and its surroundings.[95]

The onstage fare at the New Empire was somewhat less highbrow than that of its theatrical neighbours, as a description of the first night illustrates.

---

94 The Stage – 13 July 2010

95 The ERA – 25 March, 1899

Eugen Sandow receives an ovation when his muscular figure is observed on the pedestal, and expressions of wonder are everywhere heard during the exposition of the athlete's marvellous physical development. In a scene representing a Roman amphitheatre, Sandow afterwards takes hold of bar-bells and dumb-bells of extraordinary weight, one of which he balances on his knees while on another a stalwart attendant is swung to and fro. Other astounding feats are performed by this modern Hercules, who, later, seated on the haunches of a horse, bends backwards, lifts a man from the ground up over his head, and seats him astride on the horse's back. As a specimen of finger-strength Sandow tears in halves one and two packs of playing cards, his last effort being to separate no less than 154 cards. Sandow is encored again and again, and his performance is discussed with eager astonishment long after he has left the stage. [96]

As well as the above feats, the enthusiastic audience were treated to singing, burlesque, ventriloquism, piano playing and a farcical sketch. Such variety was presumably on offer until the Empire Palace was bombed in 1940, the building eventually being demolished.

The variety and music hall style may have been to local taste, but post-war this too was in decline. Theatre goer Pat Francis recalled her visits to the East Ham Palace when interviewed for the British Library Theatre Archive Project,

---

96 Ibid

describing a downward spiral that saw the number of chorus girls dwindle from several down to two, then to one who was drunk. Then it shut down, a lone drunken chorus girl stumbling around on the stage obviously not good box office.[97]

Although cinema was also starting a slow post-war decline, it was still more popular than the theatre and variety hall, and perhaps more to the point cheaper. Cinema offered a much more instant form of escape, and in the austere and grey 1950s its power hadn't yet dimmed. However, increasingly television was making its impact felt, and as cinemas were converted into bingo halls the challenge of enticing people to pay to watch live performance was even more pronounced. Knowing as we do that early audiences for Theatre Workshop performances often numbered barely into double figures, it is tempting to come to the conclusion that anyone without Joan and Gerry's passion would have thrown in the towel, and the theatre would have been lost in the demolition of the late sixties.

If television was keeping their parents indoors, then the thing that offered a sense of excitement and release for young people was increasingly music. The birth of rock'n'roll and the subsequent pop explosion changed the cultural landscape. As well as pop culture there was also an increasing consumer culture, and the birth of the teenager threw the two together. Our perception of this era, thanks to television and the nostalgia industry, tends to be somewhat selective: as if

97 British Library Theatre Archive Project. 2007

overnight young people became hip, swinging things and life was a perpetual, brightly coloured party. In reality the shift from an old world to the brave new one was less clear cut. A photograph in the Newham Archives brings this home quite neatly.

The photograph depicts a parade of pearly kings, queens, princesses, young children and pets at the congregation of a pets' service at Durning Hall on 26th June 1955. The practice of wearing suits adorned with pearl buttons has roots in the 19th century, and the Pearly Society was formed in 1911. A phenomenon peculiar to London, it has always been charitable, but as a signifier it is all about tradition. In the background of the picture can be seen a sign poking out from a small hedge. It advertises the Forest Gate Jive Academy; in the mid-fifties this is what passed as a nightclub.

The Jive Academy was located in a large house on Earlham Grove. A reel-to-reel tape recorder in the bay window would play the hits of the day. Pre-rock 'n' roll, this would have meant big band swing music and the sounds of Count Basie, Woody Hermann and other jazz bands. Patrons would jive or dance the 'creep' downstairs, while upstairs was a cloakroom and seating area. Until an alcohol license was obtained, a quick dash to the nearby Railway Tavern for refreshment was necessary. Saturday nights would often start in this pub, by Forest Gate station, and more often than not would involve a sing-song round the piano. The choice of venues increased with the opening of The Lotus, which was above a furniture store on Woodgrange Road. Further afield for regulars of these two dancing venues was Stratford Town Hall, though this tended to be ballroom dancing.

Of course it wasn't long before the idea of starting a band became feasible for young people. The Small Faces started life when Plaistow-born Ronnie Lane met Steve Marriott in 1965, when Marriott was working at the J60 Music Bar, Manor Park. They drafted in friends Kenney Jones and Jimmy Winston from Stratford, rehearsing at the Ruskin Arms. Winston would be replaced by Ian McLagan after two singles and would move down the road to work with Joan Littlewood, helping out with 'The Nutters' – the local n'er do-wells who Littlewood decided would do less damage all round if they were given a space to express themselves. The Small Faces went on to considerable fame, of course, and eventually mutated into The Faces with Rod Stewart and Ronnie Wood. In their original guise their sound, heavily influenced by American rhythm and blues, and lack of pretension made them a favourite of working class youth, who felt that psychedelia offered them little. It is no surprise that they, along with The Who, were two of the few bands given any credit by The Sex Pistols, who covered The Small Faces *Watcha Gonna Do About It*.

It is surprising just how few bands have come from this part of London; aside from The Small Faces, Iron Maiden and The Cockney Rejects, the roll of honour is a short one. The Rejects hailed from Canning Town, forming in 1978. Their brand of punk, influenced by Sham 69, would help to influence its own sub-genre, *Oi!* Their first demo, *Flares and*

Slippers, was picked up by Walthamstow independent label Small Wonder Records, and they were subsequently signed to EMI. They made it onto Top of the Pops in 1980 with their version of the West Ham terrace anthem *I'm Forever Blowin' Bubbles*, the sales of which were boosted when underdogs West Ham beat Arsenal in that season's F.A. Cup final, thanks to a rare headed goal by Trevor Brooking.

One of the venues that played a key role in the early career of the band was the Bridge House in Canning Town. From 1975 to 1982 this venue, with landlord Terence Murphy at the helm, played host to a variety of live music in an attempt to stop the locals disappearing up West. The list is an impressive one: Dire Straits and U2 played their first UK dates here, while Depeche Mode were signed to Mute Records on the strength of a gig alongside Fad Gadget. Mick Jagger was once told to stop dancing as the venue didn't have a dance license, and other bands treading the boards included Tom Robinson, Paul Young, Annie Lennox, Iron Maiden, Wasted Youth and Alison Moyet. One regular was Plaistow-born Ray Winstone, who had starred in Scum and Quadrophenia and was advised by Murphy to give up boxing and concentrate on acting.[98]

Iron Maiden may have played the Bridge House and Ruskin Arms in East Ham, but the venue that is synonymous with their birth is the Cart and Horses in Maryland, Stratford. Band founder Stephen Harris was born up the road in

98 Legends of the Bridge House; The venue everyone loved. Pierre Perrone. The Independent. Friday 11 January 2008

Leytonstone, and after leaving school had trialled for West
Ham United. An early line up of the band, with Paul Mario
Day on vocals, played at the pub and pretty soon started
building up a following. Day wasn't deemed to have enough
charisma and was replaced by Dennis Wilcock. Over the next
couple of years there were numerous comings and goings of
personnel, but one night in 1978 Harris was introduced to
Paul Di Anno in the Red Lion in Leytonstone, and armed with
his raspy voice a settled line up went from gigging at the Cart
and Horses to much wider fame in a relatively short period.

Other venues of musical note include The Princess
Alice in Forest Gate, which was host to the first Rock Against
Racism gig in 1976 when Matumbi and Carol Grimes
performed.

Local rock and pop stars are thin on the ground, but Matt
Johnson, who in the 1980s had success as The The, grew up
in The Two Puddings pub on Stratford Broadway. His father,
Eddie, became the landlord in the winter of 1962, and during
a snowstorm a woman knocked on the doors looking for a
job. This was Maxine Daniels, and Eddie took her on as a
singer. Daniels, sister of Kenny Lynch, was a jazz singer who
had worked with Humphrey Lyttleton. The customers at the
pub loved her. The Two Puddings had a bit of a reputation
for violent incidents, but also attracted a famous clientele: the
likes of Bobby Moore, Martin Peters, the Krays and The Small
Faces all drank there. Jackie Charlton supposedly dropped by
for a pint the night England won the World Cup, and Harry
Redknapp met his wife there. Above the pub was a club which

played host to the 'Devil's Kitchen' nights in the sixties, the club being done out in ghoulish day-glo murals.

I remember going there in 1991 when I had first arrived in London, and enjoyed a drink on the lively karaoke nights when the large crowd would let the aspiring singers know what they thought of them in no uncertain terms. As I recall there were only ever one or two singers of any note, so the cat-calls, heckling, laughter and booing were fairly constant. The cheers for one particularly golden-voiced woman, however, shook the walls. The Two Puddings closed down in 2000, reopening not long after as *The Latin ¼*, but without Eddie Johnson in charge.

One day that he can remember is the Sunday in February 1967 when The Beatles arrived in Stratford to do some work on a promotional film for Penny Lane. The film shows them riding white horses through an alleyway from a car park onto Angel Lane, and also includes shots of Lennon walking down the street and meeting the rest of the group by the Theatre Royal. Much to Eddie's chagrin the fab four used a rival pub, The Salway Arms, as their base that day, so he didn't even get to see them. Such would have been the shock of pop stars appearing in the vicinity, it is probable that many locals who did see them were left rubbing their eyes in disbelief. The swinging part of the sixties hadn't made many inroads this far East. When the demolition of the Angel Lane area got under way, it would have been tempting to think that the sixties had never happened.

CHAPTER 7

Bronco Bullfrog and Angel Lane

"Not much to do round here is there?"

Del Quant (Bronco Bullfrog)

The further we get away from them, the more unique the 1960s appear to be as a time in history. Near full employment and the introduction of the Welfare State after the war had provided opportunities for the working classes as never before. At the same time, class barriers, while not disappearing, were having holes poked through them as working class actors, photographers and pop stars were introduced to middle and upper class society via their managers and industry insiders. Similarly, the increase in working class access to higher education meant that the lines between working and middle class were increasingly blurred.

But it would be a mistake to think that the sixties was swinging for everyone. Young working class people of the East End could be forgiven for thinking that the good times were happening on another planet. The white heat of technology had ignored Stratford, where the dark scars of industrialisation were still very much evident in the decaying environment. It would seem that the real winners in this decade of plenty were those who had successfully made the transition from working to middle class, along with the existing middle classes, who had easier access to the heart of the elite inner circle of the swinging scene. The benefits to the working classes are harder to fathom; although there were undoubted increases in standards of living, this was often at the expense of the communities that had sustained them for generations. When the dust had settled from the slum clearances of this decade, the impact on the sense of community was immediately apparent, particularly when new housing stock consisted of high-rises. With the benefit of hindsight the impact seems much more profound, though the seismic economic shocks of the 1970s clearly delivered the coup de grace – one that access to debt has kept hidden until our recent crash.

One man keen to document the flip-side to the sixties was Barney Platts-Mills, the son of QC John Platts-Mills who had defended the Krays and the Great Train Robbers. With the advice of the producer and director – and family friend – Lewis Gilbert ringing in his fifteen year old ears, Platts-Mills secured himself a job as an assistant trainee editor on Gilbert's *The Greengage Summer* at Shepperton Studios. After working on Kubrick's *Spartacus* and Schlesinger's *A Kind of Loving*, he then moved to working in television editing, and was involved in series such as Anglia Television's *Survival* and Granada's

World in Action. This being the sixties, and with a pocket full of Granada's change, Platts-Mills then opted to take a long holiday. This indirectly led him to Marlene and John Fletcher, who had just set up Dateline Films and were shooting a short drama with the boys from the Paddington Youth Club. This was a watershed moment for Platts-Mills, as the idea of accessible, independent, working class cinema formed in his mind. In 1966, along with film director Adam Scott and editor and cinematographer Adam Barker-Mill, he set up Maya Films.

The first two short films produced by Maya Films were *Love's Presentation* (1966), on the work of David Hockney, and *St Christopher* (1967), on Rudolf Steiner schools in Bristol and Botton Village, Yorkshire. He was asked to put in some time editing a documentary film that Joan Littlewood was trying to make in support of her Fun Palace project. Following Joan around as she failed to shoot the film gave Platts-Mills access to the Play Barn in Stratford, where in the evenings local teenagers, 'The Nutters', were given free reign to express their lives and fantasies, guided by Peter Rankin and ex-Small Faces keyboard player Jimmy Winston. The result was *Everybody's An Actor, Shakespeare Said.*

This thirty minute documentary trained its camera on these local teenagers inside the Play Barn, improvising scenes based on their own lives. It is a fascinating film for a number of reasons, not least of which is that a moment in time is captured in the sort of detail that memory alone cannot provide, often revealing things that even the film maker wasn't necessarily conscious of shooting. Exterior shots of Angel Lane and the streets round the theatre clearly show just how devastated the area looked. For an East End still scarred by Word War Two bombs, this urban decay must have seemed a constant, particularly in an environment as industrial as Stratford's still was. But the particularly interesting aspect of the film is that although it captures moments in time from the sixties, it points much more closely to the approaching seventies.

In 1968, when the film was made, the pop music explosion had long been sidetracked by psychedelically enhanced experimentation, distancing the music from many working class youth. While the middle class were turning to hippy fashions of kaftans, bells and incense, the style of the boys caught by the camera of Platts-Mills' film is something entirely different. In January of '68 Prime Minister Harold Wilson endorsed the 'I'm Backing Britain' campaign, which encouraged people to work an extra half hour each day without pay – the first sign, perhaps, of the approaching economic strife ahead. The student riots in Paris that year clearly demonstrated that something was wrong in paradise, but the working class youth of the East End were far removed from such concerns. For them the future wasn't a question of political and intellectual choices, but of low paid manual labour and boredom. While the beautiful people in the West End were exploring their inner psyches, people like Del Walker, Sam Shepherd and Roy Haywood were trapped within much narrower horizons.

At one point in *Everybody's an Actor...*, Platts-Mills interviews Walker, a sixteen year old apprentice plumber. Asked why he comes to the Play Barn, he replies, 'It's better than hanging about the streets.' When he is asked if that is all he ever did before, Walker throws a look that momentarily captures the gulf between the upper-middle class world of the director and the working class lives of his subjects, before replying with a wry smile, 'It's all I've ever done. Stratford, Plaistow, Greengate, East Ham, Leyton, Chingford, everywhere.' The smile then disappears and he adds, 'Get a bit sick of it.' Later in the film he points out that when they hang about the streets they 'get done for loiterin'.'

The clear absence of anything to do or anywhere to go, and the accompanying scenes of urban decay with high-rises in the distance, position this moment less in the sixties and more as an early manifestation of seventies ennui, when tower blocks and boredom were two of the great signifiers of punk. The cheeky banter and exuberance of the boys as they act out their scenes make this an invigorating film, and you can't help but think that in different circumstances some of them may well have formed bands themselves. But punk was eight years away, a lifetime for a teenager, and in this sense they were perhaps unfortunate to have been in the right place at the wrong time.

It is a funny film too. There is a great scene where the lads are playing football on the sort of thick, muddy pitch that only people of a certain generation will remember, with a ball the colour of mud and the weight of a house brick. Set to a soundtrack of The Small Faces' *Lazy Sunday*, it is much shorter than, but every bit the equal to the famous football scene in Ken Loach's *Kes*. By the final scenes we learn that the Play Barn has closed, partly due to the boys' own destructive behaviour. But Platts-Mills kept in touch, and they suggested he make a 'proper film'. The result, shot over a six week period in 1969 and with a budget of £18, 000, was *Bronco Bullfrog*.

In cinematic terms, Bronco Bullfrog was a critical success but not a commercial one. Penelope Gilliatt, writing in the New Yorker Review, admired its gritty realism and, though she paints in broad strokes, is able to pick up on the pervading sense of boredom. Other critics were equally impressed. Derek Malcolm, writing in The Guardian, thought the film to be honest, serious, funny, and generally more far reaching than most British offerings of that year.

The film garnered the Screenwriters Guild Award for 'Best Original Screenplay' at Cannes, and gained additional publicity when it was pulled from The Cameo-Poly on Regent Street in October 1970 after only eighteen days, to make way for the royal premiere of Laurence Olivier's *Three Sisters*. As a result, 200 members of the Beaumont Youth Club in Leyton turned up to protest, jeering the royal guest, Princess Anne, as she walked the red carpet. Sam Shepherd, who played the eponymous role wrote a letter of apology, offering an explanation of the hecklers' chagrin. Remarkably, Princess Anne took up his offer of coming to see the film at 'their' local Mile End ABC. This screening took place on November 23rd and attracted a significant crowd – not just for the film, but also to witness what might have been the first royal visit to the East End since the Blitz, putting Shepherd one-up on the Krays who had been disappointed by Princess Margaret several years earlier. He also got a firm talking to from the constabulary after he broke protocol and kissed Princess Anne's hand. However, the extra publicity didn't provide the film with the impetus it needed to become a wider success, and it soon disappeared from view and into an obscurity that made it not just a cult film, but one hardly anyone had ever heard of, let alone seen. For a while the Nutters, and Shepherd in particular, enjoyed small trappings of fame. Platts-Mills even sent Del Walker and Roy Haywood to collect the Writers Guild Award from Richard Attenborough. Soon, though, their brief flirt with the dramatic arts was over.

The film centres on the character of Del Quant (Del Walker), an apprentice welder who meets and romantically pursues fifteen year old Irene (Anne Gooding). The main thrust of the plot from hereon concerns their frustrated attempts to get some time and space alone – a neat reminder that the sexually permissive sixties didn't reach everyone at the same time. Working class youths were often economically impotent, and marriage was frequently seen as the only way of gaining the independence necessary for any kind of sex life. Both sets of parents are less than sympathetic to the budding romantics, and it is down to Bronco Bullfrog, fresh out of Borstal, to help them by offering them his pad for the night. Even then, however, they are thwarted.

Weaved into this skinny plot are scenes that capture perfectly what life was like for working class teenagers in the East End in 1969. There is a rare trip up West, and the gift of a motorbike that enables Del and Irene to escape into the country for a day (the bike is purchased from Stratford Motorcycles on Romford Road, which was still there as late as 2006 when I lived round the corner on Aldworth Road but is at the time of writing a shop-to-let). There are fights too, and the constant threat of them from a gang based in neighbouring Forest Gate. If you want to see what life in Stratford was like over forty years ago, then *Bronco Bullfrog* is pretty much your only option, but as well as serving as an insightful historical document, it is also an entertaining, frequently funny and ultimately poignant film.

It is also a useful document of the era's street style. The actors wore their own clothes, not those chosen by a wardrobe department, and so authenticity is a given. Before consumerism replaced street culture, fashion was one of the few ways that working class youth could forge a sense of identity. In this case it is a look that would become known as 'suedehead', eventually spawning one of those Richard Allen pulps (by which time the original suedeheads had long moved on – in fact when you check Sam Shepherds hair in the photographs of the Mile End screening the transition is obvious). Suedehead was a move on from the 'skinhead' look, which clearly had nowhere to go fashion-wise, but both were working class responses to the psychedelic frippery that had infected the mod bands. Even The Small Faces were guilty of dabbling in psychedelia. It was clear to a lot of young people that the swinging sixties was a party to which they weren't invited. With the hippy look anathema to the average fashion conscious lad from the streets, it was no hardship to accept that the cheap thrills of the pop explosion – maximum R'n'B, as The Who put it – were over.

Del's look in the film, with his longer hair and penny collar, is particularly interesting for style historians as it points to where 1970 was heading. In an age when 'cool' is available off the shelf for everyone, it is worth remembering that in our pre-consumerist days, cool couldn't simply be bought (and perhaps it still can't). You either had it or you didn't. It was elusive. And if society wasn't going to provide you with much, then cool was all you had left, until you got older and had kids. So our boys in the film were all dressed up right, but there was nowhere to go. This is demonstrated to glorious effect in the scene where Del and the boys retire to some sort of den in, presumably, one of the derelict houses resulting from the demolition programme. A camping lamp is lit to illuminate their decidedly low-rent hideout. The light reveals soft-core porn pin-ups on the walls, a manifestation of their sexual frustration. Del suggests they all stay the night, for a laugh, but one by one the other lads give their excuses and their night is over. For the remainder of the film Del tries to find somewhere to go with Irene. A trip to the cinema in the West End falls flat when they can't afford the Leicester Square prices, and a longer venture out into the country to visit an uncle proves fruitless. No matter what Del tries to do in the film, his horizons remain limited and shrink all the time, both physically and mentally.

Thanks to the films of Barney Platts-Mills, we can see glimpses of what Stratford was like before the last major regeneration project took place at the end of the sixties and beginning of the seventies. The building of the Stratford Shopping Centre and extension of the Great Eastern Road changed the

map of central Stratford quite considerably. Angel Lane was the
most significant loss, a bustling market street full of shops and
cafes that, together with The Broadway, made Stratford the prime
shopping centre of the East End. Angel Lane began at roughly
where the Broadway entrance of the Stratford Shopping Centre is
today. Its slightly curved trajectory continued for over a quarter
of a mile, over the railway lines, before it met Leyton Road.
Actually it still does, as the top end of Angel Lane survived the
rebuilding project, though the railway bridge has been replaced
by a newer one more suited to the current rebuilding project. If
you enter the shopping centre at the Broadway entrance you can
roughly follow where Angel Lane was by walking to the middle
of the centre, then veering left and walking along the corridor
of shops that includes Barclay's Bank and the indoor market.
When you reach the exit at the end you will be just yards away
from the Theatre Royal and what now passes for Salway Road.

The roll call of missing streets includes Martin Street,
where the Play Barn was located, and which ran roughly parallel
with Angel Lane. Between Martin Street and Angel Lane was
small cluster of streets forming a square; Broad Street, Cullum
Street, which formed two sides of the square, and Earl Street.
This area was known locally as 'The Shoot'. Jim Pickard, who
was born in 1906, grew up here and put his memories into
writing for the Newham Story, an online historical archive.
There were three outlets, one by the road leading to Martin Street
and two Courts or alleyways as they were known Reeves Court
leading to Angel Lane, the local market place and Broadway
Court (formally known as Cat's Alley), leading to Stratford

Broadway. This Court was the rendezvous for all the local boozers, both male and female from the various pubs in the Broadway, there being at that time ten Public Houses in less than half a mile. The houses were originally built for the workers of the LNER Workshops in the New Town of Stratford[99]

Unsurprisingly this small area was a poor one. Many families were on Parish relief, the welfare of the day, which carried a social stigma that meant the actual assistance was always double-edged. Of course, although the streets were poor and most likely dirty from pollution, there was a theatre right in the middle of them.

The old Theatre Royal in Angel Lane was a Mecca for children. Such horrors as Maria Martin in the Red Barn etc were real blood curdlers to the kids, who used to hiss the villain, and cheer the hero and heroine. During the midweek when audiences were very small, crowds of children used to gather at the gallery entrance, whilst one member of the gang used to purchase a ticket the rest would march up the stairs. For the price of a pint of beer, the ticket collector, who used to live in our street, allowed about a dozen to enter on one ticket. We used to consider this a form of game. I found out, years later, that the management knew of this, but closed his eyes to it, as it always provided an enthusiastic audience for the empty seats.[100]

---

99 The Newham Story

100 Ibid

Similar tricks were played to gain free access to the cinema. If you start to imagine the harsh, polluted environment that children like Jim grew up in, it's easy to appreciate just how magical the dark confines of a cinema showing films must have been to this generation. Aside of sneaky cinema or theatre visits, entertainment, unlike today, was self-generated. This might mean swimming in the River Lea, or simply window gazing at the department stores on Broadway, like Boardman's. All kinds of children's street games were played, and when imagination failed to deliver there was always song.

Crowds of children used to sit on the pavements and someone would start a song, in no time at all the whole of the street was singing the chorus, songs such as Nellie Dean and other favourites of the Music Halls, this went on until about midnight when cups of tea were passed around made by the various neighbours, it just seemed like one huge happy family. There were rows and fights, especially where some people were the worse for drink but all and sundry tried to help in patching things up between husbands and wives. [101]

Memory, of course, is both subjective and selective. If Jim's reminisces paint a somewhat glossy picture, then contemporary news stories can offer a more objective, though equally selective, view. One particular episode involving inhabitants of 'The Shoot' – who were, as Jim puts it, 'worse for drink' – happened in August 1893.

---

101 Ibid

James Wright, thirty-eight, a seaman, late of Cullum-street, Stratford, was charged on an extradition warrant, at West Ham Police-court on Tuesday, for that he did kill and slay George Pryke, a labourer, aged forty-eight, at Cullum-street, Stratford. It appears that on the night of Aug.18 the prisoner, the deceased, and a man named Robinson were seen arm-in-arm passing down Cullum-street. They were in altercation, and when they got to a dark part of the street Wright and Robinson attacked Pryke, who was worse for liquor, and he was knocked down and kicked. Pryke succumbed to blood poisoning, at West Ham Hospital, the result of the injury to his leg (which was broken in three places, the two small bones protruding through the flesh), on Sept. 12. Prisoner, who made no statement, was committed for trial to the Central Criminal Court. Wright and Robinson were each sentenced to three month's hard labour at the Central Criminal Court on Wednesday.[102]

This is just one news story, but is well worth our consideration lest we get carried away with the idea that this part of the East End was just full of lovable rogues who wouldn't hurt a fly. Like any working class environment rooted in industry, Stratford's history is tough and it bred tough characters. Sometimes, cheeky as they may well have been, they didn't do nice things.

Bronco Bullfrog portrays the flavour of the environment and its people as well as any film has ever done when setting out to capture a time and place. When Roy and Del are beaten up

---

102 The Newsman – Saturday, November 18, 1893

in separate incidents, the violence is unexpected, but thankfully undramatic. The actual choreography of the fights is a bit wooden, but better this than glorified, and it renders the violence more realistic. It just happens. It is over quickly. Life on these streets is mean. When Del has his motorbike driven over and wrecked by a lorry, he tells a passing policeman it isn't his to avoid getting caught up in any awkward questions (at this point in the film he is on the run). Rather than worry about his bike, all he can do is walk away, and it is as a consequence of this that he gets beaten up in the foot tunnel that runs under the Thames from Greenwich to Island Gardens. When it rains, it pours.

In fact, Del's day is about to get even worse. By the end of the film he is backed into a smaller and smaller corner, from which you can sense no real way out. However, rather than ending on such a downbeat note, Platts-Mills decides to freeze-frame on the face of the two ill-fated lovers, as they find themselves with nowhere left to run, down by the river. Perhaps not the most subtle of stylistic touches in 1969, but the director does somehow capture in that still image the illusive and unfathomable force of youth. In an age when working class teenagers were beginning to settle down and start families as early as 18, that fleeting sense of freedom (mostly denied to poor Del) is captured on the screen, as precious and fragile as a butterfly's wings.

Bronco himself is free to run, and at this point we see that he alone has any hope of escape, now that circumstance has forced it upon him[103]. All the other characters, by being

103 Bronco has assaulted the police officer who arrives at Bronco's flat,

passive, are seemingly at the mercy of events beyond their control – much like the area itself was at the mercy of town planners who had chosen redevelopment. Not only were the streets surrounding the Theatre Royal being demolished in readiness for the new development, but more high-rises were being built around this period. The scenes in the flat (Green Point on Water Lane) that Irene shares with her mother are filmed to vividly communicate the sense of isolation that high-rise living can bring. But any ideas that such housing was going to be seen as the answer were dealt a fatal blow at Ronan Point, a high rise block on the Kier Hardie Estate, Canning Town. Just two months after it was ready for occupation, a gas explosion demolished a load-bearing wall and a whole top corner of the tower block collapsed like a house of cards.

The blast was caused at 6am in an apartment on the eighteenth floor, when 56 year old Ivy Hodge lit a match to light her stove for a cup of tea. Mrs. Hodge was blown back by the explosion, which also blew out the opposite corner walls of the apartment. Ronan Point had been built using the Danish Larsen-Nielsen system, which involved pre-cast concrete components. The design of the tower block was such that the floors of each flat were supported by the load-bearing walls directly beneath. When the walls of Ivy Hodge's kitchen disappeared, it therefore set off a chain reaction. Firstly, without its supporting walls floor nineteen collapsed. In turn this brought down floor

---

looking for Del and Irene, in order that they might escape. He has no choice but to keep on running. Physically at least, he escapes the stifling environment that Del is trapped in.

twenty, and so on upwards. Then, with the floors from above weighing down on floor eighteen, this too collapsed onto floor seventeen below, and the pattern was repeated downwards until the ground was reached. Four people died and seventeen were injured, but the death toll could have been much higher. Most tenants had been in bed at the time, and the explosion had taken out the half of each apartment that didn't contain the bedrooms. Furthermore, only one of the apartments above Mrs. Hodges was occupied.

A public enquiry into the disaster revealed worrying facts. Similar damage to the load bearing walls could occur through fire or wind damage. The building had only been designed to withstand wind speeds of 65 mph. The building codes used for Ronan Point and its sister building had not been kept up to date, and higher winds were known to occur. Architect Simon Webb recommended a fire test be carried out, sixteen years after the collapse of the south east corner, which confirmed the theory that fire could also cause a collapse. In conversation with residents, he learnt that smoke could pass up through cracks in the floors. When he was invited into some of the apartments, even more alarming things were made evident: sheets of paper, and even coins, could pass through the floor of one flat and into the one below.[104]

Webb was asked by Newham's Housing Committee to conduct a survey. This revealed that in high winds the building

---

104 Wearne, Philip. Collapse: When Buildings Fall Down, TV Books, L.L.C., USA, 2000

was beginning to break up, and was structurally unsound in several ways. Owing to these concerns, Ronan Point and nine other blocks on the estate were finally demolished in 1986.

The effect of the disaster was a change in building regulations throughout the world. It also shone a light on the sheer folly of doing things on the cheap. Inadequate building regulations, lack of skilled labour, a change in the regulations for population density, and the political need to rehouse so many so soon made for a heady brew. Although many high rise blocks were structurally sound and many occupants liked them, overall this post war experiment in high-rise living was a disaster. The image of the high-rise as a symbol of the nation's malaise in the seventies was assured.

When Del comes home after failing to persuade the others in his gang to spend the night in the derelict house, his father asks him where he has been. 'Out,' replies Del.
'Enjoy yourself?'
'Nah. Boring as usual. Nothing to do round here.'

Station Street, Martin Street, Frederick Street, William Street and Western Street were all being consigned to history. 'The Shoot' had already gone. But it was the loss of Angel Lane that was the biggest blow to the locals, particularly those who had a business there. A way of life, and a life of memories had, for many, been demolished. Wiped out. And soon the memories would be buried even further. It was, in many ways, the end of an era. What lay ahead was the seventies and a huge chunk of Stratford was turned into a construction site to make way for a new shopping centre.

CHAPTER 8

West Ham

The maw of the London Minotaur is insatiable, and none that go into the secret recesses of his lair return again.[105]

William Thomas Stead

"You want me to come on a walk just to pick up a parcel?" Angry Bob said down the phone. "On a lovely day like this?"

"Not just to pick up the parcel Bob."

"What else then?"

"We could have a look at the pumping station. There's plenty of history on the way."

"You and your history," he said, but I knew that he was going to come. Bob didn't often pass up on the opportunity for a good walk. It gave him the chance to talk, apart from anything else. Within half an hour he was at my door on Aldworth Road and we began our walk. Before we reached West Ham Lane Bob was off and running with his views on a story he

105 William Stead. The Maiden Tribute of Modern Babylon, Pall Mall Gazette, 1885

had seen in the Daily Mirror that morning, about taking finger prints off children in schools. It was only a matter of time, thought Bob, before micro-chipping would be the norm. "There's a company in America that micro-chips pets and now they're selling it as something for your kids – so you always know where they are."

"Peace of mind eh? Brilliant."

"Like, say your kid got abducted by a pervert, well, if they are micro-chipped then everything's fine."

"Yeah. Except most kids are abused by people they know. Hardly any are abducted. But hey, why let facts get in the way of profit. We live in bad times Bob, bad times."

"We've always lived in bad times. Kids disappearing is nothing new. Interesting times is what we live in," he said, before adding, "The old Chinese curse. *May you live in interesting times.*"

"Talking of the Chinese," I said, "there's some odd graffiti been cropping up lately."

"What's that then?"

"Anti-Chinese stuff. There's some on the way, you'll see it."

"There's a Chinese over there," Bob said, nodding towards its direction over the road.

"Nothing to do with them."

"You ever use it?"

"Used to."

"Why'd you stop?"

"Monosodium glutamate. Does funny things to me. I used to wake up in the night seeing everything in negative. Thought that was a good reason to stop." We had stopped to cross by the flats at Whales Yard where I had lived when I moved to Stratford.

"There used to be a great video shop back there," I said. "It had every video you could think of stuffed into two rooms with a corridor in between them that was crammed as well. There was a giant stone fountain in the back room full of koi carp."

"That's normal," Bob said.

"Weird thing is, the bloke who ran it was really friendly and the other staff and I always used to chat but I never asked about that fountain or how they got the bloody thing in there in the first place. Wish I had now. It's still a mystery."

We crossed the road and walked past the shops and launderette, then The British Lion pub and the recreation ground, discussing on the way the previous night's World Cup final and what might have made Zinedine Zidane sufficiently upset to get himself sent off. We turned down Barnby Street and round onto Arthingworth Street. Bob spotted the sign. It was why I liked to take him on walks – that ability to spot little details the rest of us walk by. The sign warned that the building was under police surveillance and that the dealing and use of illegal substances would not be tolerated anywhere within it. This was the house that Nina Mackay and other officers entered on 24th October 1997 to apprehend Magdi Elgizouli, who had breached his bail conditions. Mackay, 25, was stabbed by Elgizouli and later died from her wounds. A memorial plague stood outside the house.

I had never noticed the sign before. We couldn't help but look around to see where surveillance might be taking place from. Her killer was diagnosed with paranoid schizophrenia and was detained initially in Rampton Secure Hospital in Nottinghamshire. Tony Blair had been present when they had unveiled the memorial in 1998. Bob had no recollection of the incident. We walked on down the street until we reached the bottom and turned onto Abbey Road. Brightly coloured washing was flapping gently in the breeze on the balconies of the David Lee Point flats, and a kitchen extractor fan was sending a slow curlicue of smoke lazily into the warm air. Abbey Road is thought to have originated as a lane, or pathway, running between West Ham church and the Abbey, which lends the present road its name. It runs in a dog leg and at the top of the first section, where it meets Bakers Row before bending left, is the Bridge Road Depot, opened in 1896 as the West Ham Corporation Depot and once home to the Corporation Stables. On the gates is a small plaque that commemorates 'Black Saturday'.

'Black Saturday' was the name given to the Saturday of 7th September 1940 when the Blitz began. Although some bombs had fallen on Beckton in August, the full force of the Luftwaffe was unleashed that night, and some 300 tons of bombs were dropped on the East End of London. The Royal Docks and other wartime industries in the area were an obvious target. Iris Warren remembered this first night of the Blitz. 'On the Saturday night, that we were first bombed, I walked from Walthamstow to Maryland Point and got on a train home. Nobody was there to take your money or anything. I got off at Manor Park because I lived in East Ham.

All along the High Street was on fire. Woolworths had been bombed on Station Hill and a furniture shop was on fire.'[106]

A more detailed account of the day is provided by Ivy Alexander, a young woman from Canning Town who had chosen to go cycling in Epping Forest that Saturday with her friend, Renee. The air raid sirens began when they were in the forest, but as the raids had not been particularly intense up to this point, the two young women were at first not unduly alarmed. They returned home in the late afternoon and as they approached London mistook the huge black clouds of smoke for an approaching storm. It was only later that they discovered it was from the many fires caused by the bombing. At Stratford everything appeared to be burning, including the Leather Cloth factory, which they couldn't get near.

Attempting to reach Renee's house on nearby Manor Road, the girls were thwarted by policemen and wardens warning of time bombs and blown up roads. They took a detour along the Chanelsea cut, out onto the sewer bank and eventually reached their destination.[107] The bombing was to return every night except one, until November 14th. On Black Saturday, the brunt of the attack was felt in Canning Town and Silvertown, the targets being the Docks, Beckton Gasworks and Woolwich Arsenal. At 7.15pm the Depot took a direct hit and 13 men were killed. Nearby Turley Close is named after one of them, Sub Officer Wally Turley.

---

106 London Borough of Newham, The Newham Story, 2002

107 Ivy Alexander, Maid in West Ham, 2001

Just along from the gates of the Depot and the plaque commemorating the events of that day, we stopped at the stone statue of a lion atop a large plinth, standing outside the flats on the opposite side of the railway cottages. It was getting black and dusty, this memorial to the dead of two world wars who had worked in the factory. The factory, a huge affair, had once been a Gutta Percha Works, owned by the Hancock Brothers. Charles Hancock would join the India Rubber, Gutta Percha and Telegraph Works Company in 1860. This company, established as S.W. Silver & Company, moved to Woolwich Reach on the north bank of the Thames in 1952. The name Silvertown comes from S.W. Silver. Gutta Percha was vital to the telegraph industry, and before long the factory in Silvertown was providing submarine cables which would eventually enable 'cables' to be sent across the Atlantic. Though Silver's company became the dominant one, it was the patents and knowledge that Hancock brought from West Ham that made it possible. Prior to this, in 1725 a Parish workhouse had been built on this land, so a history of toil was established a long time ago.

Bob was reading the inscriptions on the plinth of the lion statue. "One side for each war," he mused. "Must have been a big place to erect its own memorial. I wonder how badly damaged it was that night?"

Black Saturday also saw a mass exodus from London as people tried desperately to get away. And there was one part of London they most needed to get away from. While the rich people of the West End could still move around in a world more or less unscathed from bombs, the people of the East End a few miles away were suffering the brunt of Hitler's aerial war.

Melanie McGrath's excellent family memoir, *Silvertown*, inverts the commonly held narrative of the Blitz neatly and correctly. Creating a myth about the Blitz spirit and bravery of East Enders is in some measure a convenient way of drawing attention away from the obvious fact that in war, as in everything else, the poorest suffer the most. Vivid as the official narrative is, it cannot compare to the unvarnished reality, in all its grim and frequently surreal truth, which included human flesh hanging from trees, bodies washed up on the shore of the Thames and bombs landing in cemeteries with enough force to push coffins up to the surface and reveal their contents. She also describes a direct hit on a jam factory that spread its sticky produce over a wide area attracting black clouds of flies, and the breaching of the Northern Outfall Sewer which flooded the River Lea with raw sewage, the smell of shit hanging heavy in the air for two weeks afterwards.[108] Later in the war West Ham also suffered 58 V1 and 27 V2 rocket attacks.

Bob and I crossed the road. At the crossroads ahead Bob noticed the Spread Eagle Pub, which looked thoroughly closed down. "Another one bites the dust eh?" he said. I just muttered. Abbey Road continued to the right, over the bridge above the railway lines. In the shadow of the bridge stood cottages that stand back to back with those on Bakers Row. A

---

108 Melanie McGrath, Silvertown, An East End Family Memoir, 4th Estate, 2002. p118

South African flag, ragged from the wind, was hanging from a lamp post, moving lethargically like a cow's tail swishing away flies. At the end of this row of houses was a low-rise block of flats on ground that in the distant past had been allotments.

We walked up the incline of the road and over to the other side of the bridge. To our right were the Jubilee Line and Stratford Market Depot, the latter named, with no sense of irony, in memory of the very thing its construction had caused the removal of. We followed the road around its bend by the steps that lead to the Greenway, and crossing the road I pointed out the graffiti. CHINESE PUPPY KILLERS. It was written in white chalk on a brick wall. Bob looked at it and shrugged.

"I keep seeing it everywhere," I said. "sometimes the words are a bit different but it's all about the Chinese and dogs."

"Do you think it's all the same person?"

"Don't know. I suppose you could look at the actual writing and see if its the same or not. It always seems to be in these quiet, out of the way places though."

"Kids."

"Probably, but it just seems odd."

We moved on, pondering who might have a grudge against the Chinese, or whether there really was a gang of Chinese puppy killers and were they loose in the area? We turned left near the spot where the last operating toll-gate on the eastern side of London had operated, which by the 1930s had become a private toll-gate attached to Abbey Mill. And now Abbey Road had become Abbey Lane. Here the houses built for the workers at Abbey Mills pumping station still stand, solid and magnificent some century and a half later. We strolled past, admiring the Victorian brickwork. Ahead of us the Northern Outfall Sewer straddled the road on huge steel bridges that we walked under, careful to dodge the drip, drip, drip of water. Out from under the shadowy bridge and yards up the road was a burnt out car. Just a burnt, grey metal carcass and ashes. Bob walked over and, stooping, stuck his head into where a door once would have been.

"Not seen that in a long while," I commented, stepping round to admire the destruction from the front. Bob looked up at me. "What, a burnt out motor?"

"Yeah. Used to see them round here all the time back in '91 when I moved here. Well, more over that way." I nodded in the rough direction of Manor Road. "Kids used to joy-ride all the time. It used to get on the news, remember?" Bob clearly didn't. "It was just a craze I guess. We sometimes used to stand on the balconies of the flats on Germander Way..." Bob looked on blankly, "flats over by West Ham tube station. Some of the balconies overlooked the park and at night all you would see was two headlight beams tracing a line across the park, then sometimes another set would appear from another direction and next thing it was like watching the light-sabre scene in Star Wars."

"Next day you would find burnt out cars in the park and the gates would be buckled where they had rammed them. One time one of the cars was sitting in the paddling pool. No water, just the car, with two kids about four or five jumping up and down on the roof while their mums stood with their buggies, chuffing on their fags, chatting. Just another day for them."

"Good job it wasn't a post office van," Bob said, stepping back from the car, "You might have lost your parcel. What is this parcel anyway?"

"A book of old photographs of the East End."

"More research?" I nodded. Broken glass crackled under my foot. "What are you gonna do with it all? Are you gonna write your own book?"

"Maybe. I don't know when though, now that we are moving."

"What sort of book. Just a history book?"

"Well, if I ever get round to it, sort of yeah. A bit different from a typical history book, but I'm not sure how yet."

"You're not gonna put me in it are you?"

"Nah. Why would I do that?" I smiled and as we walked away from the car pointed to our left at the high wall and the gates set into it a bit further ahead. "The pumping station," I said. Bob seemed interested and we walked over towards the gates, which were locked. Through them you could see part of the Victorian building.

"I've never seen it from down here," he said. "It's a pity you can't just go in."

"You can book an appointment to look round apparently."

"We should do it sometime. Be more interesting than picking up a parcel."

Looking at the Victorian building through the gates, with all its intricate detailing, it struck me how we take sanitation for granted

In 1855, Alfred Dickens, younger brother of the novelist Charles, wrote a report after leading an enquiry which was called as a result of a petition to the Board of Health organised by Samuel Riles, a prominent vestryman and poor-law guardian. Referring to an area around what is now Bridge Road, at a time when the Channelsea river stretched that far, he described the conditions;

The inhabitants have no water except from the filthy river. Little back yards with stinking privies. Cholera was very bad here.

There is a drain running from the Forest-gate district past the Stratford Station of the Eastern Counties Railway. At that point it is on the company's land and partly covered. The open part is very bad. It can only be let off at low water. Originally it only took surface drainage, but now it takes privy drainage as well. It empties itself into the Channelsea river at a point above where the inhabitants of the Rabbit-hutch row, and Channelsea-court dip for their water.[109]

Dickens' report had come just a year after the Broad Street cholera epidemic, which had resulted in John Snow's breakthrough into the cause of the disease. Already disbelieving of the miasma theory, which proposed that the disease was the result of noxious air, Snow was able to make the crucial link between the disease and contaminated water supply.

---

109 Alfred Dickens, Sewerage, Drainage and Supply of Water and the Sanitary Condition of the Inhabitants of West Ham, 1855

Bob stepped back from the gate and looked back at the huge pipes carrying the sewer over the road.

"So this runs all the way from Beckton?" he asked

"And keeps going. Impressive eh?"

"Yeah," he paused, looked back through the gates at the pump house. "It must have been a bit grim before they built it." I nodded, thinking about John Snow and the Broad Street Pump. "There were cholera outbreaks in West Ham back then." I said

"You have been doing your research haven't you?"

"Yeah, but that's not how I got to know. I've been teaching my students a unit on Public Health and went through the cholera epidemic in Soho, had an interactive map and everything."

"Did they find it interesting?"

"Did they heck. They all want to be nurses and midwives and social workers. They're not interested in history. Shit gets flushed away and clean water comes out the tap. Always been that way to them and always will be."

John Snow was alerted to an outbreak of cholera in Abbey Row, West Ham, by a notice in the Medical Times and Gazette, and was taken to the site by a Dr. Elliott of Stratford. Snow reported the houses to be about a hundred yards from the River Lea, though to be more accurate it was the Channelsea River that they were close to. There were 18 houses, 16 of only two rooms on top of one another with a small kitchen at the rear. They were bookended by bigger houses, the largest of which, on the river end of the row, belonged to the owner of Abbey Mill which sat on the opposite bank.

The only water which the inhabitants of these houses used was from a pump-well near the middle of the row, and across the road. Most of the men worked at a nearby silk factory. Snow described, if not the source of the cholera itself, the source of the problem that led to the outbreak at Abbey Row.

The water of the pump which supplied the houses described above, was very impure, letting fall a copious deposit of dirty organic matter on standing. The nature of this deposit leaves no doubt on any one's mind that it proceeds from the sewer and drains which pass within a few feet of the well: but whether the leakage is by percolation, or by a direct opening, has not yet been determined. There is a ditch or sewer which passes behind the pump-well, and within a few feet of it. The ditch is now covered at this spot, but Mr. Kayess of West Ham Abbey showed me a plan of it. This ditch or sewer flows into the Lea when the tide permits, but at other times the water from the Lea flows back up the ditch, as may be observed; for it is still opened in a great part of its course between the river Lea and the pump. The drains from Abbey-row pass under the road, and pass very near to this pump-well, before entering the above-mentioned tidal ditch. The five houses in Abbey-row nearest to the house of the proprietor of the flour-mill belong to that gentleman; they are each provided with a privy over a cesspool; some, at least, of these privies have an overflow drain, which pass under the house and road to reach the tidal sewer. The remaining twelve houses belong to Mr. Kayess, mentioned above, and the privies of the first eleven of these were converted

*about a year ago into water-closets, the water being however
carried from the pump and thrown down.*[110]

Six people died and many more had serious diarrhoea or
bowel complaints. There had been previous cases of cholera
in Abbey Row in 1832, 1849 and 1854, though none as bad
as the one Snow investigated.

In 1857 an article appeared in Charles Dickens's
weekly journal, Household Words. It was entitled Londoners
Over The Border, and recounted a trip to Canning Town.

*The houses are built in rows; but, there being no roads, the ways
are so unformed that the parish will not take charge of them.
We get, then, upon a narrow path of gravel raised about two
feet above the grass - such paths enable men to walk about not
more than midleg deep about the place in rainy weather - and
we come to a row of houses built with their backs to a stagnant
ditch. We turn aside to see the ditch, and find that it is a cesspool,
so charged with corruption, that not a trace of vegetable matter
grows on its surface - bubbling and seething with the constant
rise of the foul products of decomposition, that the pool pours up
into the air. The filth of each house passes through a short pipe
straight into this ditch, and stays there. Upon its surface, to our
great wonder, a few consumptive-looking ducks are swimming,
very dirty; very much like the human dwellers in foul alleys as to
their depressed and haggard physiognomy, and to be weighed by*

110 John Snow. Med. Times and Gazette, n. s. vol. 15, Oct. 24, 1857,
pp. 417-419.

ounces, not pounds. Some of them may be ducklings, but they look like the most ancient ravens.

Perhaps this row of houses is a poor back settlement - a slum of Hallsville. We go on, and are abruptly stopped by another ditch-full of stagnating corruption, bubbling as the last bubbled; while at a little distance, is another row of houses built so that they may pour all their solid and liquid filth into it in the most convenient way, and receive it back as air, with the least possible dilution. Near those houses we find a plank by which the ditch is crossed. There is a path across a patch of green, and the path is, in one place, made up of planks rotted with wet, now dried into the soil on which they float in spongy weather. The planks tell a tale, so does the bloated and corrupt body of a drowned dog that lies baking in the middle of that patch of green. We smell the marsh, dry as it is. As we go on exploring, we find the same system of building everywhere.[111]

The reason conditions were so bad in Canning Town was that it had been more or less jerry-built, such was the demand for housing the rapidly expanding workforce of the railways, docks and industry of London, east of Bow. This area had been more accustomed to receiving effluent than getting rid of it, as in the past the night soil men would have carted the human waste of the city to the farms surrounding London, to be used as fertiliser. Now the farmland was becoming urbanised, and at such a furious rate that if pavements were

111 Londoners Over The Border, Household Words, Issue No. 390, Saturday September 12, 1857.

deemed a luxury, then waste disposal wasn't even being considered. The thing that finally led to action was not death, which could be conveniently kept out of view, but smell. A smell so bad that they dubbed it the 'Great Stink'.

Part of the problem lay with the invention of the flushing toilet. It was a good enough invention, but without an accompanying sewer system to go with it, one that was slightly ahead of the curve in terms of usefulness. What it mostly achieved, aside from reducing household smells, was to add quantities of water into often already overflowing cesspits, of which there were around 200,000 in London. The overflow from these cesspits went into the surface water sewers beneath the streets which had only been designed to collect rain water, discharging it into the many small rivers and ditches that fed the Thames. The summer of 1858 was unseasonably hot, and with the Thames bloated with excess human waste, the resulting smell was overpowering. With such a stink right outside the Houses of Parliament, the politicians of the day were finally offended enough by the problem to act. They gave authority to the Chief Engineer of the Metropolitan Commission of Sewers to begin work on a solution that could make good the 1855 Act that was supposed to prevent the city's sewage flowing directly into the Thames.

Joseph Bazalgette, born in Enfield in 1819, had been inspired by a proposal made by painter John Martin in 1834 to create intercepting sewers, complete with walkways, along the banks of the Thames. His grand project resulted in hundreds of miles of underground brick main sewers, and further hundreds of miles of street sewers connecting to them.

The main sewers, running west to east, were on three levels, with pumping stations designed to lift the sewage between levels. When working out how wide to make these sewers, he calculated out a generous sewage 'allowance' per person for the most densely populated areas of the city. Then, realising that the project was a one-off, he doubled his calculations to cover for unforeseen events. In doing so he accommodated the 'unforeseen' high-rise blocks of the following century. It took nearly 16 years to complete the project, and it still forms the backbone of the current sewerage system.

It was built in a style that only the taste and vast wealth of Victorian England could have made possible. With its decorative brickwork, lantern, mansard roof, dormer windows and Moorish style chimneys projecting 90 feet into the sky, not for nothing did it become known as the 'Cathedral of Sewage'. The extravagant chimneys were demolished after bombs damaged some of the site's buildings, and the chimneys were deemed to be too visible for German aircrews trying to target the docks. The main building, which is even more lavish inside is now Grade II* listed.

The Metropolitan Board of Works report for 1866-67 dwelt with some satisfaction on the impact of Bazelgette's works. 'Already the general health of the metropolis, and especially the health of those who inhabit the low lying districts near the river, has perceptibly improved. It will be long enough before the water of the Thames is transparent, but it is certainly not half so muddy as it was two years ago, and fish are now found in those places which were previously the most polluted.'

The report also detailed how some of the sewage was being utilised on the farm lands of Essex, the remainder being distributed by the Essex Reclamation Company on the reclaimed sands of Maplin.

The sewage has proved most valuable as a manure in the growth of mangolds, potatoes, flax, cabbage, celery and strawberries. One of the most promising experiments was in the case of a wheat crop. Those parts of the field in which the sewage had been laid down could be easily distinguished from the others by the strength and length of the stalks, and the size of the ears. The grass on the company's farm is used in the feeding of 250 milch cows, and leaves a considerable surplus, which is sold to stable keepers in the metropolis.[112]

What isn't mentioned in the report is the cholera epidemic of 1866 that ravaged the East End, killing nearly 6,000, with a further 3,197 killed by diarrhoea. On no day between 21st July and 6th August did cholera claim fewer than 100 inhabitants of the East End, and the daily mortality rate didn't drop below 20 until into November. John Snow had died six years prior to the outbreak, but William Farr had taken heed of his work and was able to write a damning report that laid the blame at the East London Waterworks Company, who were found guilty of using uncovered reservoirs.

Farr had surmised that there was a probable link to the condition of the water in the River Lea and the uncharacteristically

112 The Standard, Friday, February 14, 1868

high mortality rates in the East End as early as July, but rather than act upon warnings, the East London Waterworks Company tried to absolve themselves of any blame. Company engineer, Charles Grieves wrote a letter to The Times on August 2nd in an attempt to limit the damage of the surfacing rumours. The water in the Lea, he stated, was perfectly safe. That this was untrue was one thing: that unfiltered water had passed from the Lea into the company's reservoirs was the damning other.

Mr. Greaves himself could not perhaps describe precisely what took place in July; but this is substantially what occurred : — The Lea at Old Ford was much more polluted in the summer of 1866 than it was in 1854; for, besides the sewers emptying into it on the side of East London, the whole sewage of Stratford and West Ham on the Essex side has since 1861 been discharged into the Bow Creek arm of the river at the iron bridge. This sewage is washed up and down the stream by the ebb and flow of the tide twice daily between and in close proximity to the open and the storage reservoirs of the company.[113]

What was ironic was that the proximity of the new Northern Outfall Sewer had been no defence, and in fact was a likely contribution to the epidemic.

West Ham is out of London, so, although the great metropolitan <u>*sewer passes over its main sewer at Abbey Mills pumping station,*</u>

113 William Farr. A Report on the Cholera Epidemic of 1866 in England. 1868

the Lea, instead of deriving any advantage from that circumstance, thus grew liable to further pollution by the discharge into its waters of the overflow of the metropolitan great sewer in times of storm. The East London Company had apparently no defence against the tidal waters encompassing its reservoirs round about, and growing fouler and fouler every year after 1861[114]

In fact a deputation from the Poplar Board of Works had already noted the problem of sewage in certain sections of the river and presented a memorial asking that, pending the completion of the pumping station, a plan be put forth to do something about it. The memorial was referred to the Main Drainage committee of the Metropolitan Board of Works

The Abbey Mills pumping station was opened two years after the cholera epidemic, at the same time as what was then called the Thames Embankment. A newspaper report of the day mentions the cottages that Bob and I had admired.

The cottages for the workmen are eight in number, arranged in pairs, each containing five rooms, and are fitted with every reasonable convenience; the house for the superintendent of the works, and which is situated on the other side of the outfall sewer, and near the entrance to the works, is more commodious, and fitted up in better style. The cottages are all externally relieved by coloured brick bands and arches, so as to harmonise in some respect with the larger buildings.

---

114 Ibid

This report also refers to sewage being used on a farm, in this case in Barking, and that had it not been for difficulties experienced in the money markets for the previous two years, that the whole of London sewage might have been thus applied, predicting that this would be the case in the future.

In the meantime, the sewage of London was fortunately being carried away by the intercepting sewers and the ebbing tide, so that it never returned to contaminate the inhabitants of the metropolis.

Ten years on, despite another summer of almost unprecedented heat, there was no repeat of the 'Great Stink'. However, dissenting voices were not far away.

The Abbey Mills pumping station of the metropolitan drainage system has been opened, not without the expression of strong local indignation against the costly character of the architectural decoration. The grave question of the mode in which the bed of the Thames is becoming obstructed by the discharge of sewage of the metropolis into the stream at the new outfall has been raised, but, although it has been vigorously debated and disputed, it has not been set at rest.[115]

The debate, indeed the problem, had still not been set at rest by 1878, twenty years on from the 'Great Stink'. On September 3rd of that year The Princess Alice, a passenger paddle steamer, was making a routine 'Moonlight Trip' from Swan Pier near London

---

115 The Morning Post, Thursday, January 7, 1869

Bridge to Gravesend and Sheerness. Many of the passengers had been destined for the pleasure gardens at Rosherville in Kent, where attractions included a maze, bear pit, zoo, aviary and gardens.[116] Hundreds of Londoners had paid the two shilling fare for the trip. On the return leg, at 7.40pm, the Princess Alice was close to Woolwich Pier when she collided with the SS Bywell Castle, a much larger vessel. Hit on the starboard side the Princess Alice split in two and sunk within four minutes. Over 650 people died, many of them trapped within the wreckage. What contributed to the deaths of many people, however, was the 75 million imperial gallons of raw sewage that had just an hour earlier been released into the river from the sewer outfalls at Barking and Crossness, a twice daily occurrence. The toxic combination of this sewage and industrial contaminants was what the majority drowned in.

The Royal Commission recommended the chemical treatment of sewage (though not until four years after the disaster). From 1887 the liquid effluent was chemically separated from the solid sludge, and only the liquid sewage was discharged into the sea at the sewer outfalls. The remaining sludge was carried by 'sludge boats' from Beckton and Crossness out to Barrow Deep, beyond the mouth of the Thames, were it was dumped. This practice continued until as recently as 1998. EU regulations now forbid the dumping of sewage at sea; instead it is now incinerated at Beckton and Crossness.

---

116 Winston. G. Ramsay, The East End Then and Now, Battle of Britain International Ltd. 2007 (1997)

"It's very quiet here, "Bob said, turning away from the gates. We walked over the road and past the modern-build houses around the corner. Tucked in amongst them was the Stratford Delivery Office, Abbey Lane, the place where you came to pick up your parcels should you find one of the red cards through your letter box explaining that no-one was home and that the parcel was either too big for your letter box or required a signature. One Saturday morning I caught the postman lazily sticking one of these cards through the letter box without even trying to see if anyone was at home. Because nearly everyone has to go to work in London before the post arrives, most of us retrieve our parcels in this way from whichever depot or post office serves the function in a particular area. I had became very familiar with the walk, though I hadn't spotted the police surveillance sign on Arthingworth Street before. Once I reached this street I would hardly ever see a soul the rest of the way, no matter what the weather, and very little traffic came this way either.

Inside the post office I handed my red card through the trough. After disappearing for half a minute, the whistling post office worker returned with a fat parcel that he put in the glass box, sliding down the glass door on his side of the counter so I could slide open a similar door on my side and take the parcel. It was the size of a breeze block and felt almost as heavy. We started walking back, and as we emerged from under Bazzlegette's sewer pipe, Bob started talking about a series of mysterious disappearances that had taken place around West Ham and East Ham at the end of the 19th century. Curious, I pressed for more detail, but he could offer none.

"All I know is that a lot of people disappeared around the same time, and it was around the time of the Jack the Ripper murders, or maybe just after."

"And didn't they find any of them?"

"A couple. One of them was a young girl who was found dead in a house on Portway."

"The road that runs by the park?"

"That's right. Fancy strolling down there? I wrote the number of the house down." He patted a hip pocket, as if the matter had been decided. As we walked past the houses which had been built for the Pumping Station workers, I tried to imagine people sitting inside them over a hundred years ago, reading the lurid newspaper accounts of what were then known as the Whitechapel Murders. The roads round here at that time would have been dark and quiet, lit only by a few gas lamps. How scared were people of walking those dark streets?

The epidemic of the Vanishing Londoners began in 1881, the very year in which the first arc-lights went up in the City.

The strange aspect of the disappearances, which were mostly centred about the London districts of East Ham and West Ham, was the absence of what we may call an 'age-pattern'. Young girls, young boys, middle-aged men and elderly women – all appeared to be equally acceptable as prey to whoever – or whatever – was whipping the victims away. There were, apart from the fact that the persons had disappeared, other factors linking the disappearances.

In many – though not all – cases where children had disappeared, the children had either been seen talking to an old woman (description unsatisfactorily vague in all cases where witnesses swore they had seen her) or the old woman had been noticed somewhere around the place where the child had last been seen.

Another disturbing oddity about the disappearances was that one or two of the girls seemed to have had some sort of premonition that 'something was going to happen'; but that, asked by friends why they were hanging around the streets, so near their homes, and didn't go home, they gave evasive answers, and moved off...but not to go home.[117]

Just what had taken possession of these girls? Eliza Carter had 'vanished' only to briefly reappear in an obvious state of terror, but she couldn't be persuaded to return home by anyone and she was never seen again. A blue dress, identified as hers by her mother, was found on a football field in East Ham. Was the dress returned to her mother and did she clutch at it, trying to wring out some trace of her daughter's life? 'For nine years this pattern of disappearance continued; the last victims being three girls, who were whipped away together. The date was January 1890. Of those three girls, one – and one only – was to turn up again.'[118]

---

117 Michael Harrison, London by Gaslight, Peter Davies, 1963. p133

118 Ibid. p134.

It was very dark and very damp when 15 year old Amelia Jeffs was sent on an errand to the fried fish shop on Church Street, at half past six on the evening of Friday 31st January 1890. Two weeks later her body was found in an attic cupboard of an empty house less than 100 yards from her own. The scene of the discovery was 126 Portway, one of several houses in a newly built section of terrace.

...for some weeks past stories have been current of little girls being stopped in the streets of West Ham by men, and before the disappearance of Amelia Jeffs, the tiny daughter of a respectable resident was stopped by a strange gentleman and challenged to run a race up a dark street.[119]

Two girls had disappeared from this very same road some years before, prompting the Rev. Canon Scott of St. Mary's Church, West Ham, to make an application to the judges at the Stratford Petty Sessions, in the hope that the publicity might help with the case. When this failed to shed light on Amelia's disappearance he made a further application to Mr. Baggallay at the West Ham Police-court, but no clues could be found. Eventually Detective-Sergeant Forth and Police Constable Cross went out on special duty and began searching the empty houses in the neighbourhood. It was then that she was found in the attic cupboard of 126, opposite an entrance to West Ham Park.

---

119 The Worcestershire Chronicle, Saturday, February 22, 1890

Bob and I had retraced our steps and now reached the end of Abbey Road crossing at the triangle where West Ham Lane, New Plaistow Road and Church Street meet. A drab paved area, which isn't enlivened in any way by the presence of a small brick kiosk, a lonely tree and telephone boxes, is flanked on two sides by shops. We walked across it, then on the far side turned the corner where The King's Head pub stands and carried on down Church Street towards All Saints church. This church, built, or perhaps rebuilt, in the 12th century, contains some of the last known remnants of the Abbey. These include a carved stone funerary piece depicting five skulls which has been built into one of the tower walls, and a double arched window, built into the south porch that was originally part of the Adam and Eve pub, itself built on the grounds of the ruined Abbey.

We walked through the churchyard, past the graves. George Edwards is buried somewhere here, but as the headstone has been missing for some years, nobody knows exactly where. Edwards, who was born in Stratford in 1694, became known for his illustrations of animals, particularly birds. His engravings were published in seven volumes between 1743 and 1764. When he died in 1773 West Ham was still a village, with the dwellings clustered around the church. Aside from the church not much survives from this period. Like neighbouring Plaistow, much of the history of West Ham is about what isn't here, rather than what survives. But history books don't tend to concentrate their attentions on fields, unless of course a famous battle had taken place in them. Fields are history's blank spaces.

Parks, essentially fields that have been cultivated to look a certain way, somehow stand above them in the hierarchy of historical interest, being another representation of man's presence on the land. West Ham Park, in George Edwards' time, existed as the grounds of Upton House. It was occupied by John Fothergill, who bought it in 1762, and whose interest in flora and fauna led to it being compared at one time to Kew Gardens. He populated his rock gardens with plants from all around the world and had greenhouses and hothouses built. These haven't survived, and Upton House itself is no longer standing. It was demolished in 1872 when the house and its grounds were owned by the Gurney family. Samuel Gurney, a Quaker, bought the house in 1812 and lived in it with his wife Elizabeth. Five years prior to purchasing the property Gurney had become connected with financial firm, Richardson & Overand. By 1825 he had become a partner, and was considerably wealthy as a result. The firm was now known as Overand & Gurney, and was able to bail out many City institutions who were in danger of failing at around this time. When the economy regained its balance, these firms deposited their surplus with Overand & Gurney rather than the Bank of England. At the time of Gurney's death in 1856 the firm held considerable deposits, but in 1866 speculative trading under less experienced leadership saw its own demise. When the Bank of England refused to bail out the very bank that had once bailed them out, Overand & Gurney were declared insolvent. This led to a run on London banks by country banks, and the resulting victims included the hitherto solvent Bank of London, which ended up being absorbed by competitors, and the Bank of England, which saw its note reserves shrink by a third in a single day.

Bob and I were now by the entrance to the park on Portway, having cut through the church. Bob pulled a scrap of paper from his pocket and unfurled it.

"126," he said. "Looked it up on the Internet before I set off."

"How do you know it's right?"

"It's right. It was on some forum on a Jack the Ripper website. There was a quote from a newspaper of the time."

We were on the opposite side of the road to the park, and it was this side that the houses stood. We saw the house, just a few doors past the corner of Liddington Road, the door coated in silky blue paint. We glanced up at the attic window, both thinking thoughts about murder, and wondered if the present occupiers had any idea what had taken place in their house over 100 years previously. Was there a presence up on the top floor, a ghost even?

The crime was never solved. A man from Plaistow gave what may have been vital information regarding a man he had seen in the vicinity of 126 Portway one Friday night, who was struggling with a large bundle, wrapped in white cloth, upon his back. The man, when spotted, changed direction, away from Portway towards some fencing on Liddington Road. But this wasn't reported at the time, and presumably the witness wasn't able to give an adequate description when he finally did talk to the police.

The crime did draw the attention of the press to the area, and they took the opportunity to depict it in a negative light.

The excitement throughout the borough of West Ham is intense, and the long deferred lighting of some dangerous spots, like Caistor Park, will now be insisted on by some members of the Council. It is known that there are half-a-dozen gangs of the very worst type in the district, who gave the handful of police no end of trouble, and are a source of terror to the inhabitants. It is only a short time since that Constable Greenough was half murdered by roughs in Stratford, only one of whom was apprehended. Unfortunately this man escaped with only six months' imprisonment, although the constable had his skull fractured and his brain injured by the buckle of the ruffian's belt.[120]

Quite what this had to do with the murder of Amelia Jeffs is hard to discern, and appears only to have been included because the publication was the *Illustrated Police News*. The three characters under most suspicion were members of the same family, and all three were key-holders to the property. Grave suspicions were cast upon one of these men, but for want of evidence no arrests were made.

---

120 The Illustrated Police News, February 22, 1890

Not wishing to draw attention to ourselves by gawping for too long, Bob and I retreated across the road and entered the park. After Samuel Gurney's death the house and grounds had passed down to his son, who only outlived his father by a year, then to his grandson. Two years after the 1866 crash, he decided to put the whole estate up for sale, eventually being persuaded to sell to the local Board of Health at a reduced price, so that the local people could gain the benefits of the green, open space. Two years after the house was demolished the park opened, on July 20th 1874.

This park was thrown open yesterday to the people, and made their gift for ever. There are not, we suppose, very many of our readers who often wander among the flat lands which lie around Plaistow, of which this park may almost be said to form a part. Yet there are beautiful neighbourhoods around Plaistow and Barking. In fact, the poor left bank of the Thames is so much outshone by its sister in Kent that people imagine that there are no beauties at all on the Essex shore. This is however a grave mistake, as those who visit the new West Ham Park will see. It is not very undulating – that was not to be expected from the locality – but it is beautifully timbered in groups and knolls of noble trees, which yesterday cast a most grateful shade over the many visitors. Of course all the neighbourhood was en fete, and flags and banners streamed from every point.[121]

---

121 The Standard, Tuesday, July 21. 1874

We walked through this flat park, observing as we went the antics of a dog that staged a one-mutt pitch invasion, pushing the ball with its snout as it ran rings round the young men kitted out in boots, shorts and shin-pads.

What had happened to all those people, all those years ago? Did they have anything to do with an incident recorded in 1879?

Jacob Darken, twenty-eight, labourer, of Brewer's-road, Plaistow, was charged with indecently assaulting Mary Caroline Poulson, aged six years, in West Ham-park, also with attempting to stab Frederick George Partridge, also with assaulting Eliza Wither. It appeared from the evidence that as Mr. Partridge was passing through the park he saw the prisoner assaulting the girl Poulson. He acquainted Fuller, one of the park keepers, with the matter, who went towards the prisoner, and told him he should take him into custody, when the prisoner said he knew nothing about the charge. On the way the prisoner managed to escape, and being pursued threw some bricks at Partridge, and attempted to stab him. After a struggle he was captured and locked up. The Bench did not think the evidence strong enough with regard to the assault on the child, but for the attempt to stab the witness, he would be sentenced to two months hard labour. The other charge was then gone into, the little girl Wither stating that on the 19th of March she was going home from school when the prisoner took her into an empty house, poured something down her throat, and assaulted her. She picked him out at the station from thirteen other men. The Bench did not think the evidence sufficient, and dismissed the case – a decision against which the parents of the children loudly protested.[122]

Was Jacob Darken offered protection by the letter of law, or was someone looking after him? He has been swallowed up by history, the remainder of his life a mystery, but the incident is another bleak brush stroke in the picture of an area that appeared to be living in the shadow of the dark satanic mills that Blake famously wrote of.

In April 1881, two years after Darken was charged, Mary Seward went missing. The following January it was Eliza Carter's turn.

It is remarkable that both girls resided in West Road, West Ham – Seward at No.98 and Carter at No. 25 – and it has been ascertained that in the eastern part of the metropolis, including West Ham and Leytonstone, a suspicious gang of foreigners have been going about, no one can say on what business. The conclusion arrived at by parties engaged in the work of tracing the whereabouts of the missing girls is that they have been abducted by the foreign agents of an infamous trade to the Continent, and their fate will never be known.[123]

It needs to be taken into account that at this time there was a tendency for writers in the press and elsewhere to blame

---

122 The Illustrated Police News, May 10, 1879.

123 Sheffield Independent, Monday 27 March, 1882

foreigners for most of the ills of the East End, a menace that if unchecked threatened the very Empire itself. Perhaps the more important detail is that 'infamous trade' – one that the delicate sensibilities of the Victorian readership couldn't have named for them. Even in 1963, when writing about the disappearances, there was a reluctance to spell it out.

Witnesses, searching their collective memory, recalled having seen a woman talking to the three girls who had vanished from Portway; and assuming that this woman was the same as that 'unprepossessing woman with a long ulster and a black frock' who had been seen talking to Eliza Carter, seven years before, the coroner delivered himself of a judgement which, perhaps commonplace to us, must have startled some of the Victorians.

'Women,' said the coroner, 'are as susceptible to the lowest forms of mania as men.'

It rather sounds as though Mr Coroner knew more than he was saying – daring, by 1890 standards, though his statement was.

But what did he know? And what exactly was that 'lowest form of mania' which snatched persons of both sexes and all ages out of this world, over a period of ten years?[124]

Was there a need to link foreigners to these disappearances in order to nip in the bud any suspicion that paedophilia could possibly exist in British society? Or were the girls indeed being

---

124 Michael Harrison, London by Gaslight, Peter Davies, 1963.

procured for persons abroad, or forced into prostitution – the 'white slave trade', that was capturing the attention of social reformers and the press? The two were in fact linked, as at the time of the disappearances the age of sexual consent was just thirteen. Consequently, Victorian notions of child sexual abuse were different to our own, if only in terms of legal definition. The work of social reformers in changing this would be rewarded, but not without controversy.

On 12th February 1884, the London Daily News printed a letter sent to them by a man claiming to have a clue to the Eliza Carter mystery. He had seen a girl matching her description being dragged past him at the recreation grounds, Portmouth, on Sunday 29th January 1882, by 'a short, thick-set, repulsive looking woman, aged about 45 years, height about 5 feet 2 or 3 inches, rather shabbily dressed, and broad across the shoulders. From the rapid strides taken and other reasons, I now think it possible that this person may have been a man in disguise of dwarfish stature.'

Carter, Seward and Jeffs all lived within shouting distance of each other, all three by the park where Jacob Darken was apprehended and Carter's blue dress was found. On 21st January 1882, a week before Carter went missing, a young girl was assaulted in the park by a man, an incident mentioned in the London Standard when reporting on the Carter disappearance that February.

On 5th July 1882 Florence Elizabeth Dowse, aged 15, was reported as missing from her home in Leabon Road, just round the corner from the road that Carter and Seward disappeared from. Clearly, as industrialisation rapidly crept over the parish of West Ham and new buildings appeared at a rate of knots – houses in various stages of construction, houses that were complete but lay empty with patches of waste ground between them – something very dark was lurking in the shadows. The talk of foreigners wouldn't go away, and what was referred to as the 'decoying of girls' was becoming a popular explanation for the mysterious disappearances.

Working men, holding good positions in the Victoria Docks, assert that for many years they have heard of cases of girls, the children of men employed at the docks being met by strange men and women who have endeavoured to get them away under the pretence of being able to find them good situations abroad, and some of them narrate instances where girls have been missed for years. With regard to Mary Seward, the father states that he had received information from a woman who positively alleges that she knows a man by sight who has on various occasions visited the place for the express purpose of procuring young girls to go abroad. She further, he says, is assisted by a woman, and always seems to have plenty of money, and that he will pay a good price for assistance, or for the girls, and that he prefers obtaining girls from 12 to 15 years of age. She describes the man as being well dressed, but having common, coarse features, and in appearance like a foreign gypsy. She is certain he was in the neighbourhood the week before Easter.[125]

125 The North Devon Journal, June 9, 1881

The notion of foreigners being responsible may have lent the crime a comforting sense of 'otherness', but realistically such a 'trade' would have involved various parties, including perhaps local people who were receiving payment for ensnaring or procuring the girls, before passing them on. Might Amelia Jeffs have been an attempted procurement that went wrong? Or was her murder unconnected to the earlier disappearances?

With Jeffs' case there are no reports whatsoever of suspicious people seen at the time of her disappearance, unlike the cases of Carter and Seward, where references to a woman and various descriptions of men crop up repeatedly. The decoying of girls that some press reports mentioned refers to the system whereby the girls are snared on the pretence of some gain. Quite often the decoy would be a woman, presumably as she would represent less of a threat than a strange man. The decoy woman would entice the victims to a place where she would essentially be imprisoned. West Ham locals talked of a decoy involving a man who would offer girls a small monetary reward to deliver a letter to a nearby house. Upon arriving they would be enticed inside on some pretence, perhaps to receive their reward, and their fate would be sealed.

Journalist and social reformer William Stead described the decoy system in a series of long articles he wrote for the *Pall Mall Gazette* in 1885. The articles went into great detail about child prostitution in London and included a claim that a girl called Lily had been bought from her parents for £5. This was in fact true. The girl, however, hadn't been 'decoyed' but was secreted away into a Salvationist family, eventually being returned to her real family. The whole act had been designed by Stead and his confederates to highlight just how simple it was to procure young girls for prostitution, with the aim of forcing the government to raise the age of sexual consent. Stead's action may have been the significant factor in the age of consent being raised from 13 to 16 years of age in an Act of Parliament that same year. However, when it transpired that the character who had procured Lily had been none other than Stead himself, he was charged with unlawfully kidnapping a minor and sentenced to three months in Holloway Prison. He was later to play a role in the success of the Match Girls Strike and became friends with Annie Besant. In 1912 he accepted an offer to speak in America at an international conference on world peace, which is how he found himself on board the fateful voyage of the Titanic. He wasn't one of the survivors.

It is curious that all of this was happening at the same time as the young girls disappeared from West Ham: perhaps their fate was the same one Stead had written about in his infamous article. Child prostitution was a reality in Victorian times, with the poorest in society naturally those most likely to suffer this fate. In between the disappearance of Emily Carter and Mary Seward and the murder of Amelia Jeffs was the short but brutal reign of Jack the Ripper, another unsolved crime. Somewhere in this labyrinth of repressed Victorian sexuality and strait-jacket morality, the attitudes of the rich to the poor, and the use of foreigners as scapegoats at a time when insecurity over the Empire was rising, lies the truth. Or at least the true identity of the beast.

Bob and I were more than halfway across the park now, heading towards the exit on Ham Park Road. It was hard to contemplate the extravagance of such a large piece of land once being one man's property. Nowadays, anyone in the area lucky enough to have their own garden can most likely spit from one end to the other without wind assistance. Grand personages like Fothergill and Gurney would have been aware of the poverty around them – West Ham was always a poor parish – but they were insulated from it.

Other notable residents in the period before industrialisation altered the map of West Ham include the prison reformer Elizabeth Fry (the sister of Samuel Gurney) and Joseph Lister. Lister was born on Upton Lane, where Bob and I were about to discover that the Old Spotted Dog pub was now boarded-up. Another Quaker, he discovered that using carbolic acid on instruments, dressings and wounds to sterilise and cleanse led to a significant reduction in post-operative fatalities. At the time of Lister's breakthrough the prevailing belief was that infection was caused by miasma, and so surgeons not only neglected to wash their hands before operating, but also often wore blood-encrusted frock-coats, with the level of gore a sign of their experience and skill.

After wondering for a short while who might have killed Amelia Jeffs and what might have happened to the disappeared girls, Bob continued his macabre musings by telling me about a series of crimes known as the Thames Torso Murders. They took place between 1887 and 1889, stretching a year either side of the famous Whitechapel murders. I had never heard about these grisly murders which, as their name implies, involved a number of victims who quite literally had to be pieced together from body parts that were found at different times and locations.

It seemed something of a relief when we reached the Old Spotted Dog, where we were hoping to have a drink – only to find that it was closed down. The surprise at seeing this historic inn boarded-up brought the talk of gruesome Victorian murders to a close. Bob seemed somewhat stunned by the closure of this pub, which had been serving ale since the 16th century and was where the merchants of the City of London held their exchange during the plague years of 1665-1666. I was equally as surprised to see that a football ground was tucked up right beside it, the home of Clapton FC. Originating, as the name would suggest, in Clapton, Hackney, the club relocated to their Old Spotted Dog Ground at Upton Lane in 1888, the year that Jack the Ripper stalked the streets of Whitechapel. Clapton's honour roll includes five FA Amateur Cup victories, the last of which came in 1925, the same year that three of their players were selected to play for England. Perhaps their greatest claim to fame, however, is that they are recognised by the Football Association as being the first English side to play on the Continent, in 1892 when they beat a Belgian XI in Antwerp. As the club was formed in 1878 it means that their history is longer than that of both Leyton Orient and West Ham United.

By the time Clapton FC had relocated to West Ham, its population was expanding rapidly.

In 1851 it had been 19,000, but by 1910 it had grown to around 180,000, many of this number having migrated east over the border represented by the River Lea. As the Essex side of the Lea was not bound by the Metropolitan Buildings Act, all manner of dangerous and noxious industries from slaughterhouses to chemical works took advantage. As the workforce expanded, so the necessary housing stock was hastily built. Before long the once distinct villages of Stratford, Plaistow and West Ham were joined together by urban sprawl. In 1871, when the population of West Ham was 63,000, the police force numbered 99. Yet ten years later when the population had doubled to 127,000, the number of men policing the area had only risen to 162. This fact was raised in parliament by Colonel Makins, but was met with a rather indifferent response. Criticism of the police over disappearing girls was voiced, but the vanishings seemed to cease around the time Amelia Jeffs was found folded into an attic cupboard. Meanwhile the waves of people kept coming, washing over the history of the place, obliterating it at the same time as they became the next layer.

CHAPTER 9

Stratford Peculiar

O ne Saturday morning in October 1864, *at about twenty minutes before seven o'clock, there occurred at a certain spot on the southern bank of the Thames, near Belvedere, and distant about one mile above the church of Erith, and the same distance below the reservoir and Outfall of the whole main drainage of that side of the river, an explosion of a quantity of gunpowder which appears to have far exceeded in the amount that of any explosion in time of war, whilst the sound and concussion reached to places at a distance of eighty, ninety, or approaching one hundred miles. The quantity is estimated to have been 1040 barrels of 100 lbs each, or in all nearly 46.5 tons.*[126]

---

126 Journal of the Franklin Institute 1864, vol 78 p 301

Warnings had been uttered about the dangers to the metropolis of storing such large quantities of gunpowder, even in places as distant as Belvedere, Plumstead and Purfleet, but they went unheeded. People were far more wary of the accumulation of petroleum and other combustibles in buildings amongst the streets of London. The immediate human cost – confined, it appeared to the immediate area – was difficult to ascertain, such was the devastating effects on skin and bone. The police were finding 'portions of human frames about the locality' days later, and one such portion was limited to a pair of feet with toes of such peculiar shape that the son of the man they had belonged to was able to identify him thus, along with the marks on the toe-nails.[127]

Further away from the explosion the damage was limited to buildings, but it was extensive and widespread. 'At Stratford the window shutters of many of the shops fell out of their places, the window sashes were projected, doors were burst open, and a great quantity of glass was broken in several places.'[128] One of the window shutters affected belonged to the house in Maryland, Stratford, where Sarah Hope lived, opposite the railway station. Some years later, on Tuesday 2nd April 1872, an inquest was held in The Cart & Horses into the death of this woman;

whose body – a perfect skeleton – was fond in a house at Stratford, known for many years as the "mysterious closed house." This is

---

127 London Standard, Tuesday, 4 October, 1864

128 Essex Standard, Wednesday, October 5 1864

situated in one of the busiest market thoroughfares of Stratford, having a large shop front and large flourishing shops on each side. The shutters, which are black with the scorching of many a hot summer's sun and the grime of nearly a quarter of a century, have not been taken down for twenty-one years, and the last time they were known to come down was when they were blown down by the Erith explosion.[129]

Her brother John, who also lived in the house, 'did not fetch a doctor to her before because he would rather have the devil in the house than a doctor at any time; he did not belong to the Peculiar People, but he was peculiar on that point, that there should be no doctor in his house if he could help it.'

'When the deceased was discovered last week she had long unkept locks, with nails like eagle's claws on her toes, which measured 2¾ inches long.'[130] After the discovery, many hundreds of people visited the house to gaze at it, to wonder, gossip and tittle-tattle about the woman who stopped eating. The Peculiar People, so named after an alternative translation of the phrase "Chosen People", were viewed with suspicion. They didn't believe in medical intervention and were often accused of child cruelty and neglect because of it.

Maryland Point appeared on a 1696 map of Essex, published by John Oliver. The name is believed to have come from a rich local merchant who bought land and built in the

---

129 London Standard, Wednesday, 3 April, 1872

130 Ibid

area having returned from the American colony of Maryland. Sitting at the top of The Grove, Stratford, it was also at the foot of Stratford New Town, an area hastily developed to accommodate the influx of workers resulting from the expansion of the railways. Mistrustful of the cultish ways of the Peculiar People, the inhabitants were straight-laced in their views, and deviation from the norms wasn't likely to be met with tolerance. For example;

No little excitement has been created at Stratford New Town from the fact of a married man eloping with a married lady residing in the same neighbourhood. The parties were traced to Norwich. An effigy of the man has been paraded through the streets, preceded by a rough band, and followed by hundreds of persons. Ultimately the police were called in, and but from their aid no doubt a very serious disturbance would have taken place.[131]

The excitement continued to simmer in the air long after the police dealt with the crowd.

A year later, some of the men from the Stratford Railway Works formed a co-operative society. By 1870, just before Sarah Hope starved herself to death, they had 439 members and a shop at the junction of Falmouth Street and Maryland Street. Maryland remained at the heart of the co-operative movement as it grew, and the accompanying spread of the

---

131 The Essex Standard, Wednesday October 2, 1861

socialist movement in the area made many in power view this part of the East End as being alive with 'restless natives'.

Daniel Defoe made note of the existence of Maryland in 1724, on his Essex journeys.

The village of Stratford, the first in this county from London, is not only increased but, I believe, more than doubled in that time, every vacancy filled up with new houses, and two little towns or hamlets, as they may be called, on the forest side of the town, entirely new, namely Mary-land-Point, and the Gravel Pits, one facing the road to Woodford and Epping, and the other facing the road to Ilford; and as for the hither part, it is almost joined to Bow, in spite of rivers, canals, marshy ground, etc[132].

Gravel Pits is not named on any map, but there were gravel pits along the Ilford Road (now Romford Road), so we can guess that he was referring to an area near Stratford Green.

Stratford Green was formerly called "Gallows Green" from the circumstances of a person who resided there having been murdered and the offender executed in front of the house in which the crime was committed. The body of the murderer was afterwards hanged in chains in Stratford Green, not far from the Pigeons Inn. The custom of hanging murderers where the crime was perpetrated was not uncommon during the past century.[133]

---

132 Daniel Defoe, Tour of the Eastern Counties, 1724

133 The Essex Standard, Friday, October 29, 1858

Strange it would be to see the murderer of your husband, wife, brother or sister hanging from a gallows outside your house, surrounded by a shimmering black cloud of flies.

Stratford Green has long since disappeared. It used to stretch from Water Lane to where St. John's church now stands. This church was opened in 1834, built as a result of the growth of the area and the belief of the Vicar of West Ham that a church of this size was thus needed. In 1879 the Martyrs Memorial was built to commemorate the thirteen men and two women burned in Stratford-atte-Bow in 1856 during the reign of Queen Mary, who had almost 300 religious dissenters burned at the stake in the Marian Persecutions. It has long been disputed where exactly these executions took place. As Stratford-atte-Bow was mentioned in historical documents, many believed that Bow was the location. Katharine Fry, writing about it in her history of East and West Ham, begged to differ.

There has been much controversy on the question of locality, whether the martyrdom took place at Stratford-le-Bow, or Stratford in Essex. Fox in his "Martyrology" uses the two names interchangeably, but if we take into consideration, that twenty thousand persons attended the great burning of the thirteen martyrs, we must look for a place capable of holding such a number. At that time and even within the memory of men, there was an open space, where now St. John's Church stands. Doubtless this open space was a portion of "Stratford Green," the memory of which is still preserved in the grass field surrounded by gentlemens's houses and gardens on the

*Romford Road, known as "Stratford Green," whose ancient
name was "Gallows Green."*

*The reader will remember, that in 1275 Richard de
Montfichet, or his father, when Sheriff of Essex, had licence to
"erect there a gallows in his lordship of Hamme." This green
or common appears to have been a place of public execution,
while the place near Stratford Church, at the junction of the two
turnpike roads, was unquestionably the place of the burning.*[134]

More recently one theory has suggested Fairfield Road, Bow
is the more likely site, and so the debate continues.

Between Defoe's journey, and the erecting of the Martyrs
Memorial, The Three Pigeons Inn was built (1796). It was rebuilt
in 1896 and known simply as The Pigeons. It has now joined
the lengthening list of Dead Pubs, currently existing as a Tesco
Metro, with a development of flats in the pipeline for the upper
floors. Looking at floor plans and illustrative photographs of the
flats was an oddly dislocating experience, as the last time I was
there was for an after hours club night in 1992. The dark interior,
thick drapes and carpeted floors are all gone; soon someone will
be sleeping, cooking, or perhaps entertaining friends where the
long bar used to be. In the pub's early life, before it was rebuilt,
a windmill had stood next to it.

I experienced a similar feeling in 2005 when I looked
around the half-finished flats in a building that previously

---

134 Katharine Fry, History of the parishes of East and West Ham. (ed.
G.Pagenstecher) 1888

housed the University of East London (UEL) student union (and had once been a tobacco factory). Walking into the dark and dusty interior, I couldn't help but try and visualise where the bar and dance floor had been. When I came to London in 1991 I stayed with an old school friend in a flat above a cafe on Manor Road, West Ham, right next door to the tube entrance (this has now disappeared thanks to the redevelopment of West Ham station). He was in his final year at UEL, which had been North East London Polytechnic when he actually started his course. We would sometimes come to Maryland for a drink, stopping off at the Bacchus Bin before heading over to the student bar for cheaper drinks.

Stratford was, as ever, going through growing pains in the early nineties. The area that forms the apex of Romford Road and The Grove was boarded-off. On the corner where there is now an Ibis hotel and Nando's restaurant, used to be Young & Marten, a building and decorating merchants founded in 1872 by William Young. He was later joined by H.H. Marten, and the company had its own railway sidings between Maryland and Stratford so they could transport building materials to their warehouse on Grove Crescent Road. The warehouse is now an apartment block.[135] The shop was a large affair, stretching a good way down Romford Road, and can be seen in Bronco Bullfrog during the scene where Del rides off on his new motorbike. Just a couple of years after this was filmed, Young & Marten had to move out to

---

135 Newham Archives

make way for the Borough's new civic offices, including a pyramid-like block that itself is now history.

We would sometimes drink in The Two Puddings, still open for business in '91, and where Saturday nights would see a raucous karaoke session that would test the nerve of prospective crooners. Gentle encouragement wasn't really on offer for anyone torturing *New York, New York*, and the verbal abuse, laughter and booing were more entertaining than the singing. Good singers, however, rare as they were, would get a response as loud as a football terrace after a goal. The Swan, nestled on the island between Tramway Avenue and West Ham Lane, was another option for refreshment, but it was always quieter here. Established as long ago as 1631 and rebuilt in 1921, it was a popular destination to watch football in its last few years, but in 2005 it too joined the ranks of Dead Pubs of London when it was converted into a betting shop.

A few doors up from The Swan, opposite St. John's church, is the King Edward VII, better known as the Eddie. It was established in the eighteenth century as the King of Prussia, but by 1925 existed under its present moniker. When I first visited in 1991 it was popular with locals and students alike. Its three bars were smokey and noisy, but some nights it wasn't busy at all. In fact Stratford was often eerily quiet, and on a Saturday it felt like the nightlife was happening elsewhere. When I moved to Stratford in 1998, the pub had lost its sticky carpets and most of the students, but retained its low ceilinged charm in the front bar. Capturing a window table was always a bonus, particularly on a winter's day when you felt the full benefit of the big iron radiators. One night each week a local fantasy gaming club would meet in the upstairs bar at the rear, and their tables would be full of odd shaped dice, cards with fantasy figures, coloured counters and other paraphernalia. Quiz nights in the front bar were popular but often so noisy that, despite using a microphone, the quiz master was often lost in the din.

A pub that no longer exists on The Broadway, because of the Stratford Shopping Centre development, is The King's Head. It was here in the past that inquest and post mortems would be held. Reading about these reveals a lot about life in the area in the 19th century. There were frequent deaths – at the railway yards, for example, often involving workers being crushed by trains or goods wagons. Suicides were common and it was often the waters of the River Lea that claimed the victims – usually the poor and love-lorn. In 1896 Harriet Lacey was found dead in the Channelsea, and at the King's Head inquest none could agree how this came to pass. The Foreman was of the opinion that she hadn't simply fallen in, and that the state of the water was diabolical, thick as it no doubt was with industrial pollutants and detritus. 'The verdict was that "The deceased was found drowned but that how she got into the water there was not sufficient evidence to show.'[136]

Of the intent and cause of death of fifty year old Ann Victoria Johns, the wife of a house decorator in Walthamstow, there can be no doubt. It is a long walk from Walthamstow to

---

136 The Newsman, Saturday, September 26, 1896

Stratford and many people must have seen Ann John passing them. Perhaps they even noticed an unhappy look on her face. Or maybe it was troubled, or just determined. Walking with her decision heavy inside her, weary and unable to find a quiet place, she finally gives up; on Stratford High Street she swallows a bottle of carbolic acid. She had been circling around this momentous act for some time according to her husband, and a letter was found on her person that is full of mystery and sadness.

I hope when you receive this I shall be no more. Give my love to my dear brother and sister. Look well after daughter; be very kind and gentle with her. Alf knows what I would say to him. Be kind to his dad. Don't make any fuss; it will only be a nine days' wonder. Look after my cats and the fowls. I am tired to death walking about. Can't find a quiet place. Pity my weakness, my evil behaviour, I am leaving in weakness my sins to my Saviour. Good night. God bless you. Excuse scribble; I have come without my dear old glasses. No-one to touch me but mother.[137]

The things she chose to bring with her on this journey – probably the last things she read – were love letters from her husband, tied in bundle.

By the time of these sad events Stratford had grown considerably. It happened at such a rate that older people in particular must have felt a considerable sense of loss, as

---

137 The Newsman, saturday, July 4, 1896

memories were built upon and obscured. In the middle of the nineteenth century;

the neighbourhood of Stratford abounded in fields and country lanes. All along the Leytonstone road there were farms on both sides, interrupted only by a few cottages. Turning down Angel Lane, you soon entered upon a country road, running between high banks topped with hedges. Now the fields are gone into the hands of building societies or speculative builders.[138]

In 1853 The Hertford Mercury reported that some land on Leytonstone Road, Stratford, had realised upwards of £600 per acre. The area was known for hay making, and had higher than average yields,[139] but this particular plot was sold for building purposes. Land once clear of people because it was more profitable to use it for intensive farming and sheep grazing, was now proving more valuable for the purposes of bricks and mortar.

An 1800 map of the parishes of East Ham and West Ham shows Stratford as a small settlement on the edge of marshland. Not too far distant, north east, lies the western most tip of Epping Forest at Forest Gate. It was a gate here that kept the cattle in the forest that gave the area its name. The area between Epping Forest and Hackney Marsh to the west, where Temple Mills, Leyton and Leytonstone lie, is

138 History of East & West Ham, Dr. Pagenstecher, 1908

139 The Hertford Mercury, Saturday, June 18, 1853

clearly shown as agricultural land. Chobham farm is depicted, just above an area called Hop Ground that is bound to the east by Angel Lane and Leyton Road.

By 1833, although there had been growth, it wasn't spectacular.

Stratford is a populous hamlet and ward, in the parish of West Ham, and hundred of Becontree; about three miles from Whitechapel church, London. It is the first place you come to after leaving Middlesex, from which county is it divided by the river Lea, crossed by means of Bow-bridge; on this stream are situated extensive flour-mills, and many manufacturing establishments, print-works, distilleries, chemical works, &c., some of which are upon a very large scale. Stratford itself is greatly improving in appearance, which will be heightened when the projected new church (which will occupy an eligible site in the Broadway) is completed. In the parish of West Ham are several schools for gratuitous education; one of these, for the parish generally, has a revenue derived from benefactions, amounting to above £3,000; and another, founded by Mrs. Bonnell in 1761, is also well endowed. There are also some almshouses, and two chapels for dissenters. The land around here is very fertile, well wooded, and the scenery pleasing; great numbers of the inhabitants are employed in agriculture, which the vicinity of Stratford, to the metropolis renders a profitable pursuit. By the parliamentary returns for 1831, the hamlet of Stratford contained 6,686 inhabitants.[140]

---

140 Pigot's Essex 1832-3 Trade Directory

If you look at the 1867 Ordinance Survey map, however, a dramatic change has taken place. Hop Ground has been swallowed up by George Hudson's Stratford Works, the railway works he established some twenty years earlier, and the streets and houses of Stratford New Town, originally called Hudson Town. There are still fields on the map and urbanisation of the area is clearly a work in progress. Above Chobham Road, and to the east of Leytonstone Road, Stratford Nursery is depicted: beyond it, more fields. In a little over 30 years, there had been significant expansion of the railways and a total obliteration of green space. The hay making days of Leytonstone Road were well and truly over.

The Stratford railway works eventually covered an area of over 132 acres, the various buildings used as workshops for the construction or repair of engines. These included foundries for casting, forges, fitting rooms, braziers' shops, carpenters' shops, and saw-mills. The principal erecting shops were about 120 yards in length by 60 in breadth. One shop alone contained 100 or so machines for the performance of the most delicate work, and the smiths' shop contained a hydraulic riveting-machine. These huge warehouse-like shops were stuffed full of heavy iron machinery, huge wheels and cogs with teeth the size of chair legs. A web of girders in the ceiling diffused the light coming from outside, which would have been further smothered by the output of all the heavy work taking place.

Women too were employed at the Works, sitting in long rows in the sewing machine room in white smocks, far enough apart to make talking to each other difficult in all the din. Or in the polishing shop of the carriage department – dull and monotonous.

In 1878 it was recorded that about 500 engines, 3,000 carriages, and 10,000 wagons were kept in constant repair.[141] The same publication also noted the growth of the town built by Hudson to house his workers.

The new town which has sprung up in the neighbourhood of the works is the residence of several hundreds of skilled employees—engineers, drivers, and others. At first it was called Hudson Town, in compliment to the "Railway King;" but when he lost his crown, the name fell into disuse. In 1862 the New Town numbered some 20,000 souls; and now probably the population has nearly doubled itself. The town, it may be added, has its literary institution, a "temperance" public-house, besides numerous places of worship.[142]

The smoke belched out by all these locomotives coming into and out of Stratford must have been a sight to behold, though not a good one for any of the senses, let alone the lungs. Added to the smells and pollutants thrown into the air by the various noxious industries in the land below the railway works and in West Ham, the fire and smoke must have given Stratford,

---

141 Edward Walford, Old and New London:Vol. 5, 1878

142 Ibid

on overcast or rainy days, the sort of hellish appearance that had inspired William Blake when writing Jerusalem. In total, Stratford Works built 1682 locomotives, 5,500 passenger vehicles and 33,000 goods wagons. In 1891 workers there managed to build an entire steam train in an unsurpassed record time of 9 hours 47 minutes. The Works feature in Barney Platts-Mills *Bronco Bullfrog*, in the scene where Del and Roy join Bronco and his accomplice in a raid on the goods yard at night, relieving one of the goods wagons of as much of its contents as they can carry. A panning shot revealing the scale of its industrial landscape appears in Platts-Mills' short film *Everyone's An Actor, Shakespeare Said*. By this time, the late 1960s, the heyday of the railway works was gone; a decade and a half later the Wagon works and Temple Mills closed down, before the last section was closed in March 1991. It is on the ground where the Works was sited that much of the Olympic Park is now situated.

Many of the railway workers who had formed the Stratford Co-operative Society in 1861 would have lived to see its growth, but few, if any, would have been around to see the formation of the London Co-operative Society, which came as a result of merging with the Edmonton branch in 1920. The premises on Maryland Street remained its central point of operations, despite being bombed in 1941. In 1954 they bought J. R. Roberts department store on Stratford Broadway and built their own department store on the site. At the same time a new office block was completed at the Maryland headquarters. By 1969 the London Co-operative Society, having taken over various other societies, had a membership of over a million and annual sales of £38 million.[143] Not a bad return from such modest beginnings.

What a lot of people didn't know about the unassuming building on Maryland Street in the 1960s, was that in its basement was a well-secured vault packed with safety deposit boxes containing cash and other valuables. Those who did know were members of the East End criminal scene, a selection of villains who saw the vault as an ideal place to keep money, jewels, bullion and guns away from the prying eyes of the police and taxman. With alarms, a reinforced door with steel bars and a vault door that was 60cm-thick hardened steel, it was also deemed secure enough for any of said criminal fraternity to steer clear, as any attempt to use explosives would bring the building down.

On Saturday 11th November 1967, Richard and Vivien Tucker were married and had booked the Co-operative Society function suite for their knees-up reception. As they and their guests drank and danced, and the band played on, downstairs in the basement a gang had broken in and were busy using a home-made thermic lance to burn through the 60cm of steel. It was the first time any such device had been used in a crime in Britain, and detectives believe it took up to 16 hours. Such was the jollity upstairs that even if anyone heard the alarm above the din, they didn't feel in any way inclined to bother about it.

---

143 W.R. Powell (ed) A History of the County of Essex: Volume 6 (pp. 76-89) 1973

When Co-op staff returned to work on Monday morning they found, amid an acrid smell of burning, a vault ankle-deep in loot the gang had left behind. Only 120 of the 600 boxes in use had been opened, which suggested the time it had taken to cut through the vault door had been longer than they anticipated. It was estimated that the gang had got away with between £1 million and £2 million, but the actual amount was difficult to ascertain because so much of what was taken belonged to criminals who were hardly going to disclose details of illicit property.

The investigation went on for a year, but despite many tip-offs from the underworld, nobody was brought to justice. Then in 1968 a filling-station manager walking his dog in East Horndon, Essex, stopped to admire a green Mark X Jaguar parked outside a restaurant. Noticing his dog sniffing excitedly at one of the doors, he peered in to discover a tarpaulin covering something inside. When police arrived they opened the car to find the blood-stained body of East London car dealer, Tony Maffia, who had been shot twice in the head at point blank range.

Maffia, reputedly London's wealthiest 'fence', was thought to be the driving force behind the robbery. He was not a hands-on criminal which had helped him escape arrest throughout his criminal career, with the exception of a brief period inside after being convicted of helping burglar Alfie Hinds in one of many escape attempts from prison. Maffia lived in a six bedroom house in Buckhurst Hill, Essex, and also owned property in the Channel Islands and Europe. As well as the Jaguar that had caught the filling-station manager's eye, he owned a luxury yacht. But though the police couldn't get their hands on the man they knew was guilty of handling such large amounts of stolen property, the criminal underworld clearly decided that when it became clear none of his deposit boxes were touched in the raid, it was time for Maffia to go. Small time crook Stephen Jewell was convicted of Tony Maffia's murder. At his trial Jewell claimed he had simply been in the wrong place at the wrong time, and that Maffia had been executed by East End rivals who he had double-crossed. But a detective on the investigation firmly believed that Jewell had been a hired man, and that he was he who had pulled the trigger.[144]

Two other criminals whose notoriety was earned further west than Stratford were the Krays. But they were not unfamiliar with the locality, and were vigilant enough to notice a drinking club at Maryland Point, called The Maryland (actually 127 The Grove and now a chemist), which they thought was too close to their own Double R club. A firebomb was quickly despatched through a window of The Maryland, and before long it was under their protection. Stratford's biggest crime story of this era, though, was probably the killing of two police officers, Inspector Philip Pawsey and Sergeant Frederick Hutchins, who were shot in Tennyson Road on Saturday June 3rd 1961.

A man called John Hall had called at West Ham Police Station on West Ham Lane on 2nd June to hand himself in

144 Real Life Crimes and How They Were Solved. No.98, Eaglemoss Publication Ltd. 2004

after attacking his wife, Sylvia, with a chair when he went to collect her from her mother's in Tavistock Road. He had also attacked her sister and mother. At the station, agitated at being asked to empty his pockets, he pulled out a Luger and shot at a police officer, narrowly missing. He then ran out of the station and, presumably because it is opposite the entrance, down Aldworth Road in the direction of Tennyson Road, where he was tackled by Sergeant Hutchins whom he fatally shot. Inspector Pawsey, who had been driving back to the station, heard a radio report asking for officers to look out for an armed man. On spotting Hall on Tennyson Road, he jumped out of his car and in his attempts to arrest him was also fatally wounded.

A picture of Hall was broadcast by the BBC, and a manhunt ensued in the East End. In the evening Hall phoned the Sunday Express newspaper from a call box on the corner of Lakehouse Road, Wanstead. The call was traced, and at 8pm cars from West Ham Police Station sped to the scene. The phone box was surrounded and Hall shot himself in the chest.

Memory is an illusive thing. Japanese photographer Daido Moriyama, speaking about memory, points out that people cannot be relied upon to recall how scenes from 10 or 20 years ago appeared. In talking about our memory, he talks about "landscapes" we have accumulated. But unlike photography, these landscapes change in our memories. Much detail is lost or faded. Colours sometimes change. Dates and times move around mischievously, and often two memories overlap in a way that means what we think we saw at A was really something we experienced at B. Our subjective memories are important, certainly to ourselves, but not so useful to others.

For example, I know there was something at Maryland Point, at the bottom of Leytonstone Road, before the current block of flats were built. I just can't remember what. It is as if the physical presence of what is there now has pushed what was there before beneath the surface of my mind, and only some mental archaeological dig might reveal the answer. That or a photograph.

Very few people left alive will remember the church that once stood here at Maryland Point: the Trinity Presbyterian Church of England, built by Andrew Black, who was its first minister from 1863-75. A hall was built in 1863 and the church was ready by 1870. It ceased to function as a church in 1941 and the building took on a new use as a factory. Perhaps more people will remember it thus, as the factory existed until 1953 when it was destroyed by a fire. The hall, however, escaped serious damage and continued as a factory until 1966. You can see an early photograph of the church in the Newham Archives. The date is sometime between 1870 and 1873. We know it is not later as Maryland Station has not yet been built, and instead of today's high concrete wall, there are metal railings curving round the corner. The station was opened in 1873 and the original building was replaced in 1891 when the Great Eastern Railway was widened to include four tracks.

My memory is equally obstinate when it comes to a missing building on Windmill Lane, which runs parallel with the railways lines between Maryland and Angel Lane. Angel

Cottage, a Grade II listed house that was built in 1826 and was one of the few remainders of Stratford's rural past, was illegally demolished in 2007. Pervaiz Khan, who bought the property at auction for £400, 000, was fined £15, 000 and reportedly sold on the plot at a loss for use as a car storage yard. At the time of writing it is owned by Forest Whitmore Ltd, who are planning to build an accommodation block for 102 students. Local residents, still appalled by the initial loss of the cottage, are now faced with another apartment block that they fear will overcrowd the area. One wonders what the land and property will be worth in a few years time.

Try as I might, I cannot clearly picture Angel Cottage, though I know what it looked like thanks to a photograph. When I lived in Stratford I walked down Windmill Lane on several occasions, but this bit has been erased from my memory banks. To any students living in the apartments, should they be built, Angel Cottage never existed. They will see a view out of their windows of Westfield and the Olympic Village. Standing at the end of Windmill Lane on a grey April morning in 2012, this was the first time I had seen this present view. Steam escaping from a series of vents in the huge shopping centre made it look like a giant ocean liner that had cruised slowly over land and berthed, the white blocks of the Olympic Village the ships cabins. Angel Lane now curves in an S shape, thanks to the new railway bridge, and you walk uphill with this new city-scape peeking over the cement grey wall of the bridge. As you round this bend a tall, black block of flats stands like a watchtower. With two bed apartments inside selling for £340, 000, the profit margins to be had by building upwards are plain to see.

The face of Stratford is changing so dramatically here that it conjures up the strange ghost cities that have been thrown up in certain parts of China, with an equal amount of haste and disregard for sentiment. In this respect it resembles the Railway Mania that had reshaped this landscape one hundred and fifty years or more earlier. George Hudson may have been known as the 'Railway King', but even he wasn't immune from the temptation to indulge in bad practice and bribery of MPs. On finding the financial status of his companies wasn't what he had led them to believe, shareholders were disgruntled enough to fight back, a process that was eventually to see Hudson spend time in prison.

There are still a handful of old houses left on Windmill Lane, though none as old as Angel Cottage. A short terrace of properties still stands on the same side of the road as St. Marks Mission Church, which opened in 1876, and the Railway Tavern survives on one corner while the Cart & Horses still stands on a corner at the Maryland end of the Lane. In between on both sides is mostly modern, post-war housing, including a block of shared ownership flats overlooking the railway lines.

A century ago the scene was quite different, with a coffee house and dining rooms at opposite ends and a whole host of shops in between, ranging from a greengrocers to a butchers, newsagent to tobacconist, baker to confectioner. There was a midwife at number 21 and a physician at 114. Two tailors competed for trade, and Walter Nickels at 54 could fix your sewing machine. Those fallen upon hard times could visit a pawnbrokers, and for those just wanting a temporary escape from their troubles there was a beer retailer. On the south side past the church stood the Stratford Stores of the Ind Coope brewery, an asphalt paving company and the Great Eastern Railway Cattle Depot. This was Windmill Lane in 1902; quite a community on such a short road.

Queen Victoria had died a year earlier; thus, the Victorian era that had seen such phenomenal change east of the River Lea was over. The Edwardian age, in contrast, was born into modernity. Though the residents of Stratford and its environs probably didn't notice any change, the world was only five years away from Picasso's *Les Demoiselles d'Avignon*, and twelve from a Great War that would change everything.

Of course, modernity can be subjective. In 1831 when Walter Hancock ran his "Infant" steam carriage from Stratford to Whitechapel, the great metal beast breathing steam might have been more modernity than the average onlooker could handle in one go, accustomed as they were to horse power and their own foot power. A one-off trip to Brighton took place in 1832, made lengthy in the extreme by frequent stops for water and coke, and a broken cast iron flange which required a rear wheel be fixed. On the return journey an attempt at sabotage was made, as was recorded in the Journal of Elemental Locomotion.

A word to the person by whose order fifty yards of Streatham Hill was covered with broken stones, six inches deep all the way across, 'to prevent the return of the steam-carriage.' We withhold his name; though such an exhibition of ignorance and hostility well entitles it to public exposure. We have taken upon us the duty of advocates for elemental locomotion; and, whilst we shall endeavour to discharge ourselves of the task, with courtesy to all who choose to stand up against it in the fair field of argument, we will not be slack to reprobate the conduct of whosoever resorts to any other means.[145]

Though the reporter refrains from naming names, it is safe to say that the act of sabotage was the action of persons worried about their livelihood in the face of this steam-powered competitor, which had given ample demonstration of its traction abilities the year before.

In 1831 Hancock commenced running his steam coach "The Infant" regularly for hire between Stratford and London. Before it was placed on the station it was tried in every possible way. The possibility of a steam carriage ascending steep hills had been doubted by many, and to remove if possible all scepticism on the subject, Hancock fixed a day for taking his carriage up Pentonville Hill, which has a rise of one in eighteen to twenty, and invited a numerous party to witness the experiments. He says: "A severe frost succeeding a shower of sleet had completely glazed the road, so that horses could scarcely keep their footing. The trial was made therefore under the most unfavourable circumstances possible; so much so,

---

145 Alexander Garden, Journal of Elemental Locomotion, 1832

that confident as the writer felt in the powers of his engine, his heart inclined to fail him. The carriage, however, did its duty nobly. Without the aid of propellers or any other such appendages (then thought necessary on a level road) the hill was ascended at considerable speed and the summit successfully attained, while his competitors with their horses were yet but a little way from the bottom of the hill." [146]

Despite this apparent victory over horsepower, the development of steam powered buses was on the wane by the 1840s, due in part to heavy tolls introduced by the Turnpike Act. So the proprietors of the horse drawn bus were to win out, until at least the triumph of the internal combustion engine in the next century.

In 1844 the poet Gerard Manley Hopkins was born and lived at 87 The Grove, Stratford. His experimental approach ran counter to the traditional verse of his day. He looked back to Anglo-Saxon verse in an effort to escape the more rigid rhythmic structure inherited from the Norman influence. Hopkins' exploration of sprung rhythm and vivid imagery made him more modern than his contemporaries; it is perhaps not surprising, therefore, that his greatest fame was achieved posthumously. He was eight years old when he moved with his family to Hampstead in 1852, the year that Walter Hancock died. A memorial was established in Hopkins' memory in 1994 near to the spot where he had briefly lived, unveiled by poet Seamus Heaney. A metal plaque laid into a

---

146 William Fletcher, Steam Locomotion on Common Roads, 1891

large piece of rock contained lines from stanza 21 of perhaps his most famous poem, *The Wreck of the Deutschland*:

> *Loathed for a love men knew in them,*
> *Banned by the land of their birth*
> *Rhine refused them. Thames would ruin them;*
> *Surf, snow, river and earth*
> *Gnashed: but thou art above, thou Orion of light*[147]

The poem was written in memory of the five nuns who had drowned, along with others, when the Deutschland struck a sandbank near the mouth of the Thames Estuary during a blizzard. The wreck lay grounded for thirty hours before assistance finally arrived, during which time it was raided of valuables by men from nearby coastal towns. A report in the Times indicated that corpses had been robbed of their jewellery. Four of the nuns (the fifth body was never found) were laid to rest at the priory opposite the house Hopkins was born in, where a funeral sermon was given by Cardinal Manning. Two years after the incident Hopkins, a deeply spiritual man, was ordained into the Jesuit priesthood. In December 2011 the metal plaque from the memorial was stolen, though a replacement is now in its place.

By the time that Hopkins was born, Walter Hancock's interest had turned away from steam powered buses to something that was to prove much more lucrative. In May

---

147 Gerard Manley Hopkins. The Wreck of the Deutschland. 1875

1844 his younger brother Charles registered a patent for an improved design for bottle stoppers that employed a vegetable extract, introduced from the East Indies, known as gutta percha. A Dublin chemist, Henry Bewley, became interested in these patents and together with Charles Hancock decided to develop the patent for mutual benefit, forming the Gutta Percha Company in 1846. Walter joined the company, which was based on Stratford High Street, and benefited from financial backing arranged by Samuel Gurney. Two years later Charles registered a patent for a 'Wire Covering Machine' that could coat a continuous length of wire with gutta percha, and would lead to the subterranean and submarine cable business.[148] The company fractured in 1950 due to friction between Bewley and Charles Hancock, and the Hancocks set up a rival company on Stratford High Street, the West Ham Gutta Percha Company. Two years later Walter died aged 53, and in 1856 the company relocated to Smithfield.

By this time the population of Stratford was somewhere on an upward curve between 10,000 and 16,000. Hudson's railway works, now well established, had contributed to this rise. What was about to become apparent – to an audience much wider than the people directly affected – was the appalling condition of much of the accommodation of this growing population. The 1855 report *London Over the Border* by Alfred Dickens, inspector for the Board of Health, attracted much needed attention to the levels and conditions of

---

148 Jim Lewis, East Ham & West Ham Past, Historical Publications Ltd, 2004 (pp.78-79)

poverty that existed east of the River Lea at the time. The 1857 cholera outbreak reported on by John Snow merely reinforced what was becoming known. In the same year William Cowper, President of the Board of Health, visited West Ham to see at first hand what had been highlighted by others.

'He first visited Gilby's Alley in the Leytonstone Road. No language can depict the state of these hovels. Without water supply, except of the foulest description, with small back yards only a few feet square, with accumulation of putrid matter, sodden by wet.'[149] He then visited cottages on Vicarage Lane, two room abodes with 'no accommodation for the offices of nature.'[150] For the eight cottages near Vicarage Terrace there was a shared privy that was open to the street. It was so full and overflowing that the woodwork was decayed and it was impossible to enter; Cowper described the sight and smell as 'odious'.

Under a communal pump was a drain;

which the neighbours all said was the only drain. Into this they habitually empty all the slops of their houses. They truly said they have no other place to throw them into. This sink communicates, either directly or indirectly, with the well underneath. It has long been pointed out to the local authorities as frightfully fouled by the most filthy drainage, yet the people still drink this water – they have no other.[151]

149 The Examiner, November 14, 1857

150 Ibid

151 Ibid

Women of the court were often seen filling their tea kettles from this well.

Cowper then visited Abbey Row where the cholera victims of earlier in the year had lived. All in all the Parish had 'upwards of 140 acres of open sewers or ditches, evaporation or absorption being the only outlet.'[152] If Snow's theories on water-bound disease had been taken more seriously by more people, then it is clear that the 1866 cholera epidemic that claimed hundreds of lives in West Ham might have been avoided.

Of course not everyone in Stratford and West Ham was living in such conditions. The railway works in particular demanded a certain percentage of skilled workers, and these men were likely to have lived under better conditions than their unskilled counterparts. Though by no means well-off, they were comfortable and smart enough to want to establish some firmer ground under their feet. The founding of the Co-operative Society was one example of efforts to improve the lives of workers collectively. Others joined together in altogether different alliances, such as the Equality Lodge, who would meet at the King of Prussia on Stratford Broadway.

In 1859 they attracted the attention of the Grand Lodge of Freemasons in England, who were highly perturbed by their irregular brand of freemasonry. The Stratford men followed the Rite of Memphis, previously thought to be extant only in France. Established by Samuel Honis at Cairo in 1814,

---

152 Ibid

it was imported into France the following year. It repeatedly ran into trouble with the establishment and made life difficult for its followers. The Grand Lodge in England was to treat it no differently, and wrote to all Masters of lodges warning them that any admittance of 'Memphis masons' into their lodges would lead to expulsion from the Order.

The Grand Secretary received a letter from the Stratford Lodge not long afterwards. It pointed out that many of its members were from the artisan class, who could not afford to join traditional lodges. It neglected to mention that the heads of the rite in England were French radical republicans who had fled France after the election of Prince Louis Napoleon Bonaparte as President.[153] Their argument was that many of these skilled mechanics and engineers were often required to export their expertise to Europe of the Colonies and that in this respect, belonging to a fraternity would be of great benefit.

No more is known of what happened to the Stratford Lodge, but in 1869 the Grand Lodge was still decrying the irregularities of the followers of the Rites of Memphis.

The peculiarities of this era weren't confined to arcane rites in the pub now known as the King Edward VII. The members of the 'irregular' Stratford Lodge, had they been meeting in the main room of the pub, would have looked out onto St. John's Church in the middle of the Broadway. Here, in 1858, a rather eccentric burial took place.

---

153 Bro. Ellic Howe, Fringe Masonry in England 1870-85, Ars Quatuor Coronatorum. (1972)

*Mr John Taylor, who was interred in a copper coffin in St.
John's Church, Stratford, for many years prior to his death
would frequently remark to his friends that he had obtained all
the money he possessed out of copper, and when he closed his
earthly career he wished to be buried in that metal. In order to
secure the fulfilment of his wish he had a copper coffin made
during his life-time, which was first kept at his own house and
then at his undertaker's for several years previous to his death.*[154]

At this point, roughly mid-century, the area had perhaps
reached the end of an era in its history. Though there had
been growth it was steady, but now the population was about
to explode. As if a pod had burst, scattering seeds all over
the East End, houses rose from the ground faster than maps
could keep up. People looking for employment, for a better
life for their families, or single people looking for this and
more, family and friends left behind in the towns and villages
from whence they came. Dickens' words written twenty or
so years earlier seemed more apt than ever.

'It is strange with how little notice, good, bad, or
indifferent, a man may live and die in London. He awakens
no sympathy in the breast of any single person; his existence
is a matter of interest to no one save himself; he cannot be
said to be forgotten when he dies, for no one remembered
him when he was alive.'[155]

---

154 The Essex Standard, Friday, October 29, 1858

155 Charles Dickens. Sketches by Boz, 1836

As the tide of urbanisation rushed over the River Lea, the chances of being lost amidst all this humanity only increased. Work was never guaranteed to be secure, and casual labour and unemployment resulted in a tolerance of strangers who were easy to ignore, easy to become invisible. People came and went: sailors, itinerant workers, foreigners, the misplaced, the homeless and the hopeless. The city just didn't care. It swelled, like a living, breathing thing. To the west they began to fear the swelling of Socialism that accompanied industrial growth in the East End. Soon there would be unrest amongst the poverty; strikes, scandals and ghastly murders in Whitechapel. Growth would be followed by entropy; landscape would change, communities flourish and then disintegrate, and in all this some people would suffer while others triumphed. And so it continues, but the city cares not one bit. It is not even conscious of the life within it, which gives it life in turn.

LONELY DEATH

The dead body of a man unknown was found in Temple Mills-lane, Stratford, at midnight on Tuesday. At the inquest yesterday the police described the deceased as about 30, apparently a foreign pedlar. Dr. Ashley said death was due to heart disease, accelerated by exposure and want. Verdict, "Unknown, and died from heart failure."[156]

---

156 Essex Newsman, Saturday, 27 February, 1904

Who knows where this man came from, what drove him to arrive in London and then to this eastern corner? Why did his heart fail after thirty years? Thirty years of what? What is the story of his life, or even just his name? Where were his mother and father and did he have brothers or sisters? Did they ever learn of his lonely death? We know as much now as they did at the inquest over 100 years ago.

At Temple Mills, where the body was found, there were once water mills owned by the Knights Templar who were granted a tract of meadow and marsh by William of Hastings, steward to Henry II. The mills straddled the river Lea, and so were in both Hackney and what is now Leyton. After the dissolution of the Order of the Templars, the mills passed to the Order of St. John. In 1593 they were leased to Clement Goldsmith for forty years. During this time a gunpowder mill was built, but this blew up. During the 17th century and 18th century, the former mills were used for a variety of industrial purposes. These included grinding rapeseed and smalt; processing leather; making brass kettles; twisting yarn; manufacturing sheet lead; and flockmaking. The mills, made mostly of wood, spanned the stream adjoining the White Hart in Hackney; they were pulled down by 1854. For 40 years or more the mills were not even a memory for the drinkers in the public house by the river where they once stood. They were just a name that survived their death, proving that names will outlast physical things by some distance. More ghosts haunt the spot.

*About ten o'clock on Tuesday morning, the body of a woman
unknown was discovered by a gentleman named Kennedy, at
the rear of the White Hart, Temple Mills, near the river Lea,
Hackney. Mr. Kennedy was out shooting, when he came across
the body lying in a ditch on the ice. There were impressions in
the snow as though the body had been dragged and thrown
down the bank. The body was removed to the mortuary,
where it awaits identification and inquest.*[157]

In 1897, eight years after the unknown woman was found
frozen to death, the wagon department of the Great Eastern
Railway's works at Stratford was moved to Temple Mills,
and by 1912 employed 600 men. The yard grew steadily
and after modernization in the late 1950s were the largest in
Britain and most up-to-date in the world. Within 30 years of
reaching this pinnacle of modernity, they were closed down.

Before they closed the doors – in the days when
the workers were going toe-to-toe with the Conservative
government of Edward Heath and dealing blows that made
it seem the tectonic plates of power were beginning to shift
– a group of five pickets on strike at Chobham Farm, a meat
cold storage warehouse, suddenly found themselves being
entertained at her Majesties pleasure. It was July 21st 1972,
and Conny Clancy, Tony Merrick, Bernie Steer, Vic Turner
and Derek Watkins – The *Pentonville Five*, dockers without
a waterfront – had been stitched up by private detectives

---

157 Western Gazette, Friday, 15 February, 1889

hired by the Midland Cold Storage Company. This provoked thousands of dockers and other workers to down tools, and docks throughout the country were brought to a standstill. A panicking Tory government released the prisoners, deciding – after hasty legal consultation – that perhaps they held the Unions responsible rather than individual pickets. Chobham Farm, where football matches were once played (during the same year that the unknown woman was found dead on the ice not far away), is soon to be a new housing development. It was described in the Stratford Metropolitan Masterplan as an ideal location to create a new neighbourhood. And so new homes rise out of the ground once more, along with shopping centres, sports stadiums and arenas. Land values increase, money changes hands and some people, like the evicted residents of the Clays Lane Estate which was bulldozed out of existence, suffer while others triumph. And the city doesn't care; it just keeps mutating.

CHAPTER 10

Crushed by the Wheels of Industry

If the railways were beginning to make their presence felt in the mid-19th century, another, older form of transportation was also about to make a huge impact on both the population and the land in the area. Interestingly, the architect of this change, George Bidder, was a good friend of Robert Stephenson – son of George who had built the 'Rocket' – and was involved on the London & Birmingham railway project.

Bidder, who was born in Devon in 1806, grew to become one of the finest engineers of his day, and it was his vision, skill and determination that made the construction of the Victoria Docks possible.[158] Opened in 1855 by Albert, Prince Consort, the docks would ultimately be responsible

---

158 Jim Lewis, East Ham & West Ham Past. Historical Publications Ltd, 2004. (p 63)

for wiping away all remaining traces of the rural past of its surroundings.

Docks were established in London at the very end of the 18th century to provide a sensible solution to the overcrowding of the Thames by barges on their way to quays between London Bridge and the Tower, laden with goods from ships that often had to berth as far downstream as Woolwich. West India Docks were opened in 1802 and, as the name might suggest, were granted a 21 year monopoly on trade with the West Indies. Other docks followed at Wapping and to the south of the West India docks. In 1828 St. Katherine Docks was constructed, and in the process whole streets of houses were cleared and over 11,000 residents moved without any kind of compensation. Those who worked on these docks had to live nearby, and this was usually in low-grade, unsanitary housing.[159]

As the century progressed, so too did shipbuilding technology. Ships could now be constructed from iron and steel rather than wood. These were bigger and could carry more cargo. Powered by steam rather than reliant upon wind, they could also travel further, faster. Victoria Docks was designed by Bidder to accommodate these larger vessels, which the existing docks could not do. By the time of its completion, the docks took up a large part of Plaistow Marshes. This area, once used by grazing cattle and frequented by marshmen who traversed the boggy ground by means of long poles that they used to vault from field to field, would now become a hub for trade

---

159 Ibid

and commerce. The remainder of the area would eventually be covered in houses built to accommodate the influx of workers.

In 1847 a railway line was opened that ran from Stratford Market to North Woolwich. With little industry at this time on the marshes, it was thought that the main market for this was the traffic for the ferry crossing to Woolwich. George Bidder and his colleagues, however, had grander plans and they bought most of the land between Bow Creek and Barking Creek which, as it was largely uninhabited, came at a knock-down price. Having difficulty in attracting people to the swampy environs they had purchased, Bidder hit upon the idea of building a pleasure gardens that would be the East End equivalent of Chelsea's Cremorne Gardens. It was opened in May 1851, the same month as the Great Exhibition. But before long, the North Woolwich Gardens would have one thing in common with those at Cremorne, which was an undesirable reputation. What came next, however, was a move to attract industry to the area. This was to prove more successful and much more far-reaching.

Archer Philip Crouch, writing in 1900, put Bidder's business acumen into sharp focus:

Bidder, besides being a clever engineer, possessed a far seeing capacity for business, and it was his suggestion that his associates bought the whole of the land from Bow Creek to Gallion's Reach, and from Barking Road to the River Thames. This area includes the ground now covered by the Victoria and Albert Docks, as well as the river frontage occupied by numerous thriving factories. At that time, the property, mere marshland, with only three houses on the whole extent of it, was to be had for two figures an acre. At the present day, an acre on the river front cannot be bought for less than four or five thousand pounds.[160]

Aside from shipbuilders C.J. Mare and Company, who were situated further west below what became Canning Town (and who would become insolvent in 1857 and re-emerge as the Thames Ironworks and Shipbuilding Company), there was no sign of industrial life south of Barking Road until 1851. Then the influx began. Two brothers named Howard built a glass factory and a wharf on two acres of land they had bought. A year later a more significant arrival was S. W. Silver and Co., who moved their waterproofing works over the river from Greenwich and sited themselves on land adjacent to Howard's glass factory. They initially occupied one acre of land but soon bought five more, and when the Howard brothers' enterprise failed they secured the two acres that had belonged to them.

Stephen Winkworth Silver had set up business selling clothing to the military, but by the time he was located at Greenwich S. W. Silver were manufacturing waterproof garments. Three years after the move to the North side of the thames, a spot then so remote it was known as 'Land's End', he died and the company was inherited by his sons, Stephen William and Colonel Hugh Adams Silver. It was the

160 Archer Philip Crouch, Silvertown and Neighbourhood (including East and West Ham): A Retrospect. 1900 (p 59)

latter who devised patents for spiral-winding india-rubber (caoutchouc) around a copper core, sealing it with the heat from steam, and for making ebonite (used to make insulators for overhead wires). These put the company on a sound footing in their field, but real success would come when they appointed Charles Hancock, who brought with him his patents and, crucially, a knowledge of gutta percha.

In 1864 they took over Hancock's West Ham Gutta Percha Company, and took out a patent for waterproofing and insulating materials. Deciding to enter the field of submarine cable manufacture, they established the India Rubber, Gutta Percha and Telegraph Works Co. The India Rubber and Gutta Percha departments were put under the direction of Mathew Gray, and in 1865 they laid a cable from Dover to Cap Gris Nez. Two years later they laid a cable between Havana and Key West. By this stage the Victoria Dock had been open ten years and the area was beginning to attract more industry. The eastern edge was now known as Silvertown, with several streets of houses split between both sides of the North Woolwich Road housing the workers for the Silvertown Works. In the place where this road met the curve of the Great Eastern Railway stood St. Mark's Church.

The first incumbent of this church was the Rev. Henry Boyd. The early days must have seemed like a missionary posting, such was the isolation and bleakness of the surroundings, with nothing but empty fields, docks or industry for company. But Boyd had the company and assistance of his sister Louisa.

In those days, when the neighbourhood was full of disorderly characters, the policeman conspicuously absent, and the house few and far between, it required some courage, even in a man, to walk about the ill-lighted roads after dark. Miss Boyd never allowed such fears to deter her from the execution of her parish work, though during the garotting scare she confesses to having purchased a revolver and taken a little quiet practice on the marshes as a mere precautionary measure. A difficulty arose when the fences on the way to the church had to be surmounted with a fully-loaded revolver. On such occasions Miss Talbot, who often accompanied Miss Boyd would be entrusted with the dangerous weapon till the fence had been successfully scaled.[161]

In 1863 the Rev. Boyd attended a public meeting in Colchester on behalf of the Society for Promoting the Employment of Additional Curates in Populous Places, and gave those gathered a picture of Silvertown as it then was. The event was reported on by the Essex Standard, which described the area ten years earlier as being a swamp inhabited chiefly by wild birds. Being eight or nine feet below high water mark, *"it was very damp and wanted a good deal of attention to make it a really fit place for human habitation."*[162] Boyd, and the newspaper, described the local industry:

161 Archer Philip Crouch, Silvertown and Neighbourhood (including East and West Ham): A Retrospect. 1900 (p 72)

162 The Essex Standard and Eastern Counties Advertiser, Friday, december 4, 1863

It was not a very savoury locality, for all the guano brought to London came there, and it was a great spot for storing petroleum, which was worse still. Close by was a vitriol manufactory, and worst of all, large blood manure works, which together made the locality almost intolerable. Next in order was a large sugar bakery, a brick field, and a factory for refining petroleum; then Silvertown, which was a very extensive manufactory of india-rubber goods; then a new shipyard, already employing 1,200 hands; then a manufactory of telegraph cables; then the home and colonial ale stores; and lastly, at North Woolwich, the Pavilion Gardens, which were a great resort for the East-Enders.[163]

The Reverend felt the saddest feature of his role as a clergyman in the locality was that due to a severe shortage of housing, and also preference, the better class of worker lived elsewhere. This left behind the poorest of the labourers who were *"as might be supposed a very rough and low class."* The church, which was made of corrugated iron and was thus often a noisy pace of worship, had windows broken and materials stolen, and it was suspected that adults and children alike were the culprits. Reference was also made to the 'garotting panic' that had the more respectable residents living in a state of alarm.

On the road in which Boyd lived, eight out of the twelve houses were broken into, and one man was garotted. There being no police station for three miles, a private watchmen was

---

163 Ibid

appointed with collected funds. Whether or not Miss Louisa Boyd relinquished her revolver at this point is not known.

The natural desire of those who had the means to live elsewhere doing exactly that was not just a problem in Silvertown, and it is probable that Boyd was referring also to Canning Town, to the west. After all, Charles Dickens had mentioned the very same thing in 1857:

Canning Town is the child of the Victoria Docks. The condition of this place and of its neighbour prevents the steadier class of mechanics from residing in it. They go from their work to Stratford or to Plaistow. Many select such a dwelling place because they are already debased below the point of enmity to filth; poorer labourers live there, because they cannot afford to go farther, and there become debased. The Dock Company is surely, to a very great extent, answerable for the condition of the town they are creating. Not a few of the houses in it are built by poor and ignorant men who have saved a few hundred pounds, and are deluded by the prospect of a fatally cheap building investment.[164]

Earlier in his famous article on these Londoners Over The Border, Dickens paints a vivid picture of the living conditions which, with no proper sanitation or even pavements, included damp, floods and raw sewage. The impact of all this squalor was also described:

---

164 Charles Dickens, Londoners Over The Border, Household Works, Vol XVI, 1857

A fetid mist covers the ground. If you are walking out and meet a man, you only see him from the middle upwards, the foul ground mist covering his legs. So says the parish surgeon, an intelligent man and a gentleman, by whom the day work and the night work of a whole district of this character has not been done without cost to his health. He was himself for a time invalided by fever, upon which ague followed. Ague, of course, is on of the most prevalent diseases of the district; fever abounds. When an epidemic comes into the place, it becomes serious in its form, and stays for months. Diseases comes upon human bodies saturated with the influences of such air as this breathed day and night, as a spark upon touchwood. A case or two of small pox caused, in spite of vaccination, an epidemic of confluent small pox, which remained three or four months upon the spot. "I have had twenty cases of it in one day", the doctor said. The clergyman of the parish – whose church is beyond the reach of the Hallsville people, but who is himself familiar to their eyes – told us that during a half year, when the population of Plaistow proper and Hallsville were equal, he counted the burials in each. There were sixteen deaths in Plaistow, and in Hallsville seventy two.[165]

Though a few small factories existed in Canning Town – a printing ink and varnish works, a glass bottle works and a papermaking works – most of the inhabitants worked outside the area, either in the docks or the gas works in Beckton. The Kelly's

---

165 Ibid.

Directory of 1862 reveals that apart from shoemakers, the only commercial traders were limited more or less to butchers, bakers, greengrocers and beer retailers. Being cut off from the support of the Metropolitan Local Managing Act, new streets of houses could be built without drains, roads, gas or pavement. The area by the C.J. Mare and Company's ship-building yard was dubbed Hallsville at the time Dickens wrote, but that name has long since disappeared from the lips of its residents and exists only in history.

Such was the poverty in evidence from its birth that it is unlikely that many, if any, of the Canning Town residents were making their way down stream to indulge in the pleasures of the Pavilion Gardens. The reporter for the Stratford Times, after first suggesting that only someone of questionable sanity would have dreamt of setting up a pleasure gardens in what was basically a marsh in the middle of nowhere, was impressed with what he saw when he visited in 1859, concluding that:

It is pleasant to be able to state that everything in connection with these gardens is well arranged. The hotel department is admirably arranged, and the dinners are both cheap and good; all the amusements in the gardens are excellent of their kind, and the gardens themselves are well laid out; so that there is everything to attract visitors to this pleasant retreat.[166]

But like Cremorne Gardens its reputation was to suffer. Some of the more influential landowners in the area were not happy with

166 Stratford Times, 9th September 1859

all the dancing and drinking going on out there on the river, and prostitutes were said to frequent the gardens looking for trade. Unsavoury incidents, like the one that saw William Lowe before the Ilford magistrates for causing the death his partner Elizabeth Barrett with an umbrella, didn't help. Lowe became jealous when he saw Barrett dancing with another man:

Meeting her afterwards in the grounds he accused her of 'wanting to go with other men" and struck her, the ferule of the umbrella gouging out her eye. She was removed to Guy's Hospital, but died from the effects of the wound thus received. The prisoner was apprehended by a sergeant of the K division. In addition to the previous evidence, James Heal, the gasman, who witnessed the occurrence, stated that the prisoner repeatedly accused the deceased of coquetting with other men before he struck her. The blow with the umbrella appeared to be violent and intentional.[167]

Those who found the gardens disagreeable were in the minority – albeit a minority with influence. Other reporters managed to paint a scene not of ill repute, but of nocturnal magic and daytime gaiety.

Beginning early in the afternoon the entertainments proceed without a break until "Moonlight stealing o'er the scene has blended with the tints of eve," and later still on Mondays,

167 The Hastings and St. Leonards Herald and Observer. Saturday, August 12, 1871

Wednesdays, and Saturdays, when a splendid display of fireworks by Professor Wells and an extensive and magnificent system of illumination by Mr Duffell "turn night into day" and make the North Woolwich Gardens as resplendent as a poet's dream of the East. In the daylight there are leafy avenues where lovers can walk and talk, or they can visit the maze and have their fortune told by a bronzed professor of divination, who will prophesy to their liking. They can afterwards visit the monster platform and join in a quadrille, waltz, or polka, assisted by a capital master of the ceremonies, and a band, under the direction of Mr Sidney Davis.[168]

But what was mere frivolity when compared to the patriotic pride of being an Englishman?

A stroll by the river next occupied us agreeably, and the sight of vessels passing down the river on their way to outlandish Islands of the Pacific, to quiet little coasting harbours, or to the other side of the world, filled us with pride of England's greatness and stimulated the appetite at the same time.

This was a neat little vision of the mighty empire built on trade; some of these vessels were perhaps sailing from the new docks. The opening of the Royal Albert Dock was just six years away, and would have been sooner had it not been for the bankruptcy of the contractor, Sir Morton Peto.

---

168 The Era. July 5, 1874

But all this wealth and the exotic and expensive goods from around the world were out of reach of the men who worked on the docks themselves, none more so than those who lived in Silvertown and Canning Town. The docks themselves, being on the very edge of such a huge city, were less visible than those in the north of England and Scotland. The men who worked them were out of sight and out of mind. Even the prevailing wind helped to conceal their existence and hardships from the more fortunate inhabitants to the west of the city, who didn't have to suffer the olfactory assault that greeted each day for many of those who lived 'over the border'. Men who lived in damp houses that stank of the shit festering in open sewers at the end of their streets might also be the same men who spent their days working at businesses like Mark Finch & Company at Victoria Docks, who specialised in blood manures, dissolved bones and guano.

Maybe it was such workers that those opposed to North Woolwich Gardens had in mind when they proposed that it should be closed and turned into a public park. Or maybe they were just uptight Victorians, who found a venue that whiffed of baser pleasures was too close for comfort. A fund was started for this purpose and a committee formed, under the presidency of the Duke of Westminster. With other powerful and influential figures involved, they were quickly able to raise the necessary funds to grant their own wish, and the gardens became public in 1890. This was less about Victorian philanthropy than it was about controlling space. When the pleasure gardens became a park, access may have been free for all, but access times could now be controlled and the evenings of drinking, dancing and frolicking down by the river were over.

After the Albert Docks were opened Silvertown grew rapidly. By the turn of the century there were at least 20 large firms located there, and many smaller ones. Chemical, creosoting and soap works rose up alongside the manure works. Next door to these pungent factories there was now a factory dealing in an altogether sweeter product. Originating in Liverpool, sugar refiners Henry Tate & Co. relocated to London in 1877, armed with the patent that would help secure its status.

Prior to the cube patent that Tate took out in 1876, sugar was manufactured in large cones or loaves. Grocers would buy these and use a long knife hinged at one end to cut off the amount of sugar each customer required. Apart from being a time-consuming process, it led to waste. Just how time-consuming and how wasteful is a moot point, because when Tate introduced the sugar cube the company never looked back, although there was initial opposition from different quarters:[169]

The new article encountered considerable opposition at first amongst grocers, who regarded the cutting up of sugar as a

---

169 There is some dispute about the origin of the sugar cube. Jakob Christian Rad, manager of the Daschitz sugar refinery in Bohemia, has been credited with inventing it in 1841, after his wife cut her finger whilst cutting her sugar loaf and asked why sugar couldn't be pre-cut, in the shape of cubes which would make inventory easier. According to Tate & Lyle however, the sugar cube was invented 1875 in Germany by Eugen Langen, in partnership with David Martineau. Tate bought the rights to the technology and thus introduced the sugar cube into mass production. Whichever version you prefer, there is no doubting who benefited from it.

useful occupation for their assistants when they had nothing else to do. But it was soon found out that the extra 2s. a cwt. which cube sugar cost, was more than covered by the saving of time and labour effected by it.

A patent is said to be of little use till it has been upheld in the Law Courts, and Henry Tate & Co. obtained the confirmation of their patent for cube sugar in 1882, when they won their case against the French firm of Say & Co., of Paris. Their position thus secured, an enormous business was developed.[170]

When Henry Tate died in 1899 he left behind not only a thriving business but also, thanks to his charitable work, the Tate Institute for working men in Silvertown and the Tate Gallery at Millbank, the latter housing his extensive art collection.

In 1881 Abram Lyle & Sons relocated to Silvertown from Greenock, Scotland, and armed with a loan from the Bank of Scotland designed a refinery that was able to produce golden syrup as well as sugar. The syrup was a by-product of the sugar refining process, and it was Lyle who decided that this sweet tasting substance could be put to use as a spread that could prove profitable for his business. His growing ambition is what led him to build his factory at Plaistow Wharf, a mile upstream from Henry Tate. The portability and long shelf life of its syrup were to win it huge popularity. Its distinctive tins, which haven't changed in over a hundred years, carried a design that came from Lyle's religious upbringing. The inspiration came from a

---

170 Archer Philip Crouch, Silvertown and Neighbourhood (including East and West Ham): A Retrospect. 1900

biblical story in the Book of Judges, in which Samson slays a lion and then sees a swarm of bees forming a honeycomb in its carcass. The second half of Samson's riddle – "Out of the strong came forth sweetness" – became the slogan on every tin.

Odam's Chemical Manure Works arrived at the same time as Silver, buying land next to Victoria Dock from a wealthy Bond Street butcher who owned Cumberland House in Plaistow and grazed his cattle on the surrounding marshland. When rinderpest was introduced into England in 1866 by imported cattle, Odam sensed an opportunity and bought an extra 15 acres of ground on the river front. There he made a wharf and landing stage, lairs for resting cattle and a place for marketing and slaughtering them. *"He then tendered them to the Privy Council, with the result that an order was issued compelling all foreign cattle to be landed, marketed, and slaughtered at this spot."*[171]

William Griffiths acquired a wharf and land in 1889, being supplied with granite for road-making and material for wood pavements from Australia. Their mill was capable of turning out 60,000 blocks of wood a day, and they won the contract to pave Regent Street with wood.

Next to Lyle's refinery was the Silvertown Soap Works, owned by John Knight & Sons. Known for their Primrose brand of soap, the full extent of their operation by the river was described by Archer Philip Crouch in 1900:

---

171 Ibid

Soap, although the chief, is by no means the only product of this manufactory. After being boiled, the oil of the best beef fat is separated from the stearine or solid matter by hydraulic pressure. The stearine is made into candles. The oil, such as is not retained for the manufacture of the best kind of soap, is sent abroad to be made into oleomargarine. The glycerine developed in the saponification process, which formerly was allowed to run to waste, is now recovered and used in the production of nitro-glycerine and dynamite. Resin being one of the constituents of soap, thousands of barrels are imported yearly from North Carolina. For the production of soft soap the firm make their own cotton-seed oil, importing the best Egyptian cotton seed for the purpose. The solid residue of the seed is made up into oil-cakes for animal; the oil itself is used for frying fish, and for the manufacture of butterine in France and Holland. The firm employ some 500 hands and have 80 to 90 horses in their stables.[172]

Meanwhile, across the waterfront the India Rubber, Gutta Percha and Telegraph Works Co. Ltd had grown considerably; by 1900 it was employing upwards of 2,700 men. The Submarine Cable Department had made approximately 40,000 miles of cable which now stretched under the seas all around the globe, laid by the company's own ships *Dacia*, *S.S. International* and *Silvertown*. In 1898 they completed laying the longest cable in the world, from Brest to Cape Cod, a distance of 2,800 nautical miles. Cable repairing

---

172 Ibid (pp 86-87)

was also carried out, a process that took considerable skill in mid-ocean.

But it wasn't just laying what modern observers have called the Victorian Internet that kept the company busy. As important as the cable service was to the world, young boys probably found more importance in rubber balls, and at Silvertown they were made in their thousands each year. Tennis balls, footballs and golf balls (made from gutta percha rather than India rubber) all literally rolled off the production line. And it didn't stop there: pencil erasers, tobacco pouches, rubber bands, draught tubing, bottle stoppers, thimbles, pneumatic tyres, sea boots, anglers' waders, rubber soles for sports shoes, waterproof clothing, rubber cushions for billiard tables, rubber valves and washers for industry, rubber hoses, rubber mats, rubber rings for apprentice swimmers, ebonite trays, dippers and funnels for photographers, hot water bottles and squeegees all came forth in their hundreds and thousands.

The expansion of their business led to an expansion of Silvertown itself, and soon the once desolate St. Mark's Church was hemmed in not just by the railway lines and road, but by more houses, a school, the Works itself and the jam factory at Tay Wharf.

It was said that every house in the land had something that had been produced at Silvertown, as one written account descriptively suggested:

From the time you rise in the morning to the time you retire at night you are enjoying the products of the factories in

which our people work – the piece of fragrant soap which
gives the added pleasure to your ablutions; the marmalade,
jam or syrup on the breakfast table; the sugar in your coffee;
that polished wood tray with the pretty grain; the soda used
in the household; the chemical manures on the garden and in
your conservatories, are all made or prepared by your brothers
and sisters in Silvertown.

The reference to brothers and sisters suggests this account may
have originated from someone connected with the Unions,
unless the author was co-opting the Socialist rhetoric. It was
written in 1917 – an infamous year in the history of Silvertown.

By this time the waterfront was nearly full of factories,
while the amount of houses in Custom House and Silvertown
wards – sandwiched between the North Woolwich Road and
the Victoria and Albert Docks – had expanded to accommodate
the necessary workforce. At Crescent Wharf stood the empty
Brunner Mond chemical factory. It had been established in
1893, producing soda crystals and caustic soda, but in 1912
the factory ceased production of caustic soda. Thus one half
of the plant was idle at the time war broke out in 1914.

It was famously thought that the war would be over by
Christmas, but as it dragged on and the forces involved grew
in size, the British army found itself short of munitions: in
particular high explosive shells. TNT in its unrefined state was
available in large quantities, but it needed purifying for use in
high explosive shells. A search for suitable emergency factories
took place, which resulted in Lord Moulton identifying the idle

half of the Brunner Mond factory as appropriate, even though it was in a built up area. Despite opposition from Brunner Mond, the decision was made to use the factory as a TNT plant.

The Brunner Mond chief chemist Dr F.A. Freeth, who invented the method used to process the TNT, believed it to be truly dangerous and repeatedly warned that the plant would go up sooner or later. Lord Moulton obviously thought it was worth the risk, though he wasn't living nearby, unlike the workers in the rows of houses some 200 yards away who would also have been aware of the highly combustible materials. Moulton would have known about the oil, varnish, wood, chemicals, flour and other highly combustible materials in the surrounding factories and wharfs, but he chose to ignore the almost cartoon-like levels of risk. When production levels were deemed insufficient, a new TNT factory was opened by Brunner Mond in an unpopulated area of Rudheath, Chesire. Though this was both safer and more prolific, the Silvertown plant remained in production.

At 6.52pm on Friday 19th January 1917, Freeth's fears were realised when a fire broke out in the melt-pot room. It caused around 50 tons of TNT to explode with such a force that people throughout London heard and felt the blast, which damaged between 60,000 and 70,000 properties and rendered the sky a reddish glow that was seen for miles around. In the immediate vicinity buildings caught fire, including a plywood factory and the oil tanks of Silvertown Lubricants. Several streets of houses were wrecked, as was the fire station. Fires raged in Victoria Dock and buildings all around, including St

Barnabas' Church. Silvertown had turned into a scene from Dante's Inferno.[173] J.J. Betts, a fireman on the scene, recorded his experience of the firestorm describing, *"flying showers of millions of tiny particles of light as though a sweeping storm of sleet had become incandescent. No doubt these tiny specks were the glowing ashes of a myriad grains of wheat carried up into the sky by the waves of flame."*[174]

His description of the explosion itself is no less vivid:

As we entered the factory gates we were met by the flying figure of the timekeeper, a burly Scotsman. 'Run for it, mon, we'll be gone in a minute!' he yelled to me as he almost staggered, past, hatless, distraught, his face distorted by terrible fear. They were his last words.

Then it was as though heaven had giddily plunged to meet the earth in a shattering upheaval. In one second the whole world seemed to have crumbled.

It might have been seconds, minutes, hours, before I next remembered. I was lying on my back on a piece of waste ground 200 feet from the spot where I and other firemen had been fixing the hose ready to play on the flames.

Around me was a vast plain of rubble. The factory had gone. There was fearful sounds in the air, the screams of injured women and children, the groans of those imprisoned under

---

173 Graham Hill & Howard Bloch, The Silvertown Explosion, London 1917. Tempus Publishing Limited. 2003 (pp13-14)

174 J.J. Betts, The Great War part 33, 243 'I Was There'.

the debris, the rattle of rafters and girders being feverishly overturned by rescuers who had rushed to the shattered area, the shrill resonance of ambulance bells, the imperious clang of fire alarms, the roar of flames.

On every side great fires were blazing. In all nine factories and mills had caught alight, ignited by red-hot iron girders, flung sky-high by the explosion, falling into their midst.[175]

The official announcement that appeared in the following day's newspapers was, by predictable contrast, cold and emotionless.

"The Ministry of Munitions regret to announce that an explosion occurred this evening at a munitions factory in the neighbourhood of London. It is feared that the explosion was attended by considerable loss of life and damage to property."

The official death toll was 73 (69 were killed instantly and four died later of their injuries), with 328 injured. The police also reported several hundred walking wounded. There was also the huge cost of damage to property and business; around 900 houses were destroyed or badly damaged by the blast. The low death rate was a result of the explosion occurring in the early evening. Numbers of staff at work were low, and the majority of people living in the houses nearby would have been downstairs when the worst of the flying debris hit the upper floors. An inquest was critical of Brunner Mond and The Ministry of Munitions, but any real criticism was unlikely to surface in wartime. The cause of the explosion was never uncovered.

---

175 Ibid

The aftermath of the disaster saw hundreds of people homeless and 19 schools closed for repairs. As the locality was camouflaged by the Defence of the Realm Act, which enforced measures such as strict censorship of the press during the war, the disaster and suffering afterwards were little known to the rest of the country. They may have heard the explosion as far away as Norwich, but any details would have been thin on the ground and strictly word of mouth. Local paper The Stratford Express covered things in more detail in a series of reports that ran in its Saturday editions from January 27th to February 10th. These included a report on the scenes of ruin and desolation that contained some surreal details, such as the morning after the explosion a member of the local authority finding a dead horse, which *"had been killed by a mass of falling metal, but in the yard close to the carcass there was a hen still sitting quietly on her eggs."*

Included in the reports were survivors' accounts that revealed the full extent of the horror unleashed. A Dr. Kennedy recalled a 16 year old girl who *"was burned practically all over the body. She lived until 8 a.m. on the 22nd, and then died from shock following the burns."* A mother was at home with her six children when she saw the fire. After the explosion she ran into the street with her children, but one was left behind; when she returned to the house he was found dead under a large piece of iron which, it appeared, had also cut off the arm of one of her daughters. A wages clerk ran into the safe to avoid the falling debris of the explosion and never saw his colleague alive again, though next morning he saw his scalp at the foot of the stairs. One witness spoke of seeing a 69 year old watchman who was employed near the plant. *'I told him to run for his life, but he was very bad on his feet, and had not much chance.'* A doctor told the Coroner that he had examined a charred body, which was headless and without arms and legs. It was the body of a young female under 23 years of age.' Over and over again witnesses described seeing people for the last time. The time, the place, the circumstances, the words spoken. People they could still see, going into offices, walking through doors, running down corridors. Or else they were with people when the explosion wrenched them off their feet, and when they came round the people they had been with and had been talking to – about the fire, about what to do – were nowhere to be seen, and would never be seen by them again.

The aftershocks sometimes reverberated long after everyone had forgotten about that terrible night. In 1925 'at an inquest at West Ham on Wednesday, on William Bowman Hudspeth, 42, an engineer, of Maryland Park, Stratford, who cut his throat, it was stated that he was injured in the great Silvertown explosion during the war, and that his nerves since then had been more or less shattered. A sister stated that since the explosion the deceased had attempted on four occasions to commit suicide. – A verdict of suicide while of unsound mind was returned.'[176]

For others the effects of the explosion had been instant, but it was the cure they had to wait years for:

---

176 Chelmsford Chronicle, Friday 6 November, 1925

When the Silvertown explosion occurred, about 4 ½ years ago, a Mrs. Clanwaring and a daughter and son were killed, and another son, Thomas, rendered dumb. On Thursday the latter went to Baldock, near Letchworth, and on his slate put a question as to where the baths were. The man whom he thus asked offered to take him there, and they prepared to bathe together. Clanwaring, who is a poor swimmer, mistook the deep for the shallow end and, finding himself out of his depth, was so frightened that he shouted for help. His power of speech had thus been restored by fear.[177]

Though it was considerably the largest, this wasn't the first explosion at Silvertown. One had taken place in 1880 at the works of Burt, Bolton and Haywood in the Victoria Docks. Manufactures of coal-tar products and railway timber, they acquired Prince Regent's Wharf in 1870 and were the largest acid manufacturers on the Thames. The presence of all this timber and acid – as well as creosote, tar, pitch, naphtha and benzoline – made sure that the consequences of any accident would be fairly spectacular, and so it was when a still exploded one Monday afternoon and set fire to the building. The retort of the explosion was heard for miles around and soon hundreds of people had gathered at the scene, together with large numbers of spectators from Charlton and Woolwich who watched from the opposite bank of the river.

---

177 Western Times, Monday 25 July 1921

The force of the explosion was tremendous, and the massive circular top of the still, which is said to have weighed nearly three tons, was forced to a great height, resembling, as one of the spectators expressed himself, "a balloon ascending." Pieces of it were found a considerable distance from the scene. Eleven dead bodies were recovered and six men were found to be injured.[178]

The talk around Silvertown the following day was that there were more dead who had yet to be found. Messrs. Burt, Bolton, and Haywood complained that the newspapers printed an exaggerated account of the disaster, and instructed their employees not to talk to the press. Two men were, however, quoted by the Illustrated Police News. One recalled seeing a man rushing up to the still with a *portable fire-engine* on his back, and assumed he must have been blown to pieces. Another, Benjamin Price, was on top of the still when it burst and he was blown high into the air, the top of the still being sent with him.

Several hundred persons who were on the premises rushed from their work in a panic, and immediately found that a shower of bricks, pieces of iron, and burning liquid were descending in their midst. Two men in their haste to leave the premises rushed into a building where some chemicals had caught fire, and there met their death, being overpowered instantly.[179]

---

178 The Illustrated Police News, April 24, 1880

179 Ibid

The inquest began at the Graving Dock Tavern on the Tuesday afternoon, where the remains of the victims were identified by such physical and material details as blue stockings, a belt buckle and knife, the big toe of a foot overlapping its neighbour, the shape of toes or peculiarity of ears. A solemn procession at the funeral of all the men included 250 workmen. Funeral expenses were covered by the company, and the families of each victim were allowed to choose their own time and place of burial. They were all buried on the same Sunday afternoon, however, as this was the only day working people could be guaranteed the time to attend.

An idea of what this part of London 'over the border' looked like at this time, or at least how it was perceived by an outsider, can be gleaned from a contemporary article in the Daily News in 1881.

Here, then, is a district provided with churches, chapels, and schools, but in which the roads are so impassable in bad weather that the people cannot avail themselves of their privileges. Worse even than that. In the severe weather of last winter houses were flooded a foot high on the ground floor, and some were converted into islands upon an island by the surrounding water. Women could not go to market, places of worship, and schools were out of the question. To wade ankle deep in mud when it is wet, and to be smothered in dust when it is windy, is the common experience of the inhabitants. The obvious question arises – who is responsible for this neglect? The reply is an illustration of the saying that what is everybody's business is nobody's business. The portion of Silvertown which appears to be No Man's Land belongs to a local land company, who have some sort of dispute with the parochial authorities of West Ham. The latter would willingly take it in hand and remove the reproach; but the land company, for some reason will not, it is said, consent.[180]

The article, written for no other reason than to shine a light on the hidden far reaches of the metropolis, was simple and direct in its conclusion.

Silvertown, beyond the boundary of the West Ham authorities, may be safely commended as an undoubted example to those who would learn "How not to do it." Schools, churches and chapels are excellent things, and they are provided without stint. Decent roads are excellent things, too, and they are not provided. The Silvertonians appreciate what has been done for their spiritual and mental needs, and are thankful, but I for one do not deem them unreasonable if they inquire how long they are to be left without the common elements of physical comfort.[181]

Houses resting on the boggy marsh, without roads but surrounded by mud that was often infested with human waste, were obviously seen as acceptable as long as the factories had hands to work the machinery – and those hands were

180 The Daily News, Wednesday, November 30, 1881

181 Ibid

able to come together in prayer in a house of God. In this era Christianity and temperance were seen as ways of keeping the simmering resentments and bursts of violence of the working classes at bay.

Such violence was almost always turned inward, towards either another poor resident or the self, and drink was often involved. Too often it involved men being violent to their wives. Men, bent out of shape by drink, who killed their wives with knives or guns because they were having affairs. Men killed by drunken sailors, and sailors who killed their nearest and dearest, like George Nadin who killed three of his children like pigs, cutting their throats, wounded two more, cut his wife around the arms, then slashed his own throat. A newspaper report was at a loss for why this all happened and merely stated that *"the man had been ill."*[182]

Men who killed their own fathers and men who killed each other or just reached the end of their rope and killed themselves. After drink, jealousy and robbery, the most common element seemed to be unemployment. Though there were docks and industry as far as the eye could see, there wasn't always work for everyone. Often men could only get a few days casual labour at the docks, waiting each morning 'on the stones' outside the Connaught Tavern for the privilege.

In July 1892 Henry Reed attacked Christian Gray, one of the three brothers who managed the Indiarubber, Gutta Percha and Telegraph Works Company. Gray had apparently

---

182 The Devon and Exeter Gazette. Monday November 23 1908

instructed his foreman not to take Reed on again due to Reed absenting himself from work previously. He inflicted a knife wound on Gray's throat, which was not serious, and then fled over a railway into a field. Louisa Fury, who was in these fields in front of her house, saw Reed coming towards her.

He seemed very hot and strange in his manner. He wiped his forehead, and, looking at the ditch, said, "I've a good mind to get in there: I'm in trouble. I have done a murder." He then took a razor from his pocket and the witness ran away screaming. Elizabeth Harris, the wife of a fireman, of Gray Street, corroborated the previous witness, and added that when Reed took the razor from his pocket he opened the blade and wiped it up and down on his coat sleeve. He then started cutting his own throat, and as witness picked up her little boy prior to running away she saw blood issuing from a terrible gash in Reed's throat. He then said,"Here goes," then leaped head first into the ditch.[183]

Reed had lost four fingers and part of his right hand at an accident at the plant six years before, and was thought to be mad with liquor when he attacked Gray. His wife said he was addicted to drink, that he would not give it up. He found it easier to give up his life.

Sometimes it was just the drink that did them in. Ellen Cumming's husband had left her on account of it several times,

---

and when it was once too often Ellen *"climbed from the pier over the railway and exclaiming "Good bye, all," dropped herself in the water."*[184]

Others carried on, some minus fingers or toes, whole limbs even, arms torn off at the elbow or shoulder, thanks to the dangers of the machinery in these workplaces; if drink got them by, then so be it. But as well as the church and the temperance societies, other influences were ready to fight for the rights of the workers to do more than follow God or stay sober.

The sheer concentration of industry, amid social conditions that shocked observers from Dickens to Eleanor Marx, meant that the heavily populated areas of this industrialised London (and in particular Canning Town) were ripe for the influence of Trade Unionism and Socialism to gain a hold. The match girls strike of 1888 was still fresh in public consciousness when, not 12 months later, another blow was struck for the workers, this time at Beckton.

Beckton is a dirty, grimy place situated on the borders of the Essex marshes in North Woolwich, and the extreme east of easternmost London; and at Beckton are the big works of the Gas Light and Coke Company.

On arriving at the works the first idea the casual visitor gets is one of chaos indescribable and bewildering, of undersized, albeit capable, little engines bustling hither and thither, drawing trucks crammed with coal and coke, not only

---

184 The Essex Newsman, Saturday, June 24, 1893

all around, but above as well, for an overhead iron railway is indispensable to take the coal right up to the top of the retort houses. But despite the ceaseless din and the apparent confusion and chaos, the Beckton works - and they cover an area of some three hundred acres - are most systematically and methodically arranged.

To begin at the beginning, we must go to the huge pier which runs out into the Thames, a structure big enough to berth four large steamers and one small one, the larger sized ones capable of carrying two thousand tons of coal each journey, which they bring from the collieries of Northumberland and Durham...

Outside the works proper are the mighty gas-meters and holders, the loftiest of which is some 200 feet in height, where the gas is stored away and mixed with oil and water-gas to magnify its power as an illuminant. A sight, too, are the great mains which carry the gas into the metropolis, huge pipes as thick as the trunk of a good-sized tree, while, as can be readily understood, miles upon miles of smaller ones are employed in the transit of the gas.[185]

The Gas Light and Coke Company was founded in 1812, and in 1868 began building the world's largest gas works beside the Thames between Barking Creek and the Royal Victoria Dock. The first pile on the river wall was driven in by the then Governor, Simon Adams Beck, and the following day it was

---

declared by the Directors that the site would be called Beckton. The Thames siting was ideal, and perhaps the reason why alternative sites at Hackney, Greenwich, and Bow were rejected. Two T-shaped piers were constructed which could accommodate several vessels at a time unloading coal, shipped from Newcastle and Durham, then taken by the company's own railway to the retort houses. These were carbonising ovens that were used to produce the gas, and working on them required stamina and skill. A report written two years after the gas works opened gives a sense of the scale and drama of the retort houses.

An immense hall, its roof at times hidden in the gloom of ascending vapours, its walls and flooring of coal-dust hue, has, running all along its length, a structure not unlike an organ fitted with innumerable pipes. Below the pipes are flat plates of metal some 18 inches in circumference, which may be called the organ stops, and below these again certain little patches of bright red – the glowing ash-holes of a fire that burns unseen. At first hardly anything is visible in the gloom but these little parentheses of brightness, but soon the forms of men are distinguished, grouped pygmy-wise in front of the great "organ stops" aforesaid. For music there is the sullen roar of hundreds of tons of coal in combustion within the instrument, for the stops are but the doors of so many furnace tubes in which the mineral is put "to stew." Presently some half dozen of the pygmies open one of the tubes, and in an instant far darting tongues of fire illumine all the place. The furnace has to be emptied of the exhausted coal and replenished immediately afterwards, and in the adroit management of the large scoops and rakes...is shown the stoker's art. As the men stand on tip-toe, "fishing" for coke embers in the long gulley of fire, or shoulder the Brobdingnagian shovel, which takes three of them to lift with its load of coals, they must become half blinded if not wholly confused in the heat and glare.[186]

Unrest in the gas industry over working conditions had been simmering for a few years, and in 1872 the stokers and many other men (some 500 in total) came out on strike at Beckton in support of a sacked employee. The strike leaders were dealt with harshly, losing not just their jobs, but also their liberty, sentenced to 12 months in prison. The following year 50 coal porters refused to go to work at midnight on Sunday 2nd March and were subsequently sacked.

In 1889 Will Thorne, Ben Tillett and William Byford set up a three man committee that led to the formation of the National Union of Gas Workers and General Labourers. The working day for the gas workers of Beckton was 12 hours, seven days a week. Thorne, an almost completely illiterate Birmingham-born Irishman, was supported by Karl Marx's daughter Eleanor, John Burns and Tom Mann (Burns, Mann and Tillett had organised the docks strike of the same year). He gave a speech at Canning Town Hall on Barking Road, promising to deliver better conditions to the workforce. Within 24 hours 800 workers had joined the new union, with a total

---

186 The Daily News, Saturday, December 7, 1872

of 3,000 members by the end of the first month. Thorne delivered on his promise without even need of a strike and won the gas workers an eight hour day.

Thorne went on to become General Secretary of the National Union of Gas Workers and General Labourers. He later became a local councillor, then in 1906 he was elected Member of Parliament for West Ham South. Though there had been successes for the left up until this point, the struggle for permanent work and fair working conditions was not over. The year Thorne entered Parliament was the same year that Ben Cunningham led his band of men onto the waste ground in Plaistow, in response to what he saw as the failure of the various schemes that had been put in place to deal with the growing problem of unemployment in West Ham, much of it centred on the issue of casual labour at the docks.

The previous year a meeting took place in Canning Town Hall.

The speaker was a workman out of employment:
We must make them find work for us.
A Voice: Let us have revolution. It would wake them up a bit. [loud cheers.]
Speaker: First let us try to revolutionise the political machinery.
A Voice: Let us have revolution now. [Cheers.] Standing idle like this only means a slow death by starvation. [Cheers.][187]

---

187 Essex Newsman. Saturday 30, September, 1905

Insurrectionary talk was in the air, fuelled by the plight of men trying to get any kind of work at the docks. Some 2,000 congregated early one August morning at the Royal Albert Docks. At the British India Company's section some 400 men were turned away, and similar scenes were witnessed at four or five other places at the Albert Docks. At the Victoria Docks it was even worse. At one entrance, of the 500 men waiting for work, only 35 were taken on. One man exclaimed that he had only worked five weeks in 12 months. Another, with a wife, when beckoned by the foreman pushed another man to the front and said, *"Take him on; he's worse off than I am – he's got a bunch of kids to keep."*[188] Meanwhile, the extravagance of some members of society had not gone unnoticed.

The extravagance of those rich people who spend on a single dinner or a special train enough to keep a working man's family for a year or more, was denounced on Friday at a meeting of the West Ham unemployed in Barking-road.
The Rev. De Courcey Benwell said it was complained that some of the men out of work made violent speeches. It might be so, but it was scarcely to be wondered at. "Only the other day," he added, "I read of a dinner given by a rich man that cost £120 a head. Such reckless and vulgar expenditure is disgraceful. The sum of £120 would keep a workman and his family in comfort for a year and a half."[189]

---

188 Ibid

189 Essex Newsman. Saturday 26, August, 1905

In September Will Thorne, pointing out that trade had not been so depressed in the East End for years, moved a resolution calling on the local authorities to immediately put into action the provision of the Unemployed Workmen Act. It was estimated that 10,000 men and women in the borough of West Ham were unemployed; many of them had been forced into sharing houses, leaving many homes empty. The Unemployed Committee had petitioned local magistrates to delay as far as possible evicting people from their homes. The document, signed by Charles Mowbray, Ben Cunningham and the Rev. B.W. Pullinger, was presented to the Chairman at the West Ham Police Court. At a meeting in Canning Town on September 16th Councillor Hayday *"asserted that this country is the worst under the sun so far as poverty and general conditions were concerned."*[190]

In November, Joseph Fels offered part of an estate of 538 acres in Basildon to use as a farm colony. Various parties suggested that this was an offer worthy of acceptance, but others were of the opinion that the ground would be unworkable in the winter.

On May 14th 1906 thousands of unemployed men and women took part in a demonstration through the West End of London to Hyde Park, protesting at the government's lack of action on the unemployment problem. A detachment several hundreds strong from West Ham marched with a banner in their midst proclaiming, *"The Church in West Ham; in the name of Christ we claim that all men should have the right*

---

190 Essex Newsman. Saturday 16 September, 1905

to work. " With the right to land long gone, this was the new standard. Presiding at one platform, Keir Hardie expressed his opinion that the unemployed were too patient and that the more they remained so, the more they would be neglected.[191]

Some work was being found, such as that organised by the Borough Distress Committee of East Ham – the construction of an ornamental lake in Wanstead Park – aided by money from the Queen's Unemployed Fund. However, this was not a long term solution and in June Will Thorne made his maiden speech in the Commons in a debate on the unemployment question. He spoke vehemently of the vast increase of pauperism in West Ham, where figures showed that 17,929 persons were receiving poor relief. *"Unless the Government try to grapple with the unemployed question, the unemployed will try to grapple with Government."*[192] A month later Councillor Ben Cunningham and a group of unemployed men made their doomed land grab at Plaistow.

In 1906 the Labour Party was formally constituted. Although in the years leading up to the First World War it could not command much electoral support in East London, it was increasingly seen by Trade Unions that political influence would be more profitable than industrial action in gaining improved pay and conditions.

After the First World War – which had seen near full employment in some areas – the Representation of the People

191 Litchfield Mercury. Friday 18 May, 1906

192 Essex Newsman. Saturday 2 June, 1906

Act split the borough of West Ham into four constituencies: Plaistow, Silvertown, Stratford and Upton. From here until after the Second World War, Plaistow and Silvertown were held by Labour. Will Thorne held the Plaistow seat until 1945. Labour claimed Stratford from the Conservatives in 1922 and held on to it until the boundaries changed in 1948, when West ham reverted to two constituencies which were both held by Labour for the next two decades.[193]

In 1921 two significant events occurred at Silvertown; Tate and Lyle joined forces, and the King George V Dock was opened to the south of the Albert Dock. The Port of London Authority, which had come into being in 1908, had begun a programme to modernise the docks. This resulted in the construction of the George V Dock dock, which could take ships of up to 30,000 tons. By the 1930s London had the largest maritime cargo handling business in the world, employing 100,000 men who processed 35 million tons of cargo annually. By 1939 Tate & Lyle's Silvertown refinery was the largest in the world.

At the same time as Tate joined forces with Lyle, The London writer Thomas Burke ventured 'over the border' and described what he encountered in the dock lands:

Canning Town is good East End. Its pulse and temper are deep and wayward. It drums barbarically to the rhythms of Alsatia. Here is a bit of the old untamed London: a whiff of

---

193 Jim Lewis. East Ham & West Ham Past. Historical Publications Ltd, 2004. (p 113)

Tudor Bankside; and though like all East End parishes, it has its Missions and its Settlements, it hasn't yet surrendered to them. Respectability has pricked it, but hasn't wholly blasted it. It is to-day what the nearer East was fifty years ago. Here are big-bodied, foot-fisted men and Roaring Girls. The men are slow, elephantine. The girls, lusty and comely after their rude fashion, are full of the headlong neck-and-neck spirit of the streets; and even the flirtatious females of thirteen walk like colts. Here are the "Imperial", and its adjoining cinema, which, only a year or so ago, was the last of the tavern music-halls. And here is the serpentine Iron Bridge, and the vast disordered plain of water and yards and roofs and chimneys that it bestrides...[194]

He describes shops selling food that had long since ceased to be popular anywhere else, and instruments such as accordions and the Jew's harp that wouldn't be entertained in modern households equipped with a gramophone. It was as if the present was still some place in the future, here over the border. A stack of second hand penny dreadfuls were spied in one shop, with titles like 'Wild Boys of London', 'Skeleton Crew' and 'The Black Monk's Curse' – perhaps like those found in 1895 at the Coombes residence by the police trying to fathom why young Robert had murdered his mother.

The old defunct feast of St. Valentine is also honoured, in a twisted way, in these little shops; and during the month of February their

---

194 Thomas Burke, The London Spy, A Book of Town Travels, Thornton Butterworth Ltd 1922 (p 242)

windows are made hideous by high-coloured representations of women with asses' heads or padlocked lips and other deformities. With these atrocious missives the youth of the district work off old scores against, unfriendly associates. They are stabs in the back; delivered to the poor victim with the evil glee of the anonymous-letter maniac. There are pictures of squinting eyes, of club feet, or hare lips, each with its malicious verse; and pictures of babies, with verse suggesting that father should look into its true parentage. One of these shot into a family circle, or sent to a sensitive girl, may easily poison mutual trust, or lead to extreme action. Nowhere else in London, I believe, does the custom persist; and I hope that even the strong stomach of Canning Town will soon turn against it.[195]

Evidence that this peculiar habit had some history, in the East End at least, comes from an article in the Newsman in 1896 reporting on the events at the Stratford Petty Sessions.

The sending of Valentines has not quite died out, and that it is a custom which may generate other passions than that of love. A woman named Emily Payne, of Talbot Road, East Ham, received an ugly valentine entitled "To a creepy, sly old thing." She leapt to the conclusion that it came from a neighbour named Mrs Walsh, and she forthwith made tracks to Mrs Walsh's residence, and flung a big stone through the window, smashing not only the glass but a couple of ornaments. Mrs Walsh said she knew

---

195 Ibid (p244)

nothing of the valentine, and the defendant had to pay, in all, the respectable sum of twenty-three shillings.[196]

Burke also ventured to Cyprus Place by the Albert Dock,

which bristles with scores of cranes, travelling and stationary, dilapidated sheds, and sheaves of chimneys tipped with flowers of smoke.

Cyprus Place is the supply depot of this curious colony, peopled by workers from the docks and the great gas-works. Here are fly-blown eating-houses, fly-blown "general" stores, a newspaper shop, a sweetstuff shop, a few second-hand dealers, and the Ferndale Hotel, the only pub in Cyprus. It is many years since I first took a drink at the Ferndale. It has changed little. It is still the one bright spot in Cyprus, but bright only by its glum background. It is kept today by Joe Lyons (nothing to do with tea-shops) and is a quiet, well-conducted house. There you may sit, under warm light, and listen to the night wail of industry the squalling syren, the melancholy hooter, and the gruff lullaby of the shunting engine; and with them comes the smell of smoke and steam and dust. Here gather, from the bleak corners of Cyprus, heavy, dejected men, some in the garments of work, some spruced up by a wash and a change. But all are heavy. Talk is slow; the easy interchange of gossip becomes here only grunts and nods. They are tired with the day's work, and they must be up early to-morrow.[197]

---

196 The Newsman, Saturday, February 29, 1896

197 Ibid (pp 172-73)

Burke goes on to describe, over several pages, an opium smoking session courtesy of a 'brown man' he has met in the Ferndale. This is either artistic license or an illustration that opium's smokey tentacles reached much further east than the Limehouse of legend.

Despite the opening of the new dock, and the work of men like Thorne and Hardie in representing the people of the borough, unemployment was an ongoing issue. Ivy Alexander remembers the 1920s and 1930s as being tough times for the people of Canning Town; in particular the 'Old Town' where she grew up, a D-shaped stretch of land less than a quarter mile long, hemmed in by the railway lines and Bow Creek. Life here was decidedly tough and very few people were able to escape it. Much of the work in the docks was still casual and a neighbour returning from it would complain of sore, sticky feet from unloading sugar all day. People were apathetic and accepted their lot, the height of aspiration for girls being to work in Woolworths. The women who worked in a sack factory on Bidder Street would wear sacks covering their head and shoulders in a vain attempt to avoid being covered in fine dust that smelt of pepper. Alexander describes them as being the *"most depressed"* workers she had ever come across. Ironic that such pitiful daily grind should happen on a street named after the man who gained such wealth from the area. Alexander also mentions that Gandhi made a visit to the area, but that she was never able to find any reference to it.[198]

---

198 Ivy Alexander, Maid in West Ham, 2001

Such an event did occur in September 1931 when, somewhat improbably, Gandhi met Charles Chaplin, then perhaps the most famous film star in the world. The meeting had been arranged by Dr. Chuna Lal Katial, a friend of Gandhi's, and took place in his house in Beckton Road, Canning Town. After each of the men had made their way through a crowd of onlookers, many of whom intruded through a hole in the garden wall, the meeting took place in the front room of the doctor's house. The conversation was interrupted at 7pm for prayer, and shortly after this ten minute ceremony Chaplin bid his farewell.

"I introduced the subject of machinery," said Mr Chaplin to the *"Post"* afterwards, *"because I understood that Gandhi was opposed to the use of machinery in India. I told him that I could not understand the attitude he took up on this important matter concerning the well being of the race.*
"I admit that Mr Gandhi did not see eye to eye with me. I was not able to follow him in all that he told me, but I was nonetheless anxious to impress upon him my view that machinery was a heritage of mankind and we could not wholly depart from its usefulness."[199]

Gandhi would visit Epping Forest the following day, and was apparently impressed at such a wide open space so near London. Wearing his customary loin cloth and a blanket, he was offered black berries by a man out picking them. In London to attend

---

199 The Nottingham Evening Post, Wednesday, September 23, 1931

the Roundtable Conference, he eschewed the hotels of the West End for humbler accommodation at Kingsley Hall Community Centre, Bow, where he stayed for 12 weeks. The centre was run by Muriel Lester, who shared Gandhi's outlook in life in relation to the needs of the poor and the lack of responsibility of the rich. They would take morning walks round the Three Mills area, discussing religion and politics.

Quite why Chaplin felt the need to raise the subject of machinery when the two men met is not known. The likes of Chaplin were free to enjoy its benefits, but for the working men of the East End it was an altogether more troubled relationship. Descriptions of the industries that covered the waterfront of Silvertown hardly do justice to the harsh reality. It is only surviving photographs that reveal just what a dirty and dangerous working life it was in those days.

Men busy pitch getting at Prince Regent's Wharf were dwarfed by the hellish looking skeletons of pipes, ducts, vats and valves all scarred by the pollutants of industry. The noise and smells would have been equally as oppressive. Whilst all this machinery gave them work in the first instance, it was also responsible for them losing work. Machinery, it seemed for the workers, was man's master and not the other way round. But there was no going back. The ghost of Ned Ludd and Captain Swing may have haunted the minds of many a man, but they were now totally dependent on the very metal machinery that had driven the last of them from the land only a few generations earlier. Perhaps Gandhi had a point.

Though the business coming through the docks increased in the 1920s, employment did not. The casual labour system still existed, and the capabilities of cranes, use of conveyors and altered working systems meant that although the work for employed dockers was in some cases made easier, for others it was denied altogether. The industries on the river and docks were also very vulnerable to recession. By 1927 unemployment in West Ham ran at 19 per cent, and it was to rise to 27.5 per cent within five years[200]

Ahead lay the Great Depression, and beyond that the Second World War, which for the people of Canning Town and Silvertown meant the worst that the German bombing had to offer, as the docks and surrounding industries were an obvious target. On September 7th 1940, 300 tons of bombs were dropped on the East End. Three nights later 73 people, homeless from the bombing and waiting to be bussed out of the area, were killed when South Hallsville School in Agate Street, Canning Town was hit by a bomb. By the end of the war 25 per cent of the homes in West Ham were destroyed. In areas of Canning Town such as the Beckton Road it was higher, and in Tidal Basin by the Victoria Docks 85 per cent of housing was destroyed.[201] Slum clearance had begun in the 1930s in and around 'Old Canning Town' were Ivy Alexander grew up. Hitler, they said, just finished the job.[202]

200 John Marriot, Beyond The Tower, A History of East London, Yale University Press. 2011 (p272-75)

201 Ibid. (p 320)

202 I was travelling on Beckton train one day in the early 1990s and overheard two pensioners, talking about the bleak surroundings unfolding through the window as the train made its slow haul to Fenchurch Street. "Maggie done more damage than Hitler ever did," one commented. John Major was then the prime minister, but the spectre of Margaret Thatcher was obviously hard to shake off.

A temporary solution post-war was prefabricated houses. Some of these can be seen in the background as Del admires his new motorbike on the Romford Road in *Bronco Bullfrog*. For some, these houses were a step up from what they had lived in before, and they grew a deep attachment to them; many are still standing over 50 years later in various parts of the country. Other actions by the town planners were new estates, such as the Keir Hardie Estate at Tidal Basin. High rise blocks were to come later in the 1960s, and it was on this estate that Ronan Point was built. Many people chose to relocate to new housing provided in Essex or Kent, and a migration of sorts began. The East End demographic was beginning to change.

For those who remained, either in houses that survived the Blitz or new ones, the Docks still provided work and traffic through them reached a peak in the the two decades following the war. But the seeds of decline had long since been sown. The industrial age was slowly but surely coming to an end, and early signs were visible down by the Thames. The India Rubber, Gutta Percha and Telegraph Works that had given Silvertown its name were taken over in the 1920s by the British Goodrich Rubber Co, later to become the British Tyre and Rubber Company, then BTR Industries. It survived for another 40 years before the land was sold for redevelopment and became the Thameside Industrial Estate.

After the discovery of Natural Gas in the North Sea the days of the gas works at Beckton were numbered, and it closed in 1970. The remnants of the works were used to depict Vietnam in Stanley Kubrick's film 1987 film *Full Metal Jacket*.

Scenes from *1984*, starring John Hurt, were also filmed in the old gas works buildings. The only real reminder of its past are the the covered heaps of toxic spoil known as the Beckton Alps where, ironically, a dry ski slope existed from 1989 to 2001.

But the biggest economic blow to the area came with the closing of the docks themselves. In the late 1970s, with the London Port Authority close to insolvency, drastic measures were implemented by government. New working practices led to huge job losses, and in 1981 cargo handling was transferred from the Royal Docks downstream to Tilbury. Millwall and East India Dock had already been shut down the year before. In 1982 the Royal Docks, which had remained open for vessel impounding and maintenance, were also shut down.

The Canning Town and Silvertown of old have gone through huge changes, and continue to do so. Those who remembered the long queues to get in or out of Silvertown while they waited for the swing bridge are no longer around, and the construction of Silvertown Way to solve this very problem is now just a memory preserved in photographs and books. Gone is the chemical works at West Ham. Gone too the Peggy Leggy steps, and most obviously the sight of ships and ocean liners that were once a familiar feature at the bottom of certain streets. What is abundantly clear is that the reason for the existence of both places has now vanished. Fragments survive but, amid the piecemeal regeneration, all that remains are the ghosts of the past.

CHAPTER 11

Cuckoos

Stratford Station has surely experienced more change and alteration than any other in the world these past 15 years. Gone is the old pokey entrance down by the current taxi-rank and Stanstead coach stop, with its dim ticket hall and puddles that collected on the floor on rainy days. Gone too the long tunnels of glazed tiles that stretched to the platforms and had you thinking about scenes from *A Clockwork Orange*. In 1999 the arrival of the Jubilee line extension heralded an all-brand-spanking-new station – a silver and glass marvel that for some time became TRATFORD TATION, until they located two letter Ss. Quite why they had a problem with them is anyone's guess.

The low-level platform that used to carry the North London Line now serves the latest Docklands Light Railway extension, which means travelling to Canning Town and beyond doesn't require taking the previously protracted route via Poplar. When I arrived on a Saturday in April 2012 there was a four minute wait for the next train, so I checked my camera, not wanting to get too far before realising a memory card wasn't inside. It was a new one, so I familiarised myself with the controls and menu system. The train arrived quietly and a seat wasn't hard to find. I was heading towards the Royal Docks area to record what was now there, and in doing so record what was there no longer. The Olympic ballyhoo would lead an outsider to believe that the Five Ring Circus had started the regeneration of the whole area, but the docklands of Newham had been quietly, if slowly, changing for a number of years.

When the train stopped at West Ham I looked out at the station across the tracks and Manor Road and felt, as I always did when I saw it, a sense of dislocation. This is where I lived for nearly a year in 1991 when I arrived in London with a bag of clothes and some savings, in search of work. Back then the platform was basic and merely served the North London Line. In 1991 the Jubilee line stopped at Charing Cross and wouldn't caterpillar itself this far east for another eight years, while the DLR link was even further in the future. Though the line had made its way east, it hadn't brought the benefits of the west with it. For every two stops from Westminster to Canning Town, life expectancy drops by a year.[203] To the right of the station the view was pretty much as I saw it when standing on

---

203 London Health Observatory, 2004-2008

this platform all those years ago, though the flats on Manor Road had been given a lick of paint. In 1991 many of them were rented by students at UEL who studied in Plaistow or Barking. The block on Germander Way was entirely occupied by students, and it was common for them to arrive home at night to find the door off its hinges and a reduction in their personal property. Often the perpetrators wouldn't wait for the occupants to leave, merely expecting them to run into the sanctuary of one of the rooms while the gang of thieves quickly divested the rest of the flat of easily obtainable valuables. In the days before mobile phones that weren't the size of bricks (and perhaps more useful as a weapon than for calling the police), this was a much more straightforward task.

In those days at least one entire block overlooking the recreation ground was empty and derelict, the brown stone finish stained and windows dusty, broken or boarded up, like something from New York in the late 1970s. A flat on the top floor, fitted out with a reinforced steel door, was HQ for the modern Dickensian mob. The younger gang members were responsible for terrorising the students, but were often only allowed to deliver the ill-gotten gains and not hang out in the flat itself, such was the hierarchy and its unwritten rules. On the few occasions I found myself in this flat there was a constant knocking at the door, and after a swift check through the peep hole, a new face would walk in carrying a stereo, radio, camera or whatever. One room served as the warehouse, though the next destination for the goods was an unknown. In an area famous for industry, you couldn't argue with the industriousness of this operation. Individually some of these young lads were fine and some were clearly victims of peer pressure. Some of them were clearly pretty smart. Collectively they were a different proposition, and the despair of local shopkeepers and residents, not to mention BT who gave up fixing the telephone kiosk outside the fish and chip shop, as doing so was just an invitation for immediate destruction.

Thieving, joy riding, smoking, standing outside the off-licence on the corner listening to pirate radio stations pumping out hardcore rave while the sun set on Canary Wharf Tower in the distance, occasional football matches on the recreation ground where they displayed more skill at fouling than scoring goals; this was the day to day life. Like Del said in *Bronco Bullfrog*, there wasn't much else to do round here, and there was no-one like Joan Littlewood to engage them in anything more productive or legally creative.

I sometimes wonder what happened to them all, now that the burning flames of youth have died out. What happened to West Ham station is that it was rebuilt. It was in the making that summer and the talk of the owners of the off-licence, the post office, the newsagent and the café was about what compensation package they might get. Home for me was the flat above the café, accessed by a door flush with the station entrance, just yards away from the bridge that took the trains over Manor Road. The overground trains didn't stop here, just thundered past at a speed that shook the bricks and mortar and rattled plates draining in the kitchen to the floor, where they smashed. My bed was a spare mattress on the floor of the front room. An alarm clock wasn't necessary, as the first early morning trains would make the floorboards rumble vigorously enough to wake me from the deepest sleep.

The flat was shared by Chris, an old school friend who had journeyed down from Lancashire four years previously to study at what was then North East London Polytechnic and by the time I had arrived was the University of East London, and Tony, who had come from Yorkshire. My arrival created an imbalance in this War of the Roses, but crucially I came armed with a camping stove which, as the flat didn't have a cooker, was to prove useful. There was a fridge and a bathroom suite, but apart from two sofas, two beds and a couple of bedside tables, that was it – other than the huge television that came from a rental shop in Barking not long after my arrival, and to my recollection was never returned. The carpets were grey and thinner than underlay, and as there wasn't any underlay beneath them, the only comfort gained over bare floorboards was carpet burn rather than splinters.

There was a snowstorm the Saturday night I arrived, an hour late after waiting in vain for a Hammersmith and City Line train at Liverpool Street before a member of staff put me out of my misery: they were peak hours only, and I needed to get the Central line to Mile End and jump on the District line to West Ham. Chris, Tony and a crowd of their mates were just about to leave for a night out in Stratford, so I dropped my bag off and trudged through the thickening snow along Manor Road, left onto West Ham Lane, then right onto the Broadway at the end of Tramway Avenue to arrive at the warmth of the 'Eddie'. Threadbare carpets and low ceilings, outside toilets, and everywhere dark wood. It wasn't very busy, a mix of students and locals. Outside the snow continued to descend. The recession had hit. The Gulf War had started. This was my introduction to London.

At night the tower at Canary Wharf used to glow blue and stand alone against the dark sky, like something that had arrived from the future. In between me and it, as I looked out of the flat, was wasteland, old dockland and poverty. It was like a rocket that had landed on a devastated alien planet, yet from the point of view of those on the planet, it was the alien. Down below the window and on the right a buttery glow would light the corner, falling from the off-license door. Some of the kids would still be hanging about if it wasn't cold, smoking, eyeing up cars. Manor Road was quiet, dead even. There was no reason to be here unless you lived here. The area surrounding the station was like its own little island, mostly quiet in its isolation but with random bursts of excitement, noise or sudden violence. Like the time someone strolled into the tube station with a shotgun and shot out the plate glass that, for no reason anyone could fathom, protected a display of plants, akin to a giant sized version of a bottled garden. By the time we had ventured carefully down the stairs of the flat and gingerly poked our heads round the door to see what had happened, the shooter had gone. The guy in the ticket office just looked at us, a bit stunned, and reading our faces merely shrugged. No reason. No reason at all. Not much to do round here.

Fifteen years earlier a different sort of violence occurred, when one March day in 1976 an IRA bomb exploded on a Metropolitan Line train that had just left West Ham station. The location of detonation was an accident, although the bomber, Vincent Donnelly, didn't hang around to use that as a defence. Having boarded a train at Stepney Green only to end up going in the wrong direction, he got off at Plaistow and boarded another heading west, his intended target being Liverpool Street. By this time the timer on his device had reached its own destination and the duffel bag containing it began to unfurl fingers of smoke, signalling to Donnelly its intent. Donnelly then threw the bag down the carriage, staring at it fixedly, in disbelief perhaps at how badly his day was turning out. The sequence of events he had put in motion earlier came to an end with an explosion that nearly severed his arm, and ripped the door of the carriage off with such force that it flew through the air and landed in the chemical factory beside where the train had now come to a halt. It landed on Donald Gallo, who was busy filling a tanker with nitric acid, and broke one of his legs. The blow knocked him out and when he came to he saw an old lady trying to crawl away from the train up on the embankment.

Donnelly meanwhile had jumped off the train, bleeding, and was confronted by the driver, Julius Stephen, who he shot dead. He also shot at and wounded a Post Office engineer who had chased him down the track, which, according to witnesses he ran up and down in both directions, as if trying to work out what to do next. After shooting a police car that had arrived on the scene and sensing his position was now hopeless, he decided to turn the gun on himself, shouting an obscenity about the English in the direction of police officers who were approaching him as he did so.[204] He even failed in this mission and was taken to hospital. Bombs on the tube. An old story after all.

It was a dead zone. The flats, some of the first council high rises ever built, sat like a wall with windows opposite the railway line. They eyed each other up through a chain link fence, and in the distance, when tumescent, the gas holders down by the Chanelsea were visible. The long, dull road to Canning Town, straight as the Romans liked them, stretched under the Peggy Leggy Steps towards the docks, industry and the dirty Thames. There were small sirens on top of tall poles; when I asked Chris what they were for, he explained that it was to raise the alarm if an accident happened at the chemical factory. One day a leaflet dropped through the letter box with instructions as to what to do in the event of such an incident.

"It said to wet a towel, and lie down on the floor with it over your head," he said.
"And then what?"
"Just lie there?" he shrugged, "Wishing you lived somewhere else."

The chemical factory, and its risk, were long gone. They left behind a large patch of flat waste ground.

---

204 The Guardian, March 16, 1976

Somewhere round here soul singer Linda Lewis grew up, a sweet voice on cult folksy funk albums of the early to mid-seventies, by which time she had moved to a large house in Hampstead, to live hippy commune-style and hang out with the likes of Marc Bolan, Cat Stevens and David Bowie. At the age of just three her mother had enrolled her in Peggy O'Farrell's School Of One Hundred Wonderful Children, situated behind the West Ham United ground at Upton Park, and before she knew it Linda was in appearing in small roles in films like *A Taste of Honey*. The singing career came later, but by then she had already sung onstage with John Lee Hooker and appeared in a film with Gary Cooper. She never quite broke through into mainstream success though, and in the 1980s her star began to fade.

They had pulled down the shops that had given me breakfast, newspapers, stamps and beer. In their place now was a solid brick construction, a thick, bunker like wall, part of the expanded West Ham tube station. The modern, efficient version – not like the ramshackle model of 1991 that didn't even have ticket barriers, just an exit gate where, if they could be bothered, a member of staff would stand and look at tickets flashed in his face. They could have been years old those tickets, for all anyone cared. All the stations in zone 3 were the same. There were no ticket-barriers this far out of town and so all that was needed was a sufficient turn of speed to get past any member of staff who could be bothered to ask for the non existent ticket – payment just wasn't a strict necessity. In those days even trips to zone 1 were half-price thanks to the excess fares window, where every journey from East London miraculously began from Whitechapel. The introduction of ticket barriers put an end to the psychogeographers of the District Line, and the sport of fare dodging was transferred to the DLR.

Everybody seemed to be travelling legit this morning. We passed the ExCel Centre at Victoria Dock, a vast silvery warehouse sparkling in the sun, that since 2001 has been hosting annual supermarkets of death and destruction known as arms fairs. War and death is big business and Britain is "proudly" the second biggest dealer in the world. The *Buy British* slogan seems to be working here, at least.

The irony of the most heavily bombed area in England during the Second World War hosting events that invite the same sort of destruction to be visited upon innocent men, women and children elsewhere is not lost on the local population, least of all the pupils of the Royal Docks Community School who made a video about it (you can see this at the East London Against Arms Fairs website and enjoy watching a young school girl run verbal rings round a spokesman for Defence Security and Equipment International). As one local in the video says, the fact that the arms fairs take place in this area is an insult. But then the people in this area have been insulted by people in power ever since it existed as anything other than a marsh by the river. Some of the people who live here now do so purely because of wars in other countries that couldn't have happened without arms dealers. They have fled from where the weapons of death and destruction were unleashed against them, only to arrive at the place where those same weapons are sold.

When the train pulled in at the elevated Albert Dock platform, I was the only person who got off. Down in the dock people were paddling kayaks or stepping into dragon boats, young men at the stern ready to bang on drums. Every five minutes or so another plane would appear in the distant sky, first as a pair of yellow twinkling lights, then growing, an awkward sea bird with wings outstretched, coming in to land. City Airport opened in 1987, the first significant landmark in the post industrial Royal Docklands. At first it seemed like a yuppie taxi rank for City fly boys off on another business jaunt, but later became another staging post for cheap stag-land European city breaks. Fly to Prague for £1. Cheaper than chips. A bit more to get back.

Aside from the water sport fans – parents yelling encouragement to children with names like Toby and Jasper – the place was deserted. The water in the dock puckered in the wind, planes swooped down from the sky to land in the background, and red DLR trains glided west and east on the elevated tracks. Beyond the airport the Tate & Lyle building rose up like some sea monster from a Japanese B-movie. Bought out by the Americans in 2010 and now a corporate food industry proposition where sugar seems an afterthought compared to all manner of chemical terrors, any link to its past seems tenuous when reading the various pages of its mega-corporate web site. The body of that famous building just seemed the host to a new alien presence, a simulacra of the real thing producing replicant food products. I snapped away with my camera, getting shots of incoming planes and outgoing trains. A sense of the past was hard to conjure up.

With nothing left to see and more photographs to take, I ascended the steps back up to the platform and hopped on the next train back towards Canning Town, where I could get off and wait for the train to take me on the southern side of the docks. Although I had lived just up the road from here when I arrived in London in 1991, I had never ventured into Canning Town. There was no reason to. The nearest I got was getting off the Barking night bus at the end of East India Dock Road and walking up Manor Road towards the tube station – a lonely walk at three in the morning. It was another three years before the DLR came out this way, via Poplar, and a further five for the Jubilee line to snake its way this far east.

Such rail links might have happened a lot sooner had London hosted the 1988 Olympic Games. It wasn't artistic license that had Bob Hoskins' character in *The Long Good Friday* refer to this vision. A feasibility study published in 1979 envisaged an Olympic Park on the site of the Royal Victoria Dock, which would have put Canning Town at the gateway to the Games. The budget included extending the Jubilee line from Charing Cross to Custom House. Plans also included the creation of a new town centre for the Docklands, with housing, shops, library, cinema, sports facilities and a new national stadium. Words like legacy were then just *newspeak* waiting for spin doctors from the future. In the end no bid was made. Britain hadn't thrown its hat into the five rings since it had hosted the event in 1948 – the famous Austerity Games, so called because of the post-war hardships, and knocked together on a shoestring budget. Ironically, in equally austere times, the 2012 version sees fit to spend £7 million an hour just to bookend the three week circus. The Sports Minister muttered bizarrely that spending this amount of money would leave an economic legacy, but like the best economists provided no hard data to back up his claim, which sounded as though it had been plucked from the clouds that once fascinated Luke Howard. The Sports Minister meanwhile said that it was necessary to show the world what Britain was best at, which is presumably wasting tax payers' money.

While I waited for the train I toyed with the idea of working out how much of my tax was going on all this distraction, but even if I had possessed the numbers to crunch and the brains to do the crunching, I doubt I would have found the total very funny. Particularly not when added to the much bigger amount I had involuntarily been billed for the bank bailout of 2008 – the self-inflicted economic meltdown twenty years after the phantom Dockland Olympics.

The train cruised quietly into the station, ejecting a full load of passengers before continuing on to West Silvertown where I got off. After descending yet another set of steps down to street level, I decided that the Royal Victoria Docks would be less interesting than the strip of land that lay between the North Woolwich Road and the Thames. The most intriguing story about the dock I had come across was that of Jack Love and his wife, Mary Jane, whose bodies and car (a pre-war

Wolseley) were found in 23 feet of water in 1960. They had left home for an evening out one night four years earlier, leaving their daughter behind, and it was only when the dock was being dredged that the discovery of their fate took place. It was unknown just how or why they ended up in the dock, but I couldn't help thinking of how terrible it was to plunge into that deep darkness and remain there, slowly decomposing in the rusting hulk of a car, while up above four whole years of loading and unloading of goods from around the world took place. And of their daughter, wondering where they were, not finding out for four whole years, then being given the sad details.

I walked eastward for a few yards and turned onto Knight's Road, the top of which was strewn in rubble and broken glass. A huge white factory loomed into view beyond some waste ground next to the elevated West Silvertown station. Surrounded by a white wall covered in colourful graffiti a familiar item, in giant size, was unmistakeable. The Lyle Golden Syrup Tin. The original entrance to this Plaistow Wharf factory has gone, replaced by the station I had just left. Aside from a lorry driver fiddling around by his cab, there was no sign of life except wisps of factory smoke. The road was dry and dusty, leaves on the roadside bushes grey.

Further up the road, as it turned 90 degrees to the left, was the entrance to another factory. Tall green trees flanked the open gates; beyond them were buildings and tall thin chimneys and a man in orange overalls hosing down the top of a long ramp, the fine spray igniting sparks of sunlight. This was PDM group, the site of the John Knight factory. PDM deal in animal by-products for such things as pet foods, but the smell of animal carcasses that the workers of the Tate & Lyle factory next door might remember is not in the air today.

Next door lies Atlantis Oil and Chemicals Co. Ltd, a building of broken windows and large round tanks of peeling blue paint. It looks dead, like something from the set of Mad Max. Even the sign has a big chunk missing. Round the corner there is nothing to write home about, and nothing much to photograph. I get challenged about why I am taking any photographs at all, but it is not an officious security guard, just a bloke who works in one of the small businesses on Bradfield Road and is being cautious as there has been a lot of thieving of late. Times are hard, after all.

Further down the North Woolwich Road, as it curves slowly, shadowed by the DLR, is the Thames Barrier Park. For the locals this is a nice slice of green with a playground and a small cafe, but hardly worth any kind of journey. You can, of course, view the Thames Barrier from here, but it seems smaller in reality and is somewhat underwhelming as a spectacle. More interesting is the view facing the other direction, from the elevated platform of Pontoon Dock station. Millenium Mills can be seen from all around the area. It was in the distance when I was watching the planes land at City Airport from the Royal Albert Dock, a white block poking its head up beyond Connaught Bridge. It was there in the distance when I was back on Knight's Road. It can be seen from both branches of the DLR. It stands on the edge of the Pontoon Dock, the sun coating it in light. On the near side of the water is Grain

Silo D, another abandoned white block, this time on a much smaller scale. They seem like two of the last remaining relics of the past, like extras from Kubrick's *Full Metal Jacket*. There is something strangely magnificent in their dereliction.

Built in 1905 by Vernon & Sons, and named after their famous Millenium Flour, the building suffered damage as a result of the 1917 explosion at Brunner Mond. Shortly afterwards it was taken over by Spillers, initially for milling purposes and later for the production of pet foods. It also suffered damage from the bombing raids in the Second World War and was rebuilt in the 1950s. Since the closure of the docks in 1981, the Mills and surrounding land have been subject to speculation over use, including plans for aquariums and flats. They have also been used as a backdrop in Derek Jarman's *Last of England* and the television series *Ashes to Ashes*. Jean Michel Jarre used them as a projection backdrop for his industrial themed *Destination Docklands* concert in 1988, an event that nearly didn't take place, such was the twitchiness of health and safety observers.

Nearly a quarter of a century later, the French musician's extravaganza seems to be some kind of inspiration for the use of the site for the London Pleasure Gardens – a modern take on the Pavilion Gardens that were just up the road on the bank of the Thames. The organisers, with experience of organising the late-night area Shangri-la at Glastonbury, promise to create a cultural hub with music venues, a floating cinema and artisan cafes and bars. The 2012 Bloc festival is set to take place here in July, with minimalist composer Steve Reich one of the headliners. Without the Olympics it is hard to imagine that any of this would be taking place, and compared to the entertainment back in 1988, when warehouses and fields were being taken over for illegal raves, it all seems rather commodified, a bit like having a house party with your parents in the next room.

Call me Victorian, but I prefer the bill of fare for the Pavilion Gardens' season opening day on May 30th 1853:

Mr. Henry Coxwell makes his first ascent in his beautiful balloon at six o'clock. Darby, of Vauxhall, will astonish by an extraordinary exhibition of fireworks at nine o'clock. The best orchestral band in the kingdom, under the able conductorship of W.M. Packer. Dancing commences at seven. Unrivalled equestrian entertainment. The baby artist, four-and-a-half years old. Surprising feats on the rope, by the renowned Paddington. The maze, - bowling green. Brilliant illuminations by Duffell, &c, &c. Superior Refreshments at moderate charges[205]

Coxwell, the son of a naval officer and a dentist by profession, had been ballooning since 1844. He became professional in 1848, making ascents all over Europe. Four years after his ascent from Pavilion Gardens he made a record-breaking flight, ascending from Wolverhampton Gas Works – chosen as it was far enough inland to prevent the risk of the balloon

---

205 Kentish Independent, May 28, 1853

being blown out to sea and the gas could be used to inflate the balloon. He was accompanied on the flight by the scientist James Glaisher, who was interested in what happened to water vapour as it rose in the atmosphere. As the balloon broke through the clouds, Coxwell unsuccessfully attempted to take a photograph, which would have been the first to capture cloud formation from above.

The two men were unaware of the dangers of altitude and at five miles up both experienced serious problems, with frostbitten hands, difficulty maintaining consciousness and inability to see clearly. When they were in danger of gaining too much altitude, Coxwell, unable to grip with his fingers, managed to use his teeth on the balloon's rip chord, letting air escape for a descent just in time. Glaisher, who had been unconscious for seven minutes, came to. When Coxwell explained that he could not feel his hands, Glaisher poured brandy over them, before continuing with his scientific readings in true Boys Own fashion. Their escapade took two and a half hours from take off to landing.

I needed to get back to Stratford in plenty of time for meeting Angry Bob, but felt there was no harm in jumping on the next train going further east. I got off at City Airport in order to get a look at the huge Tate & Lyle factory from street level. Looming above rows of terraced houses, it remains a vista of a bygone age when a single factory could dominate an entire area and, in this case, dwarf its inhabitants. I didn't know it at the time, but as I took a few shots with my camera a signing session was taking place inside for *Sugar Girls*, a book about the women who worked at Tate & Lyle, written by Duncan Barrett and Nuala Calvi.

On the seat of the train back to Stratford was a brightly coloured flyer for the London Holy Ghost Festival at the Excel Centre, to be hosted by Pastor E A Adeboye, a man instructed by God in 1986 to invite everyone to a Holy Ghost Service in Lagos. *"Arise & Shine"*, the leaflet proclaimed, this is the *"Festival of Life"*. Ironic that it was taking place at a venue that also holds the festival of death and destruction that is the arms fair. The service was for the followers of the Redeemed Christian Church of God (RCCG), an evangelical movement who boast of 250 branches in the UK and are planning to build a 100,000 capacity arena for their services in London. Should they achieve this ambition it would be a much larger place of worship, by several times in fact, than the proposed 'mega-mosque' in Stratford.

The RCCG believe that homosexuality is a sin, and that the Devil exists. They also believe in all the prophecies in the bible. Worldliness – under which comes dancing, drumming, drinking and pleasures of the flesh – is forbidden, as is, conveniently, rebellion against church authority. All followers have to pay tithes, and according to an article published in the New York Times[206], members raised enough money to supply Pastor Adeboye with a private jet. Anything which is not bible teaching must be ignored entirely and any followers found guilty of backsliding on this will be punished.

---

206 Andrew Rice, New York Times Magazine, April 8, 2009

Pentecostal Christianity isn't knew in Newham. There were Pentecostal denominations in East Ham and Canning Town as far back as 1915 and 1928 respectively. The real explosion of Pentecostalism, however, has occurred with the ethnic congregations that have emerged through immigration. It is now estimated that half of Newham's Christian followers are Pentecostal.

Weekend preachers remain a fixture in Stratford. At the Broadway entrance to Stratford Shopping Centre the flow of words from competing preachers weave into each other as you walk by, like an echo-chamber, resounding with words like *Jesus, sin, redemption* and *Satan*. Unlike the pastors in church services, there seems little joy in the exhortations out on the streets, just fire and brimstone.

Christianity, which accounts for the religious denomination of half of Newhams' population according to the 2001 census, has always had a strong presence, beginning with the missionary churches established in places like West Ham, Canning Town and Silvertown to capture, or cater for (depending on your standpoint), the influx of workers in the latter half of the 19th century. Quakers, most of whom regard themselves as Christian, were hugely influential in the area as it grew; famous Quakers included Samuel Gurney, Dr. Fothergill, Joseph Lister, and Elizabeth and Katharine Fry. According to the same 2001 census, Islam accounts for a further 25% of the population, with other religions and non-believers lagging behind.

The ongoing battle between good and evil doesn't stop at the weekend. It is a beautiful, sunny Saturday and the preachers are already warning the damned outside Stratford Station. Meridian Square is busy, more so now than in the past because of Westfield and the steps leading up to the railway bridge, which act as a hang out place for young people. The old shopping centre is as crowded as ever, and when I exit at the other end there are more people urging passers by to follow the word of God, reaching out hands clutching flyers. I pass St. John's church, an altogether calmer religious entity, and wait at the crossing. Over the road is my next destination.

The 'Eddie' seemed much as it had done when I last left it, several years ago, and was still in the hands of Kendall Cortes. I commented on how much had changed since I left Stratford five years earlier. Seeing it every day meant he hadn't really noticed, though he certainly noticed an increase in takings when the high security of the Olympic Park meant that coach tours could only disembark in one location – which happened to be conveniently close to the pub.

"We were getting about seven or eight a week at one point," he said. I wondered idly what things might have been like if the coach tours had taken a wrong turning and ended up in the less salubrious Princess of Wales instead. When Kendall had to deal with other customers I looked around and remembered the days and nights I had spent in here, the fog of the low-ceilinged front bar in the pre-smoking ban days, pub quizzes never won, football matches watched when a television existed in the back bar, and the constant flow of traffic outside on the Broadway.

I decided to take a walk round the corner and see where I used to live. The Queens Head, on the island between Tramway

Avenue and West Ham Lane, was still open but deserted. Cafe Mondo was still there, but with a new sign. The job centre, which had once been the site of a cinema, was still there as well. So far no change. But above and behind the Princess of Wales was a huge glass building. They had been constructing this as far back as 2006. The row of businesses opposite the flats that had been built on the site of Queen Mary's Hospital were more or less the same. When I first moved to Stratford, living in a flat in Whales Yard, there used to be a second hand bookshop here, with narrow wooden staircases up and down to rooms packed with books and magazines and the smell of old paper. The man who ran it also ran kick-boxing sessions, if memory serves me correctly. There had been another dusty old bookshop at the bottom of Romford Road, but this was turned into a greasy spoon cafe before I moved to the area. The days of these second hand bookshops, independent shops selling music equipment or toys, a record shop; all of this was history before the turn of the millennium.

On the corner of West Ham Lane and Aldworth Road, opposite the police station where a letter bomb had blown up in the hands of Sergeant Roberts in September 1973 (he survived), there used to be a hairdresser. In the windows it still had net curtains and black and white photographs of hair models that might have looked vaguely fashionable in the 1980s. Now it was Cafe 'Lympic. Originally called Cafe Olympic, they had been threatened with legal trouble if they didn't change their name. To avoid an expensive rebranding the owner simply painted over the letter O, an inspired move that not only saved time and money but left bullying lawyers without a legal leg to stand on, and represented a heart warming victory for the common man against corporate might. Other businesses with the word Olympic in their names, or those using the Olympic rings, were also dealt with swiftly. Diners in the Burger King restaurant in Stratford Shopping Centre who order onion rings might need to be careful how they are arranged on their tray, as legal teams spotting any resemblance to the Olympic logo are likely to treat them with little humour.

I walked up Aldworth Road and had just drawn level with the house I lived in for six years when Angry Bob phoned. Despite not seeing each other for a number of years he decided to skip pleasantries and open with, "Fuck me. What have they done to the place?"

"Do you mean Stratford as a whole or a specific part of it? Where are you?"

"Outside the shopping centre, underneath some bloody tree contraption."

"It's supposed to be a shoal of fish."

"Don't look like bleedin' fish to me. Since when's Stratford been famous for fish anyway?"

Rather than continue in this vein indefinitely, I told Bob to wait where he was and that I would be with him in ten minutes. I put my phone back in my pocket and looked at the door of the house in front of me, unchanged in all this time, the ornamental metal curlicues behind frosted glass. I wanted to have a peak through the net curtains but decided against it, and wondered how the present occupiers were dealing with the Japanese knotweed in the back garden. This had sprung up through the concrete by the brick wall at the rear of the garden. Each summer we would see it grow eight or more feet in a matter of days, then after enjoying a few weekends of privacy from the overlooking flats, hack it down. This was the same stuff they found on the Olympic Park. It required incredibly expensive treatment to get rid of, and word on the street is that the Terminator-like plant will be back.

I expected to feel a wave of memory and nostalgia wash over me when I walked up this road, but I couldn't connect. I recalled the man who used to walk his white terrier in the mornings and who moved out when the Olympics put enough extra value onto his house to tempt him away, having living here for years. And the man who lived on the corner who did some plumbing work for us once. He kept ferrets, and like a surrogate Northerner had one in his trousers. He also had a duck in his back yard, and one morning I found him talking in black tones about local foxes and the disappearance of his duck. Then there was the mysterious Raytel who made music in the early noughties and left it behind in the house he had lived in, a pair of CDRs with instructions that the recipient do as they please with it. And the constant night time soundtrack of police cars and helicopters, the powerful searchlights of which would sometimes land in the garden like a scene in a disaster movie. But I didn't have time to dwell on my memories. Reaching the end of Aldworth, I turned left onto Tennyson, heading in a long circle back to the train station, treading old ground.

Every week for a couple of years cards had dropped through my door in Stratford. They were all the same size, all with the same service being offered – the solution to all your problems. The cards promised to return loved ones or split bad relationships; break curses and black magic; destroy the powers of witchcraft; lose weight; succeed in exams, marriage and business; heal sexual impotency or infertility; cure depression or stress; stop bad luck or gambling (presumably good luck in gambling wouldn't require assistance); protect from bad spirits and voodoo; stop bad dreams; and help with job interviews, court cases and immigration problems. There wasn't a problem these guys couldn't fix.

Mr. Kabba could remove evil spells. Mr Daby, who was supernaturally gifted from God, would destroy your problems before they destroyed you, and encouragingly promised 100% success in few days. Mr Fatty urged you not to remain in silence as he was the answer and there would be no disappointment. Mr Houssein, who offered to guide, help and advise on all your social, family, psychological and financial problems, also offered work by correspondence. Professor Badio, perhaps aware of the vague promise of success being offered elsewhere within an unspecified amount of days, nailed his colours to the mast by guaranteeing results within six. Over time two cards from the Professor dropped onto the door mat on Aldworth Road, showing that he had moved from one address in Forest Gate to another round the corner, and appeared to change his mobile phone at the same time. And then there was Professor Kabiro, who was based in Plaistow but had, word for word, the same sales pitch on his card as his fellow professor, Badio.

I found Bob on the paved concourse in front of the station, near the bus station, looking a bit lost. The area was busy with human traffic, and we were being asked to take Jesus into our lives and consider our sins. The teenagers sitting on the steps leading up to the rust coloured bridge over the railway lines didn't seem in any rush to contemplate such matters. Jesus would have to get in touch via their Blackberries. Bob had a new phone, which he grumbled about, saying he couldn't get used to it. Bob refused to use text messaging. It just seemed wrong, he explained.

"It's a bit of a mess," he said, turning his head like an owl and sweeping an arm in an even wider circle. "I went up there," he added and nodded at the bridge, "and had a look at everything."
"And?"
"It's like a kid putting lipstick on. A mess." He shook his head. The anger wasn't there, just disappointment. After all, he lived in Kent now so what was the point getting worked up about it all? If the planners wanted to do the place up to the same standards as a child applying make-up, what was that to Bob anymore? We finally shook hands.
"So how's Kent?" I asked.
"Quiet. How is it being a family man now?"
"Noisy. Good."
"Was I still here when they were born?"

"I think you'd not long left when my daughter was born."

"You've been gone longer than me then," he said. "Mind you, you're only up the road, you've seen all this." He shook his head again, trying to reconcile the changes. "Was all boarded up when I left."

"Have you been up there for a look yet?" I said, indicating Westfield.

"Nah. Not my thing, shopping centres. Went to the one out in Thurrock once. Never again."

"Come on, lets have a look. While you're here." We headed for the steps and Bob explained how much his new, slower pace of life was agreeing with him. All this hustle and bustle, *"even worse now, look at it"*, was gone like the end of a migraine. Relief. He glanced up briefly at the flickering advertising on the exterior of Westfield, momentarily distracted from his train of thought. I decided not to inflict the interior upon him and led us along one of the outdoor 'streets'. I was aiming to take him to The Cow, the bar on the corner of one of these 'streets' that overlooked the Olympic Park. But when we got there he was aghast at the amount of plate glass (employed to make it a bar not a pub), at the prices and lack of decent ale, and at the highly dubious idea of having half the premises serving as a restaurant.

"Restaurant. Pub." He said it with two chops of his hand in the air. "They are two different things." We stood there in the bright light of the day, reflected by the light stone of the buildings all around.

"I hear they're protesting at Leyton Marshes," Bob said, as if he would be happy to stand on this spot and talk for a few hours until he had to catch his train home. I looked out over the park, at the stadium and the twisting red tower designed by Anish Kapoor. I stared down the road that headed in the direction of old Stratford, the bus station and the high street.

"Let's walk down here," I suggested. "Have a look round. I need to take some photos for the book." Bob shrugged with his eyebrows, then followed.

It was a curious walk along a brand new road with smooth concrete sides, elevated as it veered right and headed in a downward slope parallel with the railway lines. To the left, new tower blocks had risen up like knotweed. The architectural fashion appeared to be adding colours – purples, reds, greens and oranges. To the right was the Olympic Park. The stadium, Kapoor tower and swimming arena dominated here, but train lines still snaked in between them, a reminder of the area's past. Yellow diggers were dotted about, along with piles of construction equipment and portacabins. And walking up this strange road were small clusters of sightseers, tourists, armed with cameras and time on their hands. One girl held the Kapoor tower in the C-shaped grasp of one hand while her friend took the required picture. It was odd seeing tourists here in Stratford. Bob found it amusing. Build, and they will come.

In my mind, as we walked and I pointed my camera at various vistas, connections between my research and the landscape fell into place. The contaminated land, with all that toxicity, was buried under soil and plastic sheeting. The radioactive dust had long since dispersed on the winds that blew in 2007. This should have come as no surprise. That the whole area was awash with dangerous industry and contamination was well documented. When nobody was looking, some of this waste was obviously disposed of in a way only just more sophisticated than fly tipping. In 1972 a whole drum of cyanide was found in a garage off Berwick Road, Plaistow[207], and there were other reports of the same thing happening elsewhere in the country. Just where the cyanide came from and who left it was not reported.

A year after this discovery of the cyanide, Mary Peters, gold medallist in the pentathlon at Munich in 1972, appeared at an athletics meeting of Newham AC under the floodlights of the Terence McMillan stadium, also in Plaistow. Peters was below her best: hardly surprising as her coach, Buster McShane, had died the previous week. Later that year my father secured a job in Northern Ireland, and our family moved to County Down. McShane's daughter was in my sister's primary school class, and she visited the McShane house, overlooking Belfast Loch. I asked her what it was like, having learnt about Buster McShane's death and his link with Peters. She said it was big and dark. I think she found it spooky.

These random facts, and more, were colliding internally. The curious thing was that the more I knew of Newham's past, the less I recognised of its present shape. I understood how John Curwen must have felt when writing about a Plaistow that had disappeared, or Kathryn Fry, doing

---

207 The Guardian, February 29, 1972

the same when writing about East and West Ham. Here it was again, the huge wave of change, sweeping over the landscape.

"What are they going to do with all this sports equipment after the Olympics?" Bob said, meaning the various venues and arenas. They had already given the main stadium to West Ham United, then changed their minds and taken it away again. I shrugged. It was obvious that the buildings had been designed by different people, or teams of people. Some, in isolation, looked impressive, but there was no coherence. It all looked a bit messy, and critical praise felt like a case of the Emperor's New Clothes. When we eventually reached the High Street, we emerged to a cocksure outbreak of new towers and apartment blocks, existing buildings cowering in their shadows, crumbling and unloved. A bridge now carried the Greenway walk over the road, but access to it was blocked by barricades. I persuaded Bob to walk down the sewer pipe a short distance so I could grab a few shots of Bazelgette's pumping station. Once I had done this, out of curiosity I walked a little bit further to see where Abbey Road vaulted the Chanelsea River. We found the water green with algae, littered with rubbish and old tyres, a fragment of familiarity from the past that, for no good reason, cheered me up.

"About time for a pint," Bob said, turning from the polluted river. An old man sat on a bench nearby, his grey hair blowing in the wind like smoke. Old Stratford. It was as if he had been sitting there for years as the new Stratford was growing in the distance. Walking back towards the High Street was when the totality of the change could really be grasped. From the vantage point of the Greenway, Stratford was beginning to resemble one of those instant mega-cities that were built with obscene haste in China, then seemingly stand empty, like ghost cities.

All the way up the High Street there was change. The Yardley building was imprisoned by scaffolding, the flower girls looking a bit lost surrounded by all this modernity. This included 150 High Street, the 133 storey tower being built for Genesis Housing, glass and cladding slowly making its way to the top. The Builder's Arms on Lett Road was about to be attacked by a block of flats looming above it, unfolding like a Transformer toy. Everything was either new or had been given a face-lift – or at the very least a bit of spit and polish. Everything, that is, apart from number 273, The Pie Crust Cafe, which stood proudly in all its Old Stratford shabbiness. A bit of the letter E in 'Pie' was missing, so it read The Pif Crust Cafe. The sign should perhaps have gone long ago, as it was now offering Thai Cuisine. This was the cafe that Del and his mates break into in the opening scene of *Bronco Bullfrog*. Back then it was called Harry's Joker Cafe and had an Old Holborn sign hanging above the entrance. The glass window of the door that the lads put a coat-cushioned fist through had the old Brooke Bond logo on it, and through the window from inside could be seen the Green Man pub, which was demolished in 2002.

Bob had never heard of *Bronco Bullfrog*, and didn't sound overly interested the one time I mentioned it. His thing was Spaghetti Westerns, especially the ones starring Clint Eastwood. *"It's the music"*, he once said, as if that explained everything.

"They'll get kicked out," he said out of nowhere, apropos of nothing.

"Eh?"

"The protesters at Leyton Marsh, they'll get evicted." He stopped suddenly and turned, a piece of gravel scarping the pavement under his foot. We were outside the Discovery Centre. Inside, children were no doubt playing happily. Bob looked over at the buses queuing to pull into Great Eastern Road.

"You can't stop any of this."

"Any of what?" I said, looking around, fearful that what couldn't be stopped might be bearing down on me.

"This. The Olympics. Change. They want it to happen and it will happen."

I shuffled my feet, unsure if he had finished or not. It seemed like an obvious statement. I wondered if all this time Bob had harboured thoughts that maybe things like this really could be stopped – or that at least they should be stopped. Now he had left London, he was free to give up the moral fight.

Leyton Marsh has a history. In 895AD it became 'Lammas Land' after an Act made by King Alfred. The lord of the manor could grow hay on the land, but it had to be harvested before Lammas Day, August 1st, when local people were then allowed to graze their animals upon it until March 25th the following year.

Much of the land was built upon by the Great Eastern Railway company, but when the East London Waterworks

Co. tried to take over some of the land the locals, protective of the Lammas Rights they had over the remaining 176 acres, held a huge demonstration on Lammas Day, 1892. When the Waterworks tried to sue one of the protesters, the locals set up the Leyton Lammas Lands Defence Committee (LLLDC) and took them on in court. A sign commemorating their success exists on the front of the Eton Manor Athletic Club on Marsh Lane.

Since then the land has been affected by a compulsory purchase order by Lea Valley Regional Park, and slowly encroached upon by a riding school. The latest incursion, by the ODC to sequester some of the land for a training facility for the American basketball team, did the job of stirring up a new Lammas Land protest. But Bob was right. It was doomed to failure, just like the protests in Leyton in 1994 over the M11 link – the extension of the A12 that cut a swathe through Leyton and Leytonstone and saw whole streets disappear. One of them, Claremont Road, was taken over by protesters who erected scaffolding, nets and other barricades. Parties were held in the blocked-off, empty street. Rave sounds filled the air. When they were finally evicted, some of the protesters moved to a house on Fillebrook Road, near Leytonstone Station, that was promptly christened Munster House. Protesters lasted here until June 1995. But the road, inevitably, was built, as it was always going to be. Although many locals (at least the ones fortunate enough to live on streets not affected) were glad that the roads leading down into Stratford were no longer snarled up with traffic, there remained for long afterwards a bitterness that no alternatives were considered – that over 350 Victorian houses were destroyed and a sunken dual-carriageway now cut its way brutally through a community. Memories were destroyed, obliterated, and Fillebrook road now stops abruptly, like a sawn-off tree branch.

"There's someone I want you to meet," Bob said. This sounded a bit ominous. "For your book. You know, research."
"Okay. Who? What do they know?"
"Bloke called Mickey. He knows all about this conspiracy theory..." he stopped when he saw me roll my eyes. "No, no. It's all bollocks, but..."
"But what?"
"Well, it might be good for your book. You are still doing it aren't you?"

I nodded, and asked him to continue. He looked at his watch, frowned. "You'd better get a move on with it. Anyway, you've probably heard all this stuff about the Mayan calendar and how the world is supposed to end in 2012 right? Well, there's a conspiracy specifically about the Olympics. Something to do with Temple Mills."

I hadn't been to Temple Mills for 20 years. The first time I went, the year I came to London, was a strange experience. Walking down Temple Mills Lane in the fog, I wasn't expecting fields to suddenly replace the urban background we had left. When the road turned into a lane, with a travellers camp on one side and a small estate of brown stone flats at the end, I couldn't get to grips with the geography anymore. This wasn't a London that had ever existed in my imagination. We had walked all this way for a party. As this part of London was bereft of nightclubs, there was a DIY ethic that saw flats and houses, occupied or otherwise, being converted into temporary dancehalls. The kitchen-dining area of the flat we entered had been completely cleared to serve as a dance floor. Two DJs were busy on the decks, playing hardcore rave; people were beginning to move, a sweet smell in the air. Before long it was crowded and hot enough to want to suck in some fresh air outside. People were sitting on a grass bank, smoking, chatting, drinking cans of beer. Some ICF had apparently turned up.[208] One lad standing next to me had a club-sized bit of wood poking out from under his jacket. He might not have been ICF, but he didn't seem to be getting into the loved-up spirit of things, so I suggested that perhaps he didn't need any accessories on a night like this. He mulled it over, and seemed to agree. Weed, pills, hardcore rave. It was all a great leveller back in the day, and finding yourself in unfamiliar territory with unfamiliar people was par for the course. This place felt like the edge of town, some kind of no-mans land, a border land. It was, I found out much later, the Clays Lane Estate. A few parties were held in flats here around this time. On one occasion it was rumoured that the singer of rave act Expansions had done an impromptu PA. On thing was obvious: the residents of Clays Lane were a pretty accommodating bunch.

208 ICF stands for Inter City Firm, the name of the West Ham United hooligan firm

The estate was actually built on top of the old West Ham Tip, and the land was contaminated. Badly contaminated. This was toxic land that was not supposed to be disturbed as this would unleash, like some H.P. Lovecraft spectre, radioactive waste. It hit the headlines, only to meet the sort of cognitive dissonance that is the spirit of our age. Clays Lane Estate no longer exists. In 2003, before the Olympic bid was successful, the London Development Agency had already marked its card. In 2007, with the Olympics bulldozer in full effect, a compulsory purchase order sealed its fate, along with that of the neighbouring travellers. Collateral damage. Travellers, misfit residents, and later, much nearer to the start of the whole circus, just the poor and vulnerable. Some people didn't believe in the *regeneration* mantra from the start. This would be gentrification, social cleansing; the middle classes were heading east and economics would ensure that the necessary displacement would occur.

Other people just think that a fake alien invasion during the Olympics will send everyone into such a tailspin that the New World Order can be ushered into existence without any resistance, and a New Jerusalem will be founded in this green and pleasant land. This is what Rick Clay thought, at least. Until he committed suicide just after 'revealing' his convoluted conspiracy theory on a Swedish internet radio station. Or maybe he was murdered, who knows? It was Clay's theory that Mickey, a man whose face was so pockmarked a blind man could read it, explained in a tortured way over a pint in the beer garden of The Golden Grove. The starting point of Clay's ideas, or at least the bit that Mickey began with, centred on the street names surrounding the Olympic Park. Angel Lane, Temple Mills, Great Eastern Way. Each name in direct or indirect semantic fashion had some kind of Masonic significance. The theory then proceeded to spin out of control, and by the time he had finished Mickey, perhaps observing our faces, was looking a bit sheepish. For a few seconds.

"Substitute aliens for a false flag terrorist attack though, and it don't seem so far fetched."

"No," Bob said. "Still a bit pretty fucking stretched though all the same."

"I know a bloke who's quite high up in the police though and he says something will definitely happen during the games. I think he meant a real terrorist attack. But it could be something they just let happen, or even stage. If they start having a training session that involves a terrorist attack on the Olympics then you know what's gonna happen. That's how they do it. They have this operations room and when it gets out say it was a simulation for training and just a crazy coincidence that an almost identical thing happened down the road when they were doing it. Weird huh? Gets you thinking all conspiratorial like, coming up with theories."

By now I wasn't sure whose voice Mickey was speaking in, his own, or another narrator playing devil's advocate. This wasn't helped by the fact that he had clearly been drinking for some time. I shot Bob a look that suggested this wasn't really useful for my research. He just shrugged, then asked Mickey a question.

"Do you believe any of it?"

"What, the Rick Clay stuff?" He stared into the dregs of his ale and frowned. "Nah. Don't think so. But something strange is going on."

"But do you think maybe quite a few people do believe in it?"

"Oh yeah Bob, yeah. It's been all over the Internet for ages now, and you've got all the 2012 stuff."

"What's that then?"

"The end of the world. The Mayan civilisation predicted it in their calendar or something."

"The real end of the world?"

"Maybe," I offered, "it means the end of the world as we know it?" Not knowing the first thing about the supposed Mayan prophecy I was improvising a bit, but Mickey, for one, seemed impressed.

"Exactly. And then the New World Order starts. Christ, they even talk about the New World Order. Bush and other politicians. Not like they hide it."

"The Illuminati eh?" Bob said, doing a quick roll of the eyes.

"So you do believe it?"

"Believe what, the Illuminati?"

"The Rick Clay idea. The New World Order will start because of an event during the Olympics"

"Yeah, the 100 metres," Bob said, and chuckled. Mickey looked confused. Bob capitalised on this by telling him it was his round.

As he walked somewhat unsteadily back into the pub, I looked up, shielding my eyes from the glaring sky. A crane loomed high over the road, planted like a prospectors stake. Here be gold. Not maybe; definitely. It always seems to come back to land.

This area is a small part of what has now been christened 'The Island', surrounded as it is by traffic. In the Design and Access Statement document, outlining the progress and future plans for this part of Stratford, the sculpture that Bob thought was trees and others decided was fish was revealed as 'The Shoal' and had its own section. Even here there is confusion, with references to leaves in the description of its genesis but a name borrowed from the movement of a large group of fish – perhaps moving round 'The Island'? The Shoal even has its own legacy (section 7.9). Reading this document it is clear that a short term priority was to obscure the faceless, concrete ugliness of what is currently there. Future hopes for the continuing development include the creation of new, open streets – in other words, an admission that demolishing Angel Lane and the neighbouring streets all those years ago was a mistake, and now that a 'better class' of resident or visitor is wanted, the damage needs to be undone.

"So," I said, nodding in the direction Mickey had gone, "how long have you known him?"

"Mickey?" Bob pushed his bottom lip up over his top one and shifted his eyes left and right, then gave up trying to find the accurate answer. "Years. I don't know him really, apart from when I used to drink in here. Don't know how we got talking. He might have been with Pete one night. Did you ever meet Pete?"

"No." I thought about the possibility that I had for a moment, but no face came to mind. "I'm beginning to wish I hadn't met Mickey," I added with a chuckle.

"That's a bit harsh," Bob said. "He's harmless. He's not always on about conspiracies. It's just that I thought if anyone was going to know about any Olympic conspiracy theories it would be Mickey."

"Well, you weren't wrong. Do you think he actually believes it? The aliens thing I mean"

"He seems to think something will happen. His little antenna are twitching." He said this with a smile, but it was a benevolent one.

"What about you?" I asked. Bob's brow creased like two men bowing to each other before a martial arts contest.

"A fake alien attack?" He laughed and it turned into a phlegmy cough. "Now that I would like to see." He stopped and looked me in the eye. Then, as if finally unburdening himself of something he had held in for a long time, he began. Cryptically.

"The ending has already been written." I said nothing at first, but when I started shaping my mouth for words I had yet to think of, he continued.

"The Olympics is just a side show, a little distraction from the bad news."

"So what's the bad news Bob?" He looked like he was about to spill the beans, but then Mickey returned, gingerly gripping three full pint glasses in the circle of his fingers. Two of the glasses slopped beer over their sides as he clunked them onto the table. Bob waited for Mickey to sit down, then ignored the fact that he wasn't privy to the start of the discussion.

"How tall are you?" Bob said. I told him. It was a guesstimate. "Why aren't you eight foot tall, or 20 foot, 80 foot?" Mickey frowned, perhaps wondering just how the conversation had taken such an odd turn. I hadn't bothered answering. Mickey decided he needed an explanation.

"What are you on about? I've only been gone a couple of minutes and it's gone all weird." I didn't point out that it had been just as weird before he had left. Bob continued.

"You're the height you are 'cos that's as high as you can grow. A giraffe can only grow so high, same as an elephant or a flea. Everything has limits."

I looked at Mickey and his whole face shrugged. Bob looked at me, then Mickey. We looked at each other, then at Bob. It was like some kind of Mexican stand-off. Bob finally broke the spell.

"It's the economy stupid. There isn't going to be a recovery because there can't be any more growth. The debt can't be paid off."

"I thought we were talking about the Olympics?" Mickey said, still puzzled.

"We weren't actually, " I pointed out. "We were talking about conspiracy theories."

"So what's he talking about?"

"Distractions," I said. "From the main event," I added, after a pause long enough for what Bob meant to have sunk in.

In George Romero's *Land of the Dead*, the zombie hordes outnumber the majority of the world population. The surviving humans live in a walled-in, high security city surrounded by water; a bit like Docklands. The living dead are, at moments of restlessness, distracted by fabulous firework displays. Towards the end of the film, however, one of the zombies looks up at the fireworks and, instead of being awed into pacification, continues walking towards the walled city. This zombie has made a mental breakthrough. The fireworks no longer work as a distraction. The inevitable consequence for the inhabitants of the walled city is played out in the film's final reels.

We talked some more in the pub, after quickly changing the subject. Our discussion moved onto the Olympics, then sport in general, and then football. We got back round to conspiracy theories when Mickey pointed out that the dollar bill had an all-seeing-eye on it, and this was an Illuminati thing. But Bob and I had grown weary of clichéd conspiracies, and the conversation moved on again. We didn't talk about Stratford, or history. As the sun started sinking Bob started looking at his watch, and finally said it was time for him to think about his train home. Not wanting to be left with Mickey and his conspiracy theories, I offered to walk to the station with him.

As we walked along Great Eastern Road and got closer to Meridian Square, it was noticeable that a new type of person was walking around the spruced up streets. Two of them stood next to us on the small pedestrian island at the foot of the new Angel Road bridge: a young man and his girlfriend, who were discussing the merits of a hip West End restaurant. Bob looked at the man, then at me, before saying in a clear voice, "Cuckoos."

The man looked at Bob briefly, frowning, an unsure look falling across his hitherto sure expression. He looked away. The woman was still talking about the restaurant. The lights changed. Traffic stopped. The couple walked across the road ahead of us. We were all going in the same direction. "Here they come," Bob said, much quieter this time, almost under his breath, as if the words were heavy and releasing them had made him tired. He started whistling a nameless tune.

Once the land here just existed. We know that the Romans have been, and the Vikings. Both left their traces. Once noblemen lived here in grand buildings and peasants worked the fields. As the land was settled, it was put to use to support those who lived on it, then later to provide subsistence for the City of London. Its mills provided flour for the city's bread, and its grazing land fed the cattle that provided meat for its tables. Fields, orchards and market gardens provided fruit and vegetables. It became valuable for farming, growing, then grazing, and as a result there was deforestation and enclosure. Then, with industrialisation, the land became more valuable as a location for industry – particularly the dirty, polluting, noxious, dangerous and poisonous sort that wasn't wanted in the city itself. Urbanisation followed rapidly, as the workers required by all this industry were squeezed into poor quality housing. As harsh as these times and conditions were for most people, they provided the only recognisable identity the land had. This was industry. Without it, the land would have remained fields and marshes and the urban population wouldn't have existed.

Now that the industry has long gone, including the last scraps that were bought-off to enable the Olympics to distract us for three weeks, this borough is in the middle of an identity crisis. Not only has the demographic of the population undergone yet more rapid change, but the purpose of the place has been lost in the confusion. The food eaten by its residents is now grown elsewhere, usually overseas, and the products it consumes are no longer made here. It was once boasted that every household in the land contained something that was made in Silvertown. Now this accolade belongs to China.

They dreamed of building a new city here in the days when Silvertown could make its proud boast, and published the idea a year after London first held the Olympic Games in 1908.

It was proposed the other day, at the annual banquet of the West Ham Corporation Electric Supply Department, that a new city should be created in East London, and should be known as Eastminster. It was suggested that this great area, which is divided from London by the Lea, would be best served by a single government, and it was proposed that the new city should include West Ham, East Ham, Leyton, Walthamstow, Ilford, Barking, Woodford, Wanstead, Dagenham, and North Woolwich, which have a

total population of 878,268; an area of 37,865 acres and a
rateable value of £3,627,043.[209]

Change, and the idea of change, has been continual for a long
time in this restless land by the Lea. The change just flows at
different speeds, and at the moment it is flowing dramatically
fast. We are also in a different dream now, one where the
dreamers talk of legacy. But they are not in control of the
dream. They are just dreaming it, while everyone else is living
inside it. Some people will inevitably be displaced. If there is
no hope of adding them to the 'buoyant young professional
market', then they can be shipped out and incoming young
professionals will fill the gap, like the sea rushing in to fill
footprints made in the sand.

---

209 The Illustrated London News, February 6, 1909